W9-ACU-799

Beyond Training *Ain't* Performance

FIELDBOOK

Strategies, Tools, and Guidance for Effective Workplace Performance

Includes CD With Ready-to-Use Assessments and Worksheets

PRESS

Harold D. Stolovitch
Erica J. Keeps

© May 2006 by the American Society for Training & Development, Harold D. Stolovitch, and Erica J. Keeps.

All rights reserved. Printed in the United States of America.

No part of this publication may be reproduced, distributed, or transmitted in any form or by any means, including photocopying, recording, or other electronic or mechanical methods, without the prior written permission of the publisher, except in the case of brief quotations embodied in critical reviews and certain other noncommercial uses permitted by copyright law. For permission requests, please refer to the Rights & Permissions section on the ASTD Online Store Website at store.astd.org or write to ASTD Rights & Permissions, Publications Department, Box 1443, Alexandria, VA 22313-2043.

ASTD Press is an internationally renowned source of insightful and practical information on workplace learning and performance topics, including training basics, evaluation and return-on-investment (ROI), instructional systems development (ISD), e-learning, leadership, and career development.

Ordering information: Books published by ASTD Press can be purchased by visiting our Website at store.astd.org or by calling 800.628.2783 or 703.683.8100.

Library of Congress Control Number: 2004116271

ISBN: 1-56286-407-6
ISBN: 978-1-56286-407-1

Acquisitions and Development Editor: Mark Morrow
Copyeditor: Christine Cotting, UpperCase Publication Services, Ltd.
Interior Design and Production: Kathleen Schaner
Cover Design: Kristi Sone
Cover Illustration: Mark Shaver

Printed by Victor Graphics, Inc., Baltimore, Maryland, www.victorgraphics.com.

Table of Contents

Preface

Isn't it amazing how seemingly inconsequential decisions and events may turn out to make monumental differences in our lives? This is equally true for organizations as for individuals. Not too long ago, one of our clients decided to run some data analyses on the relationship between tenure—how long sales associates had been in the job—and sales results. Concerned by relatively high turnover among sales associates and convinced that the longer one sells, the more one sells, senior management had decided to invest several million dollars in a "tenure program" to retain sales personnel. To verify the precise impact of tenure on sales, our client analyzed the existing sales data on the full population of 48,000 sales associates whose tenure in the position ran from three months to 45 years.

Imagine her surprise when the analysis turned up the following results: Overall, tenure accounted for only 1.6 percent of the variance in sales. After two years in the job, tenure accounted for a mere 0.8 percent of the variance. In other words, length of time in the sales job had almost no effect on sales.

Obviously amazed—everyone in the company "knew" that the longer one sold, the better one did—our client crunched the numbers several different ways, all ending up with the same results. Based on the data, the only sane conclusion was that tenure did not predict or determine sales success. With some trepidation, she apologetically presented her findings to management. Shock . . . disbelief . . . aggressive questioning . . . and a host of explanations followed. The fallout was incredibly dramatic, and now—two years later—there is an entirely different approach to performance improvement decision making in that organization. Our client has received recognition and greatly increased authority with respect to how new training and performance enhancement initiatives are selected. The organization has also made a strong commitment to metrics and data-based decision making. Overall, the company is emerging as a recognized industry leader in terms of learning and performance.

Why are we opening the *Beyond Training Ain't Performance Fieldbook* with this story? Well, for two reasons. First, we wanted to emphasize the wonderful potential that exists for you to make a huge difference to your organization by taking small, yet very vital performance consulting steps. You can powerfully affect desired outcomes beyond a default solution when performance isn't quite right by focusing on what really matters (obviously not tenure in our example), despite all the organizational lore to support traditional decision making. And second, to share with you what we have experienced—a dramatic and unexpected result from what was an almost lighthearted decision we made several years ago. At that time we responded to a conference request for proposals with a presentation submission titled "Telling Ain't Training." The session was a success. Designed for a modest audience, we ended up with more than 500 participants who sat on the floor and stood in every available space, all practically pressed cheek to jowl. It was a "happening." From that event, the initial interactive presentation evolved into workshops, books, conferences, and a host of exciting outcomes. We have received dozens of emails and letters from around the globe with reports of how the *Ain't* books have led to major changes and results in various organizations—from military and high tech, to coffeehouses, public education, and even early-childhood learning practices. We are humbled and astounded.

The lesson for all of us is not only that small decisions and actions can have powerful, unforeseen consequences. It is also that if we leverage these decisions and actions carefully, we can increase their impact even more. This realization leads us very naturally into the reason for creating this fourth *Ain't* book, the *Beyond Training Ain't Performance Fieldbook*.

The original *Training Ain't Performance* has received positive response from reviewers and reader-users. But as was true of its predecessor, *Telling Ain't Training,* a persistent theme from correspondents has been, "Thanks, but I want more. Help me and my team turn this book into something we can use to become better at human performance improvement. Give us additional practical tools we can apply in our organization."

Well, you asked for it; you got it. *Beyond Training Ain't Performance Fieldbook* is a true fieldbook because it takes you to the next level in improving workplace performance. By "you," we mean training practitioners and professionals; new or aspiring performance consultants; managers of training groups; human resource development, human resource management, organizational development/effectiveness specialists; and all managers concerned with achieving valued results from people. Even if we haven't mentioned your specialty or position, if you seek to help people attain results that you, they, and all stakeholders value, we're thinking of and writing for *you*. Step inside this *Fieldbook*. Lay aside your preconceived notions. Let's work together to achieve these bottom-line successes we all desire.

How the Book Is Structured

Speaking of working together, while we, as authors, are responsible for the contents of this *Beyond Training Ain't Performance Fieldbook,* we are also part of a team. Together we have crafted this volume as follows:

- There are 15 chapters that contain tools, techniques, guidelines, and strategies to help you apply the principles that appeared in the book *Training Ain't Performance* (published by ASTD in 2004). In most chapters, we summarize and occasionally comment on or enlarge upon principles from chapters of *Training Ain't Performance.* Most chapters end with a summary of key points and suggestions for applying content and tools.
- We use three icons that you will encounter frequently. They are

 which signals a reference to some part of *Training Ain't Performance.*

 which identifies key things you can do to transform yourself. It is an encouragement for you to try this on your own.

 which accompanies ideas for transforming your training/performance improvement group. Where you see this icon, we're suggesting an activity in which everyone can participate.

- To make this *Fieldbook* truly application oriented, we provide a CD-ROM containing electronic copies of the assessments, exercises, exhibits, figures, tables, and worksheets that appear in the book. They are in PDF format so you can display them in group presentations or print out copies for meetings, training sessions, and project work. You will need Adobe Acrobat or Acrobat Reader software to open these files. If you don't have this software, go to www.adobe.com for a free download of Acrobat Reader.

Acknowledgments

We said that the *Beyond Training Ain't Performance Fieldbook* is a team effort. Please take a moment to meet the team members. Permit us to thank them for their invaluable contributions.

Mark Morrow, ASTD Acquisitions Editor: You are the inspiration for this volume and all of the *Ain't* publications. There are editors and then there are caring, supportive, and nurturing editors. You are a special member of the latter group. We salute you.

One of the toughest jobs in bringing out a volume of this complexity belongs to the copyeditor who transforms manuscripts to publishable products. Christine Cotting is a unique editor. Tough, fair, and totally focused on the reader-user, she has guided us with firmness and caring. Thanks, Christine; while it sometimes hurts, we feel so much better for your ministrations.

Our deep and abiding thanks and respect go out to Saul Carliner, Miki Lane, and Paul Flynn who took on the onerous task of reviewing what we produced and helped us to be accurate, clear, and relevant to readers. We sincerely thank these devoted professionals whose only reward is the assurance of a sounder publication for those who turn to it.

Jennifer Papineau is our graphic, visual, and technical guide in everything we produce. Hardly a day goes by that we don't turn to her with cries for help. We write, Jennifer sees. Thank you for being the eyes of this *Fieldbook*.

Finally, we always end up with lumps in our throats and no words to express our gratitude to Samantha Greenhill. She is truly our right—and probably left—arm. We abuse her with our scrawls. She transforms them into coherent messages. With an enduring smile, a no-problem attitude, and an unfaltering devotion to a deadline, Sam makes it happen. Heartfelt thanks, Sam!

We dedicate this *Fieldbook* to three inspiring couples, six great professionals in the learning and performance world: Darryl and Jane Sink, Dana and Jim Robinson, and Miki Lane and Marilynne Malkin. Thank you for the significant contributions you have made to the field of human performance improvement and to improving our personal lives.

We love our work. We love helping individuals and organizations achieve performance successes. We love the collaborative moments we have spent together producing this *Fieldbook*. Thanks, mate!

Harold D. Stolovitch
Erica J. Keeps
Los Angeles, CA
May 2006

Chapter 1

Introduction:
Why *Beyond Training Ain't Performance?*

This introductory chapter

- ◆ emphasizes the distinction between *knowing* and *doing*
- ◆ guides you on easing yourself and your organization out of the training mentality toward a more productive performance orientation
- ◆ points out the limits to doing it on your own
- ◆ helps with the initial steps of bringing others aboard on your journey to performance
- ◆ prepares you to institutionalize what *Training Ain't Performance* recommends
- ◆ states the mission of the *Beyond Training Ain't Performance Fieldbook* and makes a "worthy" promise to you.

Training Ain't Performance opened with a case study titled "Show Me the Money." What quickly became apparent from the two characters, Melvyn and Marna, is that the former exhibited all the normal behaviors of a successful bank loan officer and Marna appeared to be a bit odd in the role. Melvyn was neat, careful, knowledgeable, motivated, and punctual, and displayed all the other attributes that most of us believe accompany workplace success. Marna was casual in her dressing, frequently late to work, had some loan defaults, and was not always available at the bank. We know this doesn't look good.

But wait. What is it that the bank wants? Is it good behavior and neat appearance or more profitable loans and higher revenues? Looking at the details of that case, of course we figure out pretty easily that Marna, with the bigger and more profitable loan portfolio, is the better performer. But in the real world, what we discover is that behavior and appearance frequently trump results. Although we know what the right answer is in a specific case, somehow we often give into appearance and what seems to be organizationally acceptable—*form* over *function*.

It Ain't Always Easy

Why is it that making things happen when we know what is right is so difficult? Several reasons:

1. **Knowing ain't doing.** How is it that we can be part of an ongoing event, know that something is wrong, and still play along? Here are two recent examples from our own experience:

   - *The scene:* Positronics, a high-tech company, is desperate to increase comprehensive solution sales. To this end it has launched a marketing and sales campaign for its new product, FlexGrowth. As a client company's needs change and grow, FlexGrowth adapts with them. The client pays only for what it needs, but Positronics builds in the potential to scale up, scale down, or move in any direction the client requires. Contracting for FlexGrowth doesn't just buy equipment and/or software; it buys the client adaptive, flexible information technology infrastructure that seamlessly and effortlessly "flexes" with the needs of the client. It offers capacity and performance without unnecessary investment, and it includes strategizing with Positronics on an ongoing basis. It sounds great, but sales are unimpressive. The company concludes that more sales training is needed. *The problem:* In our investigations we discovered that the sales representatives were not very confident that the company could deliver as advertised. FlexGrowth was not directly integrated into their sales quotas and compensation. Customers weren't getting the concept. Competition had a sharper-edged approach. So what to do? *The proposed solution:* After a lengthy survey pointing out all of these problems, and others, management's decision was to provide more training to the salesforce, even though every one of them had already been through several iterations of FlexGrowth training. It hadn't worked before, but conventional wisdom suggested that we try it again, this time with the admonition to "Do a better job. Make the training stick!"

   - *The scene:* À la Mode is a retail boutique clothing chain positioned as a buyer's total clothing consultant: "You feel so at home with our clothing consultants that you'll want to return again and again." *The problem:* Repeat business is down. Management has determined that the main reason is "lack of customer engagement" that should result in a complete quality experience. Whereas the company's proposed solution was training on quality customer engagement, our analysis clearly indicated that the concept of "quality customer engagement" was not universally understood. To some employees (even among management), it meant "a personalized, caring, empathic, conversation during the sales transaction." To others, it encompassed engagement from the moment a shopper entered the boutique until he or she left it. Another group viewed "customer engagement" as continuing beyond the time spent in the store (via phone calls, emails).

Our investigations turned up customer concerns with what they perceived as restrictive sales promotions and a less advantageous frequent-buyer program compared with that of the competition. ***The proposed solution:*** Training on quality customer engagement gained consensus, even among the retailer's training team who had demonstrated in a workshop using hypothetical cases that they knew it was not the way to go.

It's oh-so difficult to apply what we know to what we do, often despite concrete data displayed before our eyes. In this *Fieldbook* we will return to this problem many times and work on strategies and tactics to unite our perceptions with our actions—our knowing with our doing.

2. **I don't know where to start.** Who are you and how did you get here? People in your position most commonly come from another field, and you were great at what you did there. You communicated well. Suddenly, you're part of a new team, probably within the training or human resources development (HRD) group. The expectation seems to be that you will impart what you know to others. So you train. But you see that training ain't performance. You hear other people suggest applying other interventions. But which ones? And how? Or maybe you are a training professional and you're good at it. How do you step beyond the training arena? How do you avoid traipsing into other professionals' territories (for example, human resources, organizational development, organizational effectiveness, or management)? Excellent questions. And in both, or other, cases, you may be wondering what gives you the right to step in and say "no" to what your supervisors or clients believe should be done. What's your authority? Where do you begin? Once again, these are highly relevant questions and concerns.

    To reassure you, *Beyond Training Ain't Performance* is not just a fieldbook. It is also a guidebook. Many people have been in the same position as you, raising the same perplexing issues. The short answer to all of these questions is that you have one mission: to help your clients (the direct-contact people with whom you work) and your organization achieve results they value. How you do it will become increasingly clear as you work through the remaining chapters of this book.

3. **Is this something I can do on my own?** Probably not alone. You can—and we sincerely hope will—be a key driver and catalyst for transforming the organization from a training-fixated entity to one that understands the difference between virtuous activity and bottom-line results. And through your efforts, your insight, and especially the data you gather, you will help build a team to make it happen. In this *Fieldbook* we present you with exercises and "projects" to do on your own. When you have these experiences under your belt, we recommend how to work with colleagues and clients to spread the word.

4. **What do I do to bring others aboard?** By sharing ideas, cases, and successes and by easing your colleagues and clients into a new mode of thinking, you gain allies. Remember, we are here to help. We know that your work will be so much easier as you gain credibility, trust, momentum, and demonstrable performance results. Each of the succeeding chapters will provide you with ways of achieving this. Your challenge—and, in a sense, your mission—will be to demonstrate the value of this training-to-performance transformation to

   - your own managers, by achieving bottom-line results (such as higher payoff, lower costs, improved customer satisfaction)
   - your colleagues, by displaying greater impact, credibility, professional growth, and job satisfaction
   - your clients, by focusing on their issues in a rigorous, data-based manner that solves their problems in ways they value (for example, decreased error rates, increased productivity, rapid implementation of new systems, and decreased turnover)
   - your organization, by producing more thorough analyses and systemic, integrated solutions, and by achieving business objectives and goals complete with data-based evidence.

   Use the tools in this *Fieldbook* with each of these populations in mind. As you experience successes, interest will grow and more people will hop aboard the performance train.

Institutionalizing What *Training Ain't Performance* Recommends

Let's take one step backward before moving forward. Whether you are in the "training" group or HRD, you know what a hard battle you and others have fought to attain credibility and respectability in your organization. Now we seem to be asking you to leave your hard-won victories behind and proceed into new territory. Whoa! Can't we rest on our gains and just train? After all,

   - *training is what we know.* Sorry. We're delighted that you have acquired competence and confidence in training, but we also know that a single solution in a professional's toolbox is not enough to do all that's required. Training is a means, not an end. It's time to master new skills that integrate what you know and move on.
   - *it's accepted.* Thank goodness that training is accepted. We're not asking you to dump training but to put it into perspective. As you have seen in *Training Ain't Performance* and you will again encounter in this book, you build on what has been accepted. Then you go beyond training or other single interventions and create baskets of valued solutions.

- *we've fought so hard to get this far.* Great! You've accomplished one leg of the performance journey. There are still miles to go. You've rested enough, and it's time to venture forward. New performance horizons beckon.
- *everyone understands training, but the performance message is hard to explain.* This is true. But performance is nothing more than a placeholder term for what your clients and the organization desire. Don't say "performance." Instead, say, "increased sales," "greater consistency," "more integrated solutions," or any other result that has meaning for your client. These are messages they'll understand, especially if you define them in concrete terms (and with this *Fieldbook*, you will).
- *it keeps me employed.* That's short-term thinking. If results don't improve, eventually your value will decrease. Downsizing often starts in the "soft service" sectors that do not consistently show business results (that is, revenues, market penetration, cost savings). It's in your best interest to become a performance improvement professional with a string of bottom-line success stories.

As a final argument for institutionalizing *Training Ain't Performance*, you will get to make a significant, recognizable difference for individual performers, the organization, customers, sometimes society at large, and—not in the least—yourself through expanded capabilities. This is the direction in which the training world is moving anyway. Don't be the last person to become part of it.

Setting a Mission and Making a Promise

The mission of this *Fieldbook* is to make you and your organization self-sufficient as workplace learning and performance (WLP) professionals. As you step into the succeeding pages you will acquire this self-sufficiency via the

- tasks and activities in which we engage you
- tools, methods, and work guidelines we provide
- ongoing development activities we recommend
- competence and confidence you acquire as you work through the chapters
- successes you achieve and recognition you garner from all of your stakeholders.

You will institutionalize *Training Ain't Performance* as you let go of the default decisions of the past and apply what both *Training Ain't Performance* and the *Beyond Training Ain't Performance Fieldbook* recommend.

Here is our promise to you. Undertake the activities we offer you and your organization. Use or adapt our tools to your unique context. Follow the recommendations in these pages and—we promise—you will experience performance success. Take this guarantee with you as we step into the next chapter.

How the *Beyond Training Ain't Performance Fieldbook* Works

This chapter

- ◆ describes what is inside the rest of this *Fieldbook*
- ◆ provides "getting started" self-assessments for you and your organization
- ◆ sets the focus on you and your workplace learning and performance organization, underlining the importance of critical mass
- ◆ gets you started on putting this *Beyond Training Ain't Performance Fieldbook* to work.

Tools in this chapter include

- ◆ a *Training Ain't Performance* individual assessment that helps you determine the gap between your current and desired states along seven dimensions
- ◆ a *Training Ain't Performance* organizational assessment that does the same as the individual assessment, but for your group or team.

Although this volume doesn't appear very thick, it is dense with useful items for you. These include

- ◆ straightforward, friendly guidance and explanations for transitioning from training to performance. This *Fieldbook* is a coach and guide. To completely understand everything the *Fieldbook* recommends, you should have read *Training Ain't Performance* and have it close by as you proceed. If you haven't read it and don't have it at hand, halt, head over to your computer terminal and order a copy to be shipped immediately from www.astd.org. We often refer to *Training Ain't Performance*. While you're waiting, we can still advance. We do summarize key points from its chapters, usually with a few additional comments.
- ◆ a large number of tools, templates, samples, and recommendations for application. Why reinvent the wheel?

- models, examples, and step-by-step instructions for designing performance aids, environmental and emotional interventions, performance consulting tools, evaluation tools, and alternative methods for calculating return on investment beyond those presented in *Training Ain't Performance*.
- a lexicon with almost 100 human performance improvement terms and definitions.
- practical suggestions for forming a study and work group based on *Training Ain't Performance* and this *Fieldbook*.
- a CD-ROM containing electronic versions of all of the tools in this *Fieldbook*, thus making it easy to print out for reuse, group sessions, and adaptation/customization for your environment.
- a "getting started" self-assessment for you and your organization. There are two tools. Each contains a 10-point self-assessment that you and your colleagues complete at the start of this *Beyond Training Ain't Performance Fieldbook* adventure. They let you identify where you currently are and where you want to be along a series of dimensions. The same self-assessment tools are repeated at the end of the *Fieldbook* to track your progress, given all of the material you have encountered. These tools are reusable for ongoing personal and organizational monitoring.

We do have one important caution about this *Fieldbook*: Although there are 15 chapters, they are not linked in a process flow. Taken together, however, they create a mosaic that presents a comprehensive view of workplace learning and performance. Beginning with chapter 3, we generally mirror the chapters in *Training Ain't Performance*. The final two chapters enter new territory as they prepare you for ongoing growth and development. They also help you link up with external communities aimed at attaining goals similar to yours.

Assessing Yourself and Your Training Organization

You and your organization may be entering the world of human performance improvement for the first time or you may be relatively well acquainted with the concepts, principles, and methods of this professional domain. If the former case is true, you are probably known as a *training* group. If the latter is true, you are becoming in fact, if not yet in name, a *workplace learning and performance* organization. No matter what your situation, as you are starting out with this *Fieldbook* it is only appropriate that you undergo some form of initial diagnosis. The two tools that follow, both very similar, help establish your current and desired performance states.

 The first tool (Assessment 2-1: *Training Ain't Performance* Individual Evaluation) is about you. Focus only on yourself and rate where you honestly believe *you* are and where *you* would like to be on each of the seven dimensions.

The second tool (Assessment 2-2: *Training Ain't Performance* Organizational Evaluation) is about your team, group, or organization (meaning the entity in which you work and whose mandate is training, learning, development, performance, or any combination thereof). To complete this assessment, you rate *the organization's* current and desired states. We strongly urge you to complete Assessment 2-2 with the help of your workmates, clients, and/or manager(s). The more stakeholders you involve at the outset, the more readily they will be open to your influence.

When the assessments are done, carefully examine the gaps between your personal ratings of yourself and those of your organization. These gaps will raise red flags and trigger insights about yourself and your stakeholders (including colleagues). Are your patterns similar to those of your organization? If yes, then you all have a lot of work to do together. If, on the other hand, your own personal gaps are vastly different from those of the organization, you will have to proceed with dexterity and diplomacy.

If your responses are far from those of the organization, we assume that you are probably ahead of the pack or else you wouldn't be using this *Fieldbook*. Good for you, but don't let your enthusiasm create resistance reactions. Help your colleagues, clients, manager(s), and other relevant parties grow toward your position. If (rather unlikely) you are behind the organization, jump in; stick with both *Training Ain't Performance* and this *Fieldbook*. You'll soon catch up.

Each assessment measures seven dimensions. Follow the instructions below to complete each one.

When you've completed the assessments, follow the instructions for tracing the gaps. A difference of three or more points between your or the training organization's current and desired states on any dimension suggests that there is much to be done. It also indicates that this *Fieldbook* will be useful to you in creating alignments. Of course, you will also have to obtain strong commitment for change, exhibit political dexterity, and gather whatever usable support you can find.

A difference of three or more points between how you rate your desired state on any dimension and your group's desired-state rating for that dimension clearly indicates that you will have a lot of convincing to do. You will have to recruit allies, build success examples (or find credible ones to show to your stakeholders), and engage everyone in show-me practice and insightful cases that will help your organization and its clients evolve in their thinking.

As indicated earlier, both assessments are reusable. Every four to six months, use them again to monitor changes in thinking and progress. In chapter 14 we ask you to revisit the two assessments to verify whether there have been any changes since you began this venture. That reassessment should trigger in you the motivation to do this again in the not-too-distant future.

Assessment 2-1: *Training Ain't Performance* Individual Evaluation

Dimension	State A	1	2	3	4	5	6	7	8	9	10	State Z
My mission	To train learners based on client requests, stated needs, and/or organizational decisions											To build and support performance in ways all stakeholders value
How I am viewed by management and clients	Primarily as a deliverer of knowledge and skills content											Primarily as an expert and a partner in helping achieve desired, valued performance from people
Work style	Reactive; gatherer of training requests/requirements, and deliverer of instruction according to client demands											Proactive; partner-consultant helping clients define needs, and select and apply a range of interventions that build and support performance success
Products and services	Training programs and curricula; manuals and reference guides for learning											Performance gap analyses; consulting services to improve and support performance; broad range of performance support interventions; performance evaluation
Needs assessment process	Gather leader and client perceptions of training and development needs											Front-end analyses; performance discrepancy analyses; business case/return-on-investment studies
Evaluation process	Measure learner reactions to training; provide statistics on numbers trained/certified											Demonstrate bottom-line performance, business value, and return-on-investment
Accountabilities	I am measured on how well and how many I train											I am measured on my bottom-line impact—my measurable contributions to organizational goals and objectives

Assessment 2-2: *Training Ain't Performance Organizational Evaluation*

Dimension	State A	1	2	3	4	5	6	7	8	9	10	State Z
Our mission	To train learners based on client requests, stated needs, and/or organizational decisions											To build and support performance in ways all stakeholders value
How we are viewed by management and clients	Primarily as deliverers of knowledge and skills content											Primarily as experts and partners in helping achieve desired, valued performance from people
Work style	Reactive; gatherers of training requests/requirements, and deliverers of instruction according to client demands											Proactive; partner-consultants helping clients select and apply a range of interventions that build and support performance success
Products and services	Training programs and curricula; manuals and reference guides for learning											Performance gap analyses; consulting services to improve and support performance; broad range of performance support interventions; performance evaluation
Needs assessment process	Gather leader and client perceptions of training and development needs											Front-end analyses; performance discrepancy analyses; business case/return-on-investment studies
Evaluation process	Measure learner reactions to training; provide statistics on numbers trained/certified											Demonstrate bottom-line performance, business value, and return-on-investment
Accountabilities	We are measured on how well and how many we train											We are measured on our bottom-line impact—our measurable contributions to organizational goals and objectives

An Activity for You: Instructions for Using Assessment 2-1

To complete the *Training Ain't Performance* Individual Evaluation, follow these steps:

1. For each of the seven dimensions, read the descriptions at both ends of the continuum.

2. For each dimension, use two different colored pens or pencils to place an "X" on the continuum at those points you consider to be your own *current* state (one color) and your own *desired* state (second color). Be consistent. Always use the same color for *current* and the same second color for *desired*.

3. When you have placed all of your Xs in both colors, use a ruler to join all Xs in the *current* color and then join all Xs in the *desired* color. You'll have two (probably zig-zag) vertical lines. Here is an example (current = solid line; desired = dashed line):

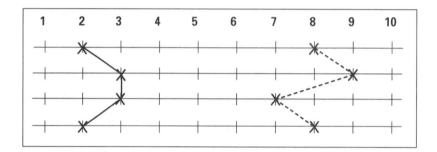

4. Note the discrepancies between the two zig-zag lines. A distance of three or more points between *desired* and *current* states on any dimension suggests that you have a lot to do to move from where you are to where you want to be.

An Activity for Your Training Organization: Instructions for Using Assessment 2-2

The instructions for completing the *Training Ain't Performance* Organizational Evaluation are very similar to those for the individual assessment. However, it is best done by a group of interested parties. Pull together fellow training team members, your manager, and, if possible, a client or two whom you regularly serve. Allow for ample discussion while making up your minds on where to place the Xs.

1. For each dimension, read the descriptions at both ends of the continuum.

2. For each dimension, use two different colored pens or pencils to place an "X" on the continuum at the point the participants believe should be the training organization's *desired* state (one color) and at the point they consider to be the training organization's *current* state (second color). Ensure consistency in the use of the two colors.

3. When all Xs have been placed in both colors, use a ruler to join the Xs in the *current* color and then join all the Xs in the *desired* color. Once more, you should end up with two irregular vertical lines. Here's an example (current = solid line; desired = dashed line):

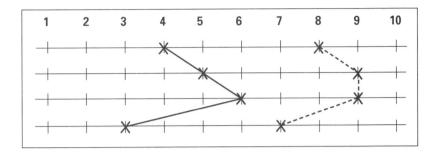

4. Note the gaps between the two zig-zag lines. A distance of three or more points between *desired* and *current* states suggests that your group (which henceforth we will refer to as the workplace learning and performance, or WLP organization) has a lot to do to move from where it is to where it would like to be.

Focusing on You and Your Workplace Learning and Performance Organization: The Importance of Critical Mass

The assessments you have just completed, although informal and based on impression and belief, are strong initial indicators of the way things probably are. They are starting points. Note the gaps—your own, those of your WLP organization, and those between you and your organization. Closing these gaps requires effort, thoughtful planning, resources, tools, and allies. Changing yourself into a human performance improvement professional while your organization remains fixated on churning out courses will only leave you frustrated. You must seek out your accomplices to make the transformation become a reality.

As you work through this *Fieldbook*, we will offer assistance and recommendations for mustering support. (You already have us as your invisible consultants.) For the moment, we have two major suggestions to make:

1. **Build your own capabilities and strengths.** If you are going to help your team/group/department grow and develop, start with yourself. Set personal goals and objectives with respect to becoming a performance professional. Learn as much as you can. Apply whatever is feasible from *Training Ain't Performance*. Above all, do all the activities we suggest. Reflect on what you accomplish. Become professionally strong.
2. **Build critical mass.** As we've said several times, seek out like-minded individuals and groups in your own and other internal departments. Show the benefits of the performance-based approach to leveraging the capabilities of people through a broad spectrum of performance interventions. Keep the focus on evolving from training order-takers to performance consultants.

As you've already seen in this chapter, we encourage you to engage others in activities, such as the organizational evaluation in Assessment 2-2. These participative activities will increase as we proceed. Get your colleagues and manager(s) involved. The more they do, the more they will learn and the more they will support you. Your critical mass will grow. Praise, reward, and reinforce all steps toward building a workplace learning and performance organization of which all can be proud.

Putting *Beyond Training Ain't Performance* to Work

The two first chapters of this *Fieldbook* have eased you into the spirit of transformation from training to performance. We've talked to you and offered you an assessment to start. Like its companion, the *Beyond Telling Ain't Training Fieldbook*, this is not a volume simply to be read. It's an activity book, a resource for you to exploit within your organization. The introduction and this chapter have led you to the beyond-training-territory borders. The next chapter puts you to work in performance country. It even teaches you the language.

Chapter Summary

This chapter did a number of things to engage you.

- ◆ You examined a brief inventory of what this *Fieldbook* has in store for you.
- ◆ You completed a personal assessment to identify what you'd like your workplace learning and performance organization to become and where it currently is. You then mapped the gaps.
- ◆ You also completed, or, more valuably, got relevant stakeholders to identify desired and current states for your workplace learning and performance organization and then noted the gaps.
- ◆ You examined the two visual portraits—yours and your organization's—of similarities and differences in perceptions. This provided you with a foundation for assessing what work needs to be done and where to start.
- ◆ Finally, you examined two challenges you must deal with: building your own "performance" strengths and fostering sufficient critical mass to effect appropriate change.

Great start! Now to work.

Working Within the Performance System

This chapter

- ◆ defines a key term for the performance professional: *system*
- ◆ defines a second key term: *human performance system*
- ◆ revisits the organizational human performance system and defines it in usable ways
- ◆ provides you with some of the most important terms in the human performance improvement language
- ◆ sends you to a glossary of terms so that you can speak and do performance improvement professionally.

Tools in this chapter include

- ◆ a checklist to help you verify that you are thinking and acting "systemically"
- ◆ an appendix glossary of human performance improvement terms to help build your workplace learning and performance professional vocabulary.

What Is a System?

We often think of a system as a way of doing things. Although that is one way of defining the term, it's not particularly helpful in the human performance improvement environment. Essentially, a *system* is a set of elements that interact with one another within a defined set of boundaries (often referred to as an *environment*) to produce a result or an output of some kind.

Here's an example: an auto engine. It has pistons, a crankshaft, various belts, and a host of diverse parts. Each element operates according to its own set of rules. But the parts also interact with one another in very different ways to produce a common result: forward or backward motion of the vehicle.

Other examples include the digestive system; a transportation system; and an orchestra comprising a musical score, a conductor, musicians, instruments, and many other elements all interacting to produce beautiful music.

Here's a quick way to see if you grasp the concept of *system*. Check off the items below that form a system:

☐ a. a nail
☐ b. a banquet
☐ c. a water heater
☐ d. a stone
☐ e. a farm
☐ f. a training session

If you checked off **b, c, e,** and **f,** you've got it! A nail and a stone are single elements. Certainly the others easily meet the system criteria.

Why is this important? Because improving human performance in the workplace usually requires a systemic way of looking at things. It is rare that you can achieve performance success through a single intervention. A *banquet* is the gathering of a large number of elements—food, utensils, menus, and decorative items. A chef preparing the banquet must think holistically, globally...systemically...if he or she is to bring it harmoniously together.

One of the rules in systems thinking is that a single element either lacking or incompatible with the other elements or the desired common result/output can decrease the efficiency and effectiveness of the end result, or even destroy it. Imagine a stew made with all the best ingredients from an excellent recipe, but either lacking salt or having too much of it. The overall result—the taste—is diminished or even destroyed.

What Is a Human Performance System?

A human performance system is composed of a large number of elements. These include the performers, managers, tasks, tools, business objectives, physical resources, work environment, culture...we could go on forever. In essence, a *human performance system* consists of all those individual elements that interact to produce "worthy" (worthwhile, valuable) accomplishments. Eliminate an element or introduce a discordant one and you can foul up the system and its results or outputs. Maintain a harmony of elements and you've got a winning formula.

Revisiting the Organizational Human Performance System

In chapter 3 of *Training Ain't Performance* (pp. 27-34), we introduced a somewhat simplified representation of a human performance system within an organization. We present it again here in Figure 3-1. We could have labeled this figure "Human Performance Improvement Country." Let's rapidly review key points of this performance portrait:

1. Each of the boxes and ovals represent important elements of an organizational human performance system. Notice that you have subsystems, such as the

Figure 3-1. An Organizational Human Performance System

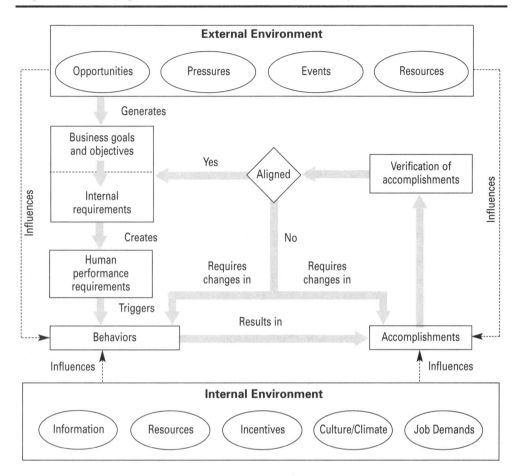

external and internal environments. We haven't shown how, within these subsystems, the various elements interact (for example, opportunities with pressures, events, and resources in the external environment) because that is not our prime focus. We've left them as independent elements that contribute to formulating business goals and objectives. Change one of these elements and the business goals and objectives can be dramatically altered.

2. The arrows suggest how the elements flow, interact, and affect other elements (for example, the behaviors of performers in the organization affect their accomplishments).

3. The entire set of elements and interactions combine to produce a common result or output: the attainment of business goals and objectives.

So this is the sandbox in which you are required to play. You have to be able to

- clearly discern and define business goals and objectives that drive any request for your assistance.
- determine in specific terms which human performance requirements may not coincide with what you are asked to do (for example, give me training).

- identify the appropriate behaviors that will most efficiently meet the human performance requirements.
- define accomplishments resulting from these behaviors, including clear success criteria and metrics.
- verify accomplishments using valid means that decision makers will find credible.
- demonstrate concretely that accomplishments successfully meet and contribute to business goals and objectives, or recommend actions to improve or alter accomplishments in the desired direction.
- perform all of the above tasks, taking into account the influences of internal and external environmental elements.

Yes, that's your job. Furthermore, you can do it. To prove this to you, we offer a case. Please keep Figure 3-1 in front of you as you work through the case. We'll give you instructions, feedback, and a checklist that you can reuse in the real world.

An Activity for You

Here is a situation facing you: The client has called you in to help her clean things up. You are a professional in what was formerly the Training Group, but has recently been renamed Workplace Learning and Performance (WLP).

Case Study—Dismal Sales at HTC

Samantha Solomon is the senior product manager for PC services at your company, High-Tech Computing (HTC), a computer and peripherals manufacturer. The new High-Availability Integrated Services (HAIS) package should be selling well. With this integrated services package, the company set goals of increasing its share of the market by 30 percent and significantly building its reputation as a high-end services provider—a critical element in its strategy to prosper in a rapidly evolving market with huge financial potential and demand.

It has taken Samantha's team almost five intensive months to sort through and pull together individual services currently being offered by HTC and its competitors. The team has carefully studied HTC's individual services; made adjustments; and bundled them into an overall, integrated, attractive PC services package. After much investigation, analysis, simulation, and argument, the team finally figured out how all the pieces fit together (for example, hardware, software, networking, communications, security, storage, and service levels). The HAIS package offers a wide choice of coverage and pricing options to customers.

Three months ago, Samantha sent out the new HAIS marketing materials, technical/reference manuals, and services and pricing options to all 400 worldwide PC services sales reps. Today, as she studies the HAIS sales figures, her mood is stormy. She anticipated 100 big-dollar sales by now. What she has is a dismal total of 15.

Samantha has summoned you to meet with her. She is firm and clear in her demand. "HAIS is not selling. Develop and deliver a solid training program and get those PC services sales reps trained. Fast! I'm thinking of a Webcast maybe or even a Webinar."

In your head a clear message of the WLP group keeps repeating itself: "Think and act systemically." Use Figure 3-1 and the following instructions to guide you in helping Samantha.

1. Begin with the external environmental elements. In the checklist below, check off those that are relevant to this case:

Opportunities	☐ A potentially big market exists out there ☐ Integrated services are in demand ☐ High-quality integrated services at a lower cost than individual services offer clients a cost saving ☐ Sales people need training
Pressures	☐ The market only wants single solutions ☐ There is probably a lot of competition for this evolving market ☐ Clients don't care about a wide choice of coverage and pricing options ☐ In a complex world, if the message isn't clean, clear, and comprehensible to the customer, you will lose his or her attention
Events	☐ The market is evolving rapidly ☐ Companies are not buying services ☐ Clients are focusing on hardware ☐ The market for high-end integrated services has expanded significantly
Resources	☐ There are not enough PC service sales reps ☐ There are many marketing and reference materials ☐ There is not enough training ☐ There are not enough potential customers

You have not been given a great deal of information in the case, so you have to make inferences. Here is how we would have responded concerning opportunities:

Opportunities	☒ A potentially big market exists out there ☒ Integrated services are in demand ☒ High-quality integrated services at a lower cost than individual services offer clients a cost saving ☐ Sales people need training

The first three items come from the case—there is a growing market and the company has set a 30 percent increase goal. Cost savings are always of interest to clients. However, sales people who need training present only an internal opportunity for a department looking to add to its training volume. It is not an external environment opportunity.

Concerning external pressure, here's what we inferred:

Pressures	☐ The market only wants single solutions
	☒ There is probably a lot of competition for this evolving market
	☐ Clients don't care about a wide choice of coverage and pricing options
	☒ In a complex world, if the message isn't clean, clear, and comprehensible to the customer, you will lose his or her attention

If a market expands, competition—especially in the technology arena—is a given. Also, confusion in highly complex matters can easily occur. If the message isn't clear, customers tune out. Nothing in the case suggests the other two items. On the contrary, selection and price are extremely important to customers.

With respect to events, here are our selections:

Events	☒ The market is evolving rapidly
	☐ Companies are not buying services
	☐ Clients are focusing on hardware
	☒ The market for high-end integrated services has expanded significantly

The case refers to the rapid evolution of the market and the potential created by high-end services expansion. There are no indications of a lack of companies buying services or of their focusing on hardware.

Concerning resources, none of the selections should be checked off. Nothing in the case indicates any lack of resources. Samantha believes training is lacking, but again this is an internal matter.

2. Based on what you have learned about Samantha's team and what they have been trying to accomplish, check off among the following items the business goals they are trying to meet:

☐ Increase market share significantly
☐ Develop trained sales reps for HAIS
☐ Establish HTC as an industry-leading high-end service provider

You probably selected "Increase market share significantly" and "Establish HTC as an industry-leading provider." These are true business goals so be sure to keep your eye on them. "Develop trained sales reps for HAIS" may be a potential means for attaining business goals, but it is not a goal in and of itself.

3. Now we turn to human performance requirements. What is it that must get done? Check your answer/s here:

☐ Train PC service sales reps to sell HAIS

☐ Ensure all 400 PC service reps have studied the marketing and reference materials

☐ Sell HAIS packages at or above target

We know you kept your eye on what is absolutely required: "Sell HAIS packages"—lots of them. That is the requirement. The others are activities that might be useful, but not required.

4. The human performance requirements generate PC sales rep behaviors and accomplishments. Which ones in each column here do you consider essential? Check them off.

Behavior	Accomplishment
☐ Define in personally meaningful terms what HAIS offers my customers	☐ Personally clear benefit message I can present convincingly to my customers
☐ Identify customers for whom HAIS is an appropriate match	☐ List of high-potential HAIS customers
☐ Develop a proposal that makes HAIS attractive to the customer	☐ A selling proposal highlighting customer benefits that are meaningful to them at an attractive price
☐ Position HAIS very competitively for the customer	☐ HAIS positioned as best in market for the customer
☐ Close the HAIS sale to the advantage of the customer, HTC, and me	☐ A profitable sale for the customer, HTC, and me

We cheated a bit here. You should have checked off all of the items. These appear to form a winning set of behaviors and accomplishments.

5. As good as the behaviors and accomplishments sound, you still have to monitor accomplishments to verify how well they are working. Which of the following indicate how well (or poorly) things are going, from a performance perspective.

☐ Our PC high-end integrated services share is steadily increasing.

☐ All of our PC service sales reps have been through the training.

☐ We are beating the competition in high-end PC integrated services threefold.

☐ The proportion of service revenues from HAIS is increasing, compared with revenues from hardware sales.

☐ Our PC service sales reps sell individual rather than integrated high-end services 70 percent of the time.

You should have checked off the following indicators:

☒ Our PC high-end integrated services share is steadily increasing.

☒ We are beating the competition in high-end PC integrated services threefold.

☒ The proportion of service revenues from HAIS is increasing, compared with revenues from hardware sales.

☒ Our PC service sales reps sell individual rather than integrated high-end services 70 percent of the time.

6. From the four checked-off indicators in number 5, which ones suggest we are aligned with the business goals and objectives? Place a Y (for yes) beside your choice/s.

    This is pretty obvious. We're sure you placed a Y beside all except "Our PC service sales reps sell individual rather than integrated high-end services 70 percent of the time." What is going on here?

7. If the indicators are all showing alignment with business goals and objectives, then you have achieved performance success. Bravo! If, despite all efforts, however, something still isn't working (for example, individual versus integrated sales) then you will have to dig deeper to uncover root causes. Here are some possibilities:

    - The commission structure favors individual sales.
    - The HAIS package is not appropriate for most customers.
    - The HAIS integration message is too complex to explain.
    - PC service sales reps are not confident that HTC can deliver as promised.
    - The benefits of HAIS are not apparent to customers.
    - Competitive service packages are better.

    You can probably find other reasons. What this suggests is that you have to analyze more deeply. Fortunately, the next chapter helps you out with this.

Summing Up the Activity

We took you through the "Dismal Sales at HTC" case for two reasons. The first reason was to make the organizational human performance system illustrated in Figure 3-1 clearer and more concrete for you. This *is* your country—where you live and work. You can take any case from your own work environment and examine it by means of this model. Doing so helps you identify all the critical elements and begin to see what has to be done to achieve performance success.

    The second reason was to give you more practice in applying the model as you focus on desired performance outcomes (by aligning behaviors and accomplishments with business goals and objectives).

You should be more confident about what your territory and your mission are, having done the "Harry's Diner" case in *Training Ain't Performance* (pp. 31-34) and the "Dismal Sales at HTC" here. This leads us to suggest an activity for your workplace learning and performance colleagues.

An Activity for Your WLP Team

Depending on the experience level of your team and the willingness of its members to evolve into true performance consultants, select either the "Harry's Diner" case from *Training Ain't Performance* or the "Dismal Sales at HTC" case you just completed and have the team work through it. Start by presenting the organizational human performance system, step by step. Then turn everyone loose on the selected case. Discuss each step to clarify major points or resolve disagreements.

At the conclusion of the case, debrief the team. Here are some useful questions to discuss:

1. As you worked through the case, was there any time when you felt like saying to the client, "Get off it. Training won't do it"? What made you feel this way?
2. Could you see for yourself what errors any of us might easily make if we were in the case situation? How might we avoid falling into conventional traps?
3. Have you ever been in a situation similar to the case, and missed the boat— did not focus on meeting business goals and objectives, but simply did what was asked? What were the consequences? If you were to do it again, what would you do differently?
4. How does using the organizational human performance system help us better understand what we have to do?

An excellent follow-up to this activity would be to select a real case from your work context and examine it in light of your case experience and discussion.

An Organizational Human Performance System Checklist

To close out this discussion of where we operate as performance professionals, here is a checklist (Worksheet 3-1) that may help you and your team stay focused. The checklist leaves space to note what you should do to be systemic and systematic in your work. Use the checklist either when a request for assistance comes to you or when you observe things "not working."

The Language Spoken in Human Performance Improvement Country

Chapter 2 of *Training Ain't Performance* (pp. 6-10) presented some key terms as a basic performance vocabulary. These terms of the trade included *behavior, accomplishment,*

Worksheet 3-1: An Organizational Human Performance System Checklist

Question	Yes	No	Actions to Be Taken
Are the business goals and objectives clearly identified and defined?	☐	☐	
Are the external factors driving the business goals and objectives clearly identified and defined?	☐	☐	
Are the human performance requirements specified?	☐	☐	
Are the performers doing what is required (expected behaviors)?	☐	☐	
Are the accomplishments of the performers being achieved as required?	☐	☐	
Are there means for validly verifying accomplishments?	☐	☐	
Are accomplishments aligned with business goals and objectives?	☐	☐	

performance, worth, value, worthy performance, valued accomplishment, and *worth analysis.* Perhaps a brief review of this fundamental vocabulary is in order. Match each term in the left-hand column below with its appropriate definition in the right-hand column. Place the number of the selected definition next to the term.

Term	Definition
_____ Accomplishment	1. A ratio of value compared with cost
_____ Behavior	2. The right price; what is expected for payment made
_____ Performance	3. The outcome of a behavior
_____ Value	4. The combination of behaviors and accomplishments is worth far more than the cost
_____ Valued accomplishment	5. Something a person does; an action in response to a stimulus
_____ Worth	6. Both the actions of a person or people and the results of the action
_____ Worth analysis	7. An analytical procedure to calculate the financial benefit for closing a gap between desired and current states
_____ Worthy performance	8. The result is viewed as desirable by all stakeholders

Here are the correct matches:

3   Accomplishment
5   Behavior
6   Performance
2   Value
8   Valued accomplishment
1   Worth
7   Worth analysis
4   Worthy performance

If you got all eight correct, you're definitely speaking the performance language. If you made errors, please review pp. 6-10 in *Training Ain't Performance*.

You now have a basic vocabulary. Advancing in Performance Country requires a more extensive mastery of the language. That's why we have included a rather extensive glossary of human performance improvement terms (Appendix A). Skip to it now. You may be surprised at some of the terms and their meanings. Check out *blended solutions, competency, learning,* and *structured on-the-job training* for starters. The more fluent you are in speaking the language of performance and using precise terminology, the more professionally at ease you and your colleagues will become as workplace learning and performance consultants.

Chapter Summary

In this chapter you covered a lot of territory:

- You defined two important concepts for performance professionals: *system* and *human performance system.*
- You revisited the organizational human performance system and then applied it to a case.
- You helped your WLP team examine the organizational human performance system model, solve a case, and then apply it to your work setting.
- You reviewed some key terms in the human performance improvement vocabulary and then came face-to-face with a glossary of WLP terms.

What a long journey this chapter has taken you on. Take a breath, relax, and then let's plunge ahead to chapter 4 and a variety of performance improvement models.

What's My Greatest Performance Block?

This chapter

- ◆ revisits Gilbert's Behavior Engineering Model, and goes beyond it
- ◆ presents other models for improving human performance to help you view the performance world from a variety of perspectives— not just ours
- ◆ guides you to apply other models to strengthen your professional skills
- ◆ concludes with a "bottom line" for investigating performance blocks.

Tools in this chapter include

- ◆ three performance models you can apply to your work
- ◆ a job aid for identifying performance blocks.

Sensitizing Your WLP Team, Management, and Clients to the World of Human Performance Improvement

Over the years we have found that the exercise we asked you to do in chapter 4 of *Training Ain't Performance*—the one titled "I would Perform Better If..." (pp. 37-41)— is one of the most effective ways to open people to the range of factors influencing workplace performance. It is a rapid means for discovering where the major performance blocks exist. To remind you, here are the basic steps in the exercise:

- ◆ First we asked if you could perform better than you are currently performing...even a little better. You answered "yes." We know this because 100 percent of the thousands of people to whom we have posed this question answered "yes."
- ◆ Then we asked, "What's holding you back?" or "Where's the block?" and we offered you six choices:

I would perform better if...

☐ 1. I knew the exact expectations of the job and had more specific job feedback and better access to information.

☐ 2. I had better tools and resources to work with.

☐ 3. I had better financial and nonfinancial incentives/consequences for doing my job.

☐ 4. I received more and better training to do my job.

☐ 5. My personal characteristics and capacities better matched the job.

☐ 6. I cared more and wanted to do my job better.

◆ Next we displayed Thomas Gilbert's Behavior Engineering Model (somewhat adapted) and showed how most people have responded to the choices. Each of the six choice numbers above corresponds to a key set of factors that affect workplace performance (see Figure 4-1).

Figure 4-1. Gilbert's Behavior Engineering Model (Adapted) with Data

	1. Information	2. Resources	3. Incentives/ Consequences
Environmental Factors 75%	35%	26%	14%
	4. Knowledge and Skills	**5. Capacity**	**6. Motivation**
Individual Factors 25%	11%	8%	6%

Basically, the exercise and model combine to demonstrate that 75 percent of the factors affecting people's performance are found in the environment and only 25 percent reside within the individual. As we pointed out, despite the potential limits and biases of self-reporting, these figures truly reflect the real world of work. Yes, 70 to 80 percent of the factors that influence workplace performance are environmental—outside of the individual. To improve performance, then, let's begin with the environment.

An Activity for Your WLP Team

Review pages 37-44, almost all of chapter 4, in *Training Ain't Performance*, and then conduct the Gilbert exercise with your team. Give each person a small sticky note on which to write the number of her or his choice (only one choice per person). Collect these and show what the results look like on a flipchart sheet (as shown in Figure 4-2).

Figure 4-2. Example of the Results of a Workplace Learning and Performance Team's Responses

	Information	Resources	Incentives
Environmental Factors 75%	40%	25%	10%
	Knowledge/Skills	Capacity	Motivation
Individual Factors 25%	10%	10%	5%

Debrief this exercise to highlight the following points (from *Training Ain't Performance*, p. 41):

- Lack of performance in the workplace is far more frequently caused by environmental factors than by individual ones.
- Nevertheless, we continue trying to fix the individual rather than the environment.
- It is cheaper and easier to fix the environment.

Ask if this has been your team members' observation in their own work. Would it really be easier to fix the environment? What would it take?

Use this exercise with client groups as well. It is a good opener to a discussion of why the default "training" solution for lack of performance seldom works as anticipated.

Beyond Gilbert's Model

Gilbert's Behavior Engineering Model is a wonderful aid to opening eyes and uncovering what affects workplace performance—pinpointing the blockages—so that people can begin to view performance more systemically. Other human performance leaders have provided us with different models for examining performance gaps. What follows are two interesting models to stimulate your thinking and practice. They are only representative of the many models that have been published, and we offer them here to expose you to a small sample of the rich variety of models available to help you deal with performance issues. In examining the ones we offer, you advance beyond *Training Ain't Performance* and strengthen your ability to help your organization attain its goals.

The PIP Model

An important name in human performance improvement (one you should use in conversation to demonstrate your knowledge of the field) is Joe Harless. As one of the pioneers in the field (and a former student of Gilbert), Harless developed his own strategy, which he labeled *PIP* (for performance improvement process). What triggered this model was the discovery he made in follow-up evaluations to training. He found that "despite the training having been well-designed in accordance with the standards..." (Dean and Ripley 1997, p. 94) and although learners performed well on tests, the skills and knowledge were not being transferred to the workplace. This prompted him to develop his PIP model, which incorporated a new process called *front-end analysis.* The model provided a foundation on which many later models have been built. Figure 4-3 presents an overview of the PIP model. Let's examine its steps and try to place it in a real-world context to help you determine how you can put it to use in your workplace.

Figure 4-3. PIP Model in Overview

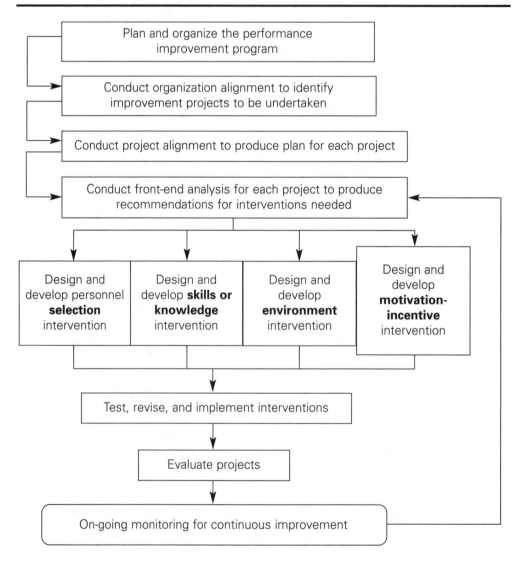

- *Plan and organize the performance improvement program.* Let's say you have received a request to train or intervene in some way. Or, you or someone else has spotted gaps between what should be (or might be) and what currently is the performance level in your organization. The analysis you conducted using the organizational human performance system in chapter 3 would be an excellent means for uncovering the gaps—the lack of alignment between business goals, objectives, and performer accomplishments. Thus, you plan and organize your performance improvement program. You obtain time, resources, and permission to proceed; gather data; and establish success criteria and metrics.

- *Conduct organization alignment to identify improvement projects to be undertaken.* Let us say you have uncovered five major gap areas. You cannot attack them all, so you have to prioritize your efforts to determine what you (or you and your team) can take on. In *Training Ain't Performance* (chapter 5, pp. 53-54), we pointed out that there are three dimensions to a performance gap:

    1. **Magnitude**—how big and all-encompassing the gap is. Is the distance between desired and actual performance very wide? Is it prevalent organization-wide or simply local?
    2. **Value**—how much the gap represents to the organization in terms of revenues, profits, or cost savings.
    3. **Urgency**—how quickly it must be resolved. What are the consequences to the organization if it isn't handled?

    Obviously, the greater these three factors, the higher the priority to close the gap. However, sometimes the organization has nonmonetary objectives. How might you deal with those?

    Harless offers a simple way of making decisions through the traditional method called *paired comparisons*. Here's how it works:

    1. Create a matrix with all the gaps labeled along the top and down the side, as in Figure 4-4.

Figure 4-4. Sample Paired Comparison Matrix

	Gap A	Gap B	Gap C	Gap D	Gap E
Gap A					
Gap B					
Gap C					
Gap D					
Gap E					

2. Darken the cell that compares each gap to itself (for example Gap A with Gap A) and all of the cells below it, as in Figure 4-5. This leaves you with empty cells that permit every gap to be compared with every other gap.

Figure 4-5. Sample Paired Companion Matrix Ready for Making Priority Comparisons

	Gap A	Gap B	Gap C	Gap D	Gap E
Gap A					
Gap B					
Gap C					
Gap D					
Gap E					

3. Start with the first cell (that is, in Figure 4-5 the cell containing an arrow). Ask, "Between Gap A and Gap B, which has the greater impact on the organization's goals and objectives?" Include clients in the decisions. Argue. Discuss. Decide. You **must** make a choice. Continue to make a decision for each cell. At the end, the matrix should look similar to the one in Figure 4-6.

Figure 4-6. Completed Paired Comparison Matrix

	Gap A	Gap B	Gap C	Gap D	Gap E
Gap A		B	A	A	A
Gap B			B	B	B
Gap C				D	C
Gap D					D
Gap E					

4. Count up the "scores" for each gap—the number of times a letter is listed as having greater impact. In the example shown in Figure 4-6, here are the scores:

Gap A = 3	Gap D = 2
Gap B = 4	Gap E = 0
Gap C = 1	

Now you have your priorities. You will start with Gap B, which has the greatest need for alignment with business goals and objectives.

+ *Conduct project alignment to produce a plan for each project.* Based on your priorities, you have identified the projects (gaps) on which to work. Now you must create a work plan for each of these projects. You may apply whatever planning process you currently use to build your timeline and identify your resource requirements.
+ *Conduct a front-end analysis (FEA) for each project to produce recommendations for interventions needed.* Harless has developed a powerful FEA methodology you can follow. Alternatively, use all of the tools in chapter 5 of *Training Ain't Performance* (pp. 47-77) to conduct your front-end analysis.
+ *Design and develop various interventions.* The front-end analysis concludes with recommendations for aligning accomplishments with organizational goals and objectives. These are all means—solutions. *Training Ain't Performance* deals with several of these means and provides guidelines for developing those interventions. *Telling Ain't Training* suggests ways to create effective skills and knowledge solutions. Chapters 6, 7, 8, and 9 of this *Fieldbook* offer additional guidance on an array of performance interventions.
+ *Test, revise, and implement interventions.* This step is self-evident. Never implement without testing and revision.
+ *Evaluate projects.* Here Harless recommends formal verification of alignment results. If you established success criteria and metrics in your front-end analyses, these will be the guideposts for evaluation. Chapter 12 of this *Fieldbook* provides guidance and job aids on evaluating results.

Before we say farewell to Harless, please examine Figure 4-7. It is part of his front-end analysis. We include it because it is one of the few published items we have found where questions are raised about a present or new business goal. Note the differences between the Diagnostic FEA and the New Performance FEA.

So we leave Harless' PIP model with you. Think about it and apply it as circumstances warrant.

We have another model to examine. When you have reviewed it, we'll recommend an activity for you and your team that will challenge you to work with the various approaches to performance improvement that you've encountered.

An Activity for You

Please revisit the "Dismal Sales at HTC" case study. We have reproduced it below for your convenience.

Case Study—Dismal Sales at HTC

Samantha Solomon is the senior product manager for PC services at your company, High-Tech Computing (HTC), a computer and peripherals manufacturer. The new High-Availability Integrated Services (HAIS) package should be selling

Figure 4-7. Summary of Front-End Analysis

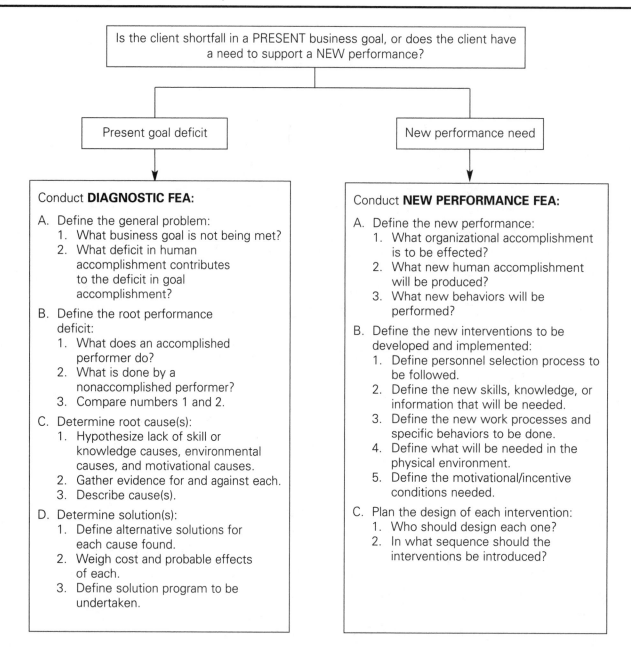

Is the client shortfall in a PRESENT business goal, or does the client have a need to support a NEW performance?

Present goal deficit

New performance need

Conduct **DIAGNOSTIC FEA:**

A. Define the general problem:
1. What business goal is not being met?
2. What deficit in human accomplishment contributes to the deficit in goal accomplishment?

B. Define the root performance deficit:
1. What does an accomplished performer do?
2. What is done by a nonaccomplished performer?
3. Compare numbers 1 and 2.

C. Determine root cause(s):
1. Hypothesize lack of skill or knowledge causes, environmental causes, and motivational causes.
2. Gather evidence for and against each.
3. Describe cause(s).

D. Determine solution(s):
1. Define alternative solutions for each cause found.
2. Weigh cost and probable effects of each.
3. Define solution program to be undertaken.

Conduct **NEW PERFORMANCE FEA:**

A. Define the new performance:
1. What organizational accomplishment is to be effected?
2. What new human accomplishment will be produced?
3. What new behaviors will be performed?

B. Define the new interventions to be developed and implemented:
1. Define personnel selection process to be followed.
2. Define the new skills, knowledge, or information that will be needed.
3. Define the new work processes and specific behaviors to be done.
4. Define what will be needed in the physical environment.
5. Define the motivational/incentive conditions needed.

C. Plan the design of each intervention:
1. Who should design each one?
2. In what sequence should the interventions be introduced?

well. With this integrated services package, the company set goals of increasing its share of the market by 30 percent and significantly building its reputation as a high-end services provider—a critical element in its strategy to prosper in a rapidly evolving market with huge financial potential and demand.

It has taken Samantha's team almost five intensive months to sort through and pull together individual services currently being offered by HTC and its competitors. The team has carefully studied HTC's individual services; made adjustments; and bundled them into an overall, integrated, attractive PC services package. After much investigation, analysis, simulation, and argument, the team finally figured out how all the pieces fit together (for example, hardware, software, networking, communications, security, storage, and service levels). The HAIS package offers a wide choice of coverage and pricing options to customers.

Three months ago, Samantha sent out the new HAIS marketing materials, technical/reference manuals, and services and pricing options to all 400 worldwide PC services sales reps. Today, as she studies the HAIS sales figures, her mood is stormy. She anticipated 100 big-dollar sales by now. What she has is a dismal total of 15.

Samantha has summoned you to meet with her. She is firm and clear in her demand. "HAIS is not selling. Develop and deliver a solid training program and get those PC services sales reps trained. Fast! I'm thinking of a Webcast maybe or even a Webinar."

Using Figure 4-7, determine whether this situation is a candidate for a Diagnostic or a New Performance FEA. Write a brief rationale for your choice in the box below. We'll meet you again when you're finished writing.

> ☐ Diagnostic FEA because _____
>
> _____
>
> _____
>
> _____
>
> ☐ New Performance FEA because _____
>
> _____
>
> _____
>
> _____

The New Performance choice appears tempting. After all, the PC service sales reps have not sold HAIS packages before. However, New Performance really refers to a very different type of performance, often involving newly designated personnel or very new roles. In our "Dismal" case study, the expectation is that PC service sales reps already sell many PC services and packages. HAIS has some new characteristics, but is still a "package to be sold" like others. In Harless' sense, new performance might include

- creation of the new position of team leader to place between managers and workers
- a new performance-consulting role—something never done before in any formal way in the organization
- establishment of an ombudsman to handle internal complaints, issues arising between the public and the organization, and whistle blowing— a radical change occasioned by the presence or threat of lawsuits.

If the performance to be required is in the planning stage, select New Performance. However, if the performance required is in the control stage once implemented, select Diagnostic.

Apply the steps of the Diagnostic FEA in Figure 4-7 to the "Dismal" case study. We realize that you can't go very far without data, but you can decide whether this Harless job aid works for you. We've applied it and found that if we actually went out and gathered evidence, it would help a great deal. We recommend that you store this valuable front-end analysis tool in your performance consulting toolbox.

An Activity for Your WLP Team

Share Figure 4-7 with your team. Show them how you applied it to the "Dismal" case. Discuss its application and requirements. Select a sample case study from your own environment and apply the front-end analysis tool as a group. Debrief the results in terms of usefulness, applicability, requirements, and shortcomings.

A Comprehensive Performance Improvement Model

Moving on from Gilbert's eye-opening Behavior Engineering Model, you can see that Harless' PIP and FEA materials help you dig more deeply into performance issues. Let's go a step farther. One of the most important milestones in the evolution of human performance improvement was the 1995 appearance of a relatively small volume—*Improving Performance: How to Manage the White Space in the Organization Chart,* written by Geary A. Rummler and Alan P. Brache. Their systemic analysis of performance profoundly influenced performance-consulting thinking. They produced a model that examines the organization as a whole and identifies key factors affecting performance at the organizational, process, and individual worker levels. Their model unites all of these levels toward a single purpose: to engineer performance success. Because this is your mission, here are two useful Rummler and Brache tools for your expanding toolbox. The first of these is displayed in Figure 4-8. Its simple title, "Nine Performance Variables," belies some deep thinking inside it.

Here's how you can use this tool. Imagine that your retail company wishes to improve sales through a very personalized approach to serving the customer. It

Figure 4-8. Rummler and Brache's Nine Performance Variables

Performance Levels	Performance Needs		
	Goals	**Design**	**Management**
Organizational Level	Organizational Goals	Organizational Design	Organizational Management
Process Level	Process Goals	Process Design	Process Management
Job/Performer Level	Job Goals	Job Design	Job Management

wants to launch its "new way of doing business" with great fanfare. As the WLP consultant for this project, you've been called in to train front-line staff and supervisors. You want to make sure that accomplishments will align with goals, so first you examine the key variables at the organizational level:

- Are the goals of the organization clear, specific, well defined, comprehensible, and feasible?
- Is the organization designed to achieve the goals? Is the organizational structure appropriate to that end? Is adequate infrastructure in place? Are resources available to support the initiative successfully?
- Is the organizational management adequate for achieving performance success? Are the right senior managers in place? Are their priorities aligned? Are they credible? Supportive?

The questions raised here are rather basic ones. Nevertheless, negative responses will certainly throw up red flags. You repeat your analysis at the process level:

- To ensure a successful performance change—from pushing our products and getting the order to a "personalized" selling and customer-handling approach—are our process goals clear? Have we specified what the outcome of our customer-handling process is/will be?
- Are our processes appropriate to the new approach? If we are to personalize our sales, will the process we currently have or have planned permit this?
- Are our processes managed in a way that facilitates a personalized approach? Do we have intermediaries (for example, invoicing, legal, and distribution service employees) who are part of the customer-handling process, but who are removed from the customer and only see him or her as an account number?

And now on to the individual job or performer level:

- Are the goals of the job and/or the performer aligned with the new approach?
- Is the job even designed to permit personalized, ongoing customer contact? (Or, perhaps when the sale is made, is the customer no longer the salesperson's responsibility?)
- Is the job/performer managed appropriately? (For example, although the new approach seeks to personalize the interaction, is the supervisor watching the clock and timing the length of each call?)

Consider applying this tool in any major performance improvement or performance change issue in your organization. It presents a highly systemic approach to examining what may be affecting the behaviors and accomplishments of the performers within your organizational human performance system.

Rummler and Brache will help you dig even more deeply through a series of questions aimed at all the major "stress points" in the human performance system. These questions can be asked at macro (large) levels within the organization or at micro levels way down inside an individual unit. Figure 4-9 presents their excellent questions in a highly visual format. All of the questions target the individual performer and the factors affecting both behaviors and accomplishments.

An Activity for You

An important mission of this *Fieldbook* is to arm you with enough of the right tools that you can build your expertise and credibility in your organization, so we urge you to review your last project. Determine what the desired and actual performance levels were, no matter what you were asked to do or what you eventually did.

Figure 4-9. Rummler and Brache's Questions Regarding Factors That Affect Human Performance

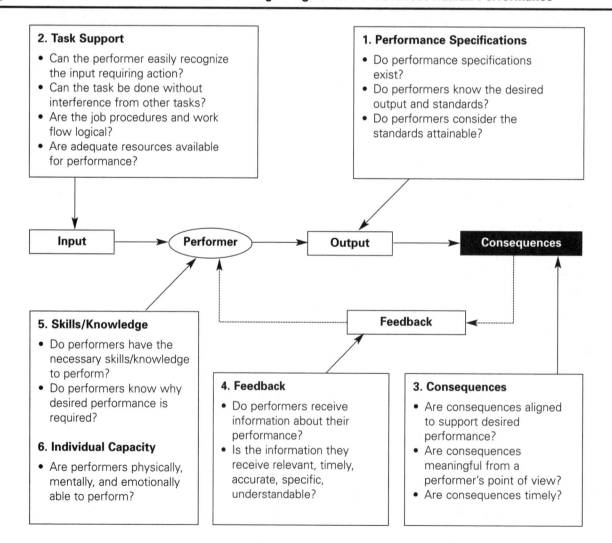

Re-analyze the project situation with fresh eyes using either or both of the Rummler and Brache tools (Figures 4-8 and 4-9). Based on your review, answer the following questions:

1. By using the tools, did I learn something new (that is, something different from or added to what I learned when I did the project)?
2. Do these tools help me approach the situation differently than before? How?
3. Now that I have these tools, would I do the project differently if I did it again? How? With what probable changes and outcomes?

An Activity for Your WLP Team

Introduce the Rummler and Brache tools to your team. Do this conceptually at first, using the explanation and descriptions we've provided in this chapter if you require them. Discuss how these tools might be applied in your work setting. Share with the team the activity you just went through employing one or both tools to your last project. Discuss implications using the three questions we posed to you. Then select a project the team has worked on in the past and do the following as a group:

*   Determine what the desired and actual performances were, no matter what the client asked for or what was actually delivered.
*   Re-analyze the project situation with fresh eyes, using either or both of the tools in Figures 4-8 and 4-9.
*   Pose the same three questions to your team that you answered in the individual activity.
*   Finally, draw conclusions about how the tools might be applied in your context.

The Bottom Line in Investigating Performance Blocks

Although we have limited ourselves to presenting only a few of the many models and tools that exist in the human performance improvement field, please realize that this is a rich, fertile domain with so much more to assist you. In chapters 14 and 15 of this *Fieldbook,* we will point you to many other resources. We stop here with those we have included so as not to create confusion for you.

What all the models and resources have in common is a systemic vision of human performance. They each endow you with means for viewing your organization and determining what factors affect desired outcomes, and what should be done to achieve accomplishments that are valued by all stakeholders.

As a performance professional, you need to broaden your skill and knowledge base continuously. To conclude, we suggest the following actions:

1. Help yourself and your team become "master craftsmen" in performance support and improvement. Like any fine craftsperson, you achieve this goal by

adding more useful tools to your professional toolbox. Apply them yourself, reflect on their utility, and share them with your team.

2. Maintain a "beyond the obvious" focus at all times. Just as was true for Alice in Wonderland, nothing is quite what it seems. Challenge—very supportively and diplomatically—the problem/solution brought to you by your clients. Never forget that training as a single solution to a performance problem is often not necessary and almost never sufficient to achieve lasting human performance results.

3. Adopt a WLP *Weltanschauung*—a way of viewing the world or a perspective on things. It's a viewpoint you and your team adopt that

   - focuses on valued accomplishments—ends and not means.
   - understands from the start that simple, one-shot solutions to complex problems don't work.
   - insists on analysis before designing and delivering interventions.
   - requires a systemic view of performance—an investigation of all likely factors that do or potentially can affect behaviors and accomplishments.

This comprehensive vision and the application of models and tools to help your organization is the true hallmark of the performance professional.

Chapter Summary

In this chapter you became acquainted with viewpoints and tools beyond those we provided in *Training Ain't Performance*. Here's how you did it:

- You reviewed the "I would perform better if..." exercise and Thomas Gilbert's Behavior Engineering Model, but with a new purpose. You prepared to use the exercise and model to show your WLP teammates, managers, and clients the importance of variables (and interventions) beyond training (skills and knowledge acquisition) that affect not only their own but others' performance.
- You studied Joe Harless' PIP model in some detail, and used some of his tools to identify and attack high-priority performance gaps.
- You applied Harless' front-end analysis job aid to the specifics of a case to determine if you should conduct a Diagnostic FEA or a New Performance FEA.
- After your introduction to Rummler and Brache's nine performance variables and their factors affecting human performance, you applied one or both of these aids to a project you had undertaken.
- You introduced these performance improvement models and tools to your team.

◆ Finally, you pulled the main points of the chapter together with what we sincerely hope is a commitment to becoming a "master craftsperson" in human performance improvement—one determined to increase the tools in your professional toolkit; keep your eye on what is needed, not simply on what is requested; and maintain a systemic worldview at all times.

Bravo! There was a lot of information in this chapter and quite a few tools. They all aimed at strengthening your holistic perception of performance. They all contribute to setting the stage for the actual operational work of engineering effective performance. That's what awaits you in chapter 5 and the chapters that follow it.

Engineering Effective Performance and Conducting Front-End Analyses

This chapter

- ◆ revisits the Engineering Effective Performance Model, focusing primarily on how your organization can benefit from it
- ◆ builds a clear link between the Engineering Effective Performance Model and your front-end analysis practices
- ◆ provides coaching notes and tips on conducting effective front-end analyses
- ◆ helps you apply the seven essential steps to a performance improvement opportunity in your organization.

Tools in this chapter include

- ◆ a job aid that provides guidelines on how to conduct a front-end analysis
- ◆ a worksheet that helps you select techniques and tools for investigating factors that affect a performance gap
- ◆ a summary worksheet that helps you pull together your findings, deficiencies, and recommended performance improvement actions
- ◆ a worksheet that helps you select appropriate economical, feasible, and acceptable performance interventions.

The Engineering Effective Performance Model

One of the most important and challenging tasks of the performance professional is to conduct front-end analyses. A medical diagnosis is probably an appropriate analogy here. If the physician can accurately pinpoint the nature of the malady and identify all influencing factors, then selecting the most suitable set of interventions is so much easier. Accurate diagnosis very significantly raises the probability of a cure. It's the same with the performance professional and front-end analysis.

In chapter 5 of *Training Ain't Performance*, we described the Engineering Effective Performance (EEP) Model in some detail (pp. 48-78). Figure 5-1 here presents the 10 steps of the model.

Figure 5-1. The 10 Steps of the Engineering Effective Performance Model

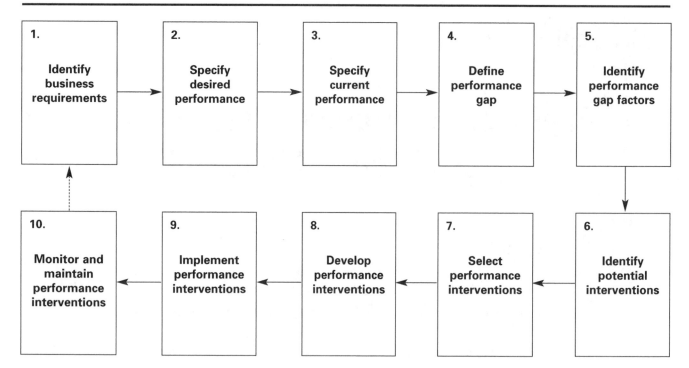

Whether you are operating in a reactive mode (that is, someone comes to you with a request for help, usually training) or proactively (that is, you initiate an intervention based on performance gaps you've spotted), you must identify the business need clearly and unambiguously. That need is the point of reference for everything that follows. So, let's begin there.

Table 5-1 presents a job aid that offers guidelines for conducting your FEA. It summarizes the detailed material for each step explained in chapter 5 of *Training Ain't Performance*, but it focuses only on the first seven steps of the model—the steps that make up the FEA process. The final three steps—intervention development, implementation, and monitoring/maintenance—are covered later in this *Fieldbook*. Table 5-1 is a useful tool for tracking FEA progress and for reminding you of what must be done.

For making your final performance intervention selections, use the matrix in Worksheet 5-2. Here are the instructions for its use:

1. List all the checked-off "Recommended Actions" from Worksheet 5-1 in the first column of the matrix—the one labeled "Interventions."

Table 5-1. Guidelines for Front-End Analysis

Step	Inputs	Key Activities	Outputs	Coaching Notes
1. Identify business requirements	• Client request and information • Existing data • Organizational changes • Information on the competition • Benchmark data • Performer comments • New business conditions • Observations	• Meet with client and/or experts: interview and clarify • Analyze data • Verify goals and objectives • Investigate, analyze, and synthesize • Verify accuracy • Observe • Review relevant documentation	• Clear, unambiguous statement of business requirements, verified and accepted by key stakeholders	• Beware initial requests. Clarify ("What triggered this request? Explain"). Verify. • Separate the business needs from frequently accompanying solution requests. • Keep your focus on the business need rather than the client want. • Verify business need and your understanding with key players to ensure accuracy.
2. Specify desired performance	• Business need • Client information • Relevant documents • Benchmark data • Results targets • Expert, customer, and/or performer information • Observations • Exemplary performer behaviors and results • Laws, regulations, contracts • Standards; quotes • Information about the competition	• Interview clients, management, and/or other key stakeholders • Review documentation • Research and analyze desired performance data • Interview/observe exemplary performers • Interview/hold focus groups with management, customers, and/or experts • Summarize findings • Synthesize desired performance findings in clear statements	• Clear, concise, and unambiguous statements of desired performance, validated by key stakeholders	• Focus on desired accomplishments first. • As required, draw out required processes and behaviors that clearly correlate with desired accomplishments. • Verify with client and major decision makers to ensure that desired performance is accurate.
3. Specify current performance	• Current/past data • Logs • Error reports • Productivity reports • Performance records • Observations of performers • Interview information	• Examine existing and past data • Review all documents, reports, and presentations on current performance • Interview performers, customers, and/or managers, as appropriate • Summarize and synthesize findings	• Clear, concise, and unambiguous statement of current performance, validated by key stakeholders	• Investigate. Don't believe what you are told. Verify current performance. • Collect data such as sales figures, work logs, revenues, and productivity figures. • Observe whenever feasible. • Verify findings to ensure currency, accuracy, and completeness.

(continued on page 46)

Table 5-1. Guidelines for Front-End Analysis (continued)

Step	Inputs	Key Activities	Outputs	Coaching Notes
4. Define performance gap	• Desired performance • Current performance • Client/organizational priorities • Cost/value information • Numbers of performers	• Determine the urgency of closing the gap (the more urgent, the higher the priority). • Determine the value of closing the gap. Calculate if numbers are available. If not, employ experts to determine/define the value. • Determine the magnitude (size) of the gap, measuring the distance between the desired performance and the current performance. • Give priority to gaps with high urgency, value, and size.	• Clear statement on the nature of the performance gap in terms of urgency, value, and size	• Defining the size of the performance gap is a collaborative venture. Review all information and data with the client. • Whenever possible, quantify value and size. • Define urgency with the client and relevant others as one of the following: critical for survival; important for achieving key goals; useful for continued success; helpful to improve current performance; not urgent.
5. Identify performance gap factors	• Data/information from all sources • Exhibit 5-1: Techniques and Tools for Investigating Factors Affecting a Performance Gap	• A critical activity in identifying performance gap factors is gathering and analyzing information on desired and current performance. Organize all gathered information into discrete categories of gap factors. Use Worksheet 5-1, Performance Gap Analysis, to assist. • Don't rely on hearsay. Make sure you obtain data or cross-validated information for each gap factor. Collect and document evidence to support each finding. • Summarize gap factors in an organized manner. • Use Exhibit 5-1 to assist you.	• Complete list of gap factors that must be addressed to eliminate or significantly decrease the performance gap	• Act as a detective. Use Worksheet 5-1 and systematically investigate each factor. • Detail your findings (evidence) for each factor and, as feasible, collect concrete evidence, such as materials, artifacts, data, documents, cases, and samples. • Summarize findings in Worksheet 5-1, and check off relevant gap factors that must be addressed.
6. Identify potential interventions	• All information and data collected in Step 5 • Worksheet 5-1	• Check off recommended actions in Worksheet 5-1 for each gap factor you determine is relevant, based on your findings. • Include all additional interventions based on findings not included in Worksheet 5-1.	• Complete list of potential interventions for closing the performance gap	• Review each gap factor you have checked off. Re-examine the findings to verify that this factor is truly relevant.

Step	Inputs	Key Activities	Outputs	Coaching Notes
6. Identify potential interventions (continued)				• Don't be concerned if there is a long list. Often, many of the recommended actions can be handled fairly simply (for example, clarify communication of expectations) or by others rather than you. • Improving performance and closing performance gaps generally require a number of combined interventions.
7. Select performance interventions	• All potential interventions • Selection criteria as described on pp. 64-65 of *Training Ain't Performance* • Worksheet 5-2, Performance Intervention Selection Matrix	• On Worksheet 5-2 list all the recommended interventions you checked off in Worksheet 5-1. • Apply the scoring system that accompanies Worksheet 5-1. • Rank-order the interventions and retain all those that are possible. (See Exhibit 5-2.)	• Set of selected performance interventions recommended for development and implementation	• Selecting performance interventions is somewhat subjective. Assign scores with client assistance. • Retain all interventions that are deemed possible. The more factors you account for, the higher the probability of performance success.

Exhibit 5-1: Techniques and Tools for Investigating Factors Affecting a Performance Gap

Technique/Tool	Advantages	Disadvantages	Sources/Targets
Existing-data analysis	• Is already available • Is factual • Is highly credible • Is generally easy to obtain • Is generally easy to investigate and report	• May require authorizations and/or technical assistance • Is static and inert; requires interpretation • Is subject to multiple interpretations • Often lacks context	• Exemplary performance data • Benchmark data • Research study data • Sales figures • Accident/incident report figures • Complaint/call-back logs • Work backlog data • Productivity figures • Revenues • Grievance reports • Error logs • Absentee data • Wastage data
Documentation analysis	• Is already available • Is accessible in hardcopy and softcopy formats • Is specific and detailed • Can be referred to repeatedly • Does not require scheduling to access	• Is time consuming to locate, sort, and review • Requires a lot of time for study • Is static and impersonal; cannot be probed • Requires considerable time to synthesize	• Research reports • Productivity reports • Company manuals • Company reports • Books • Journal articles • Examples from other departments/organizations • Industry/government reports • Grievance files • Performance reports • Minutes of meetings • Standard operating procedures and official bulletins
Survey and questionnaire	• Can be used with large samples • Is quick to distribute and administer • Is easy to tabulate and synthesize	• Generally has very low response rates • Creating clear, unambiguous items is difficult • Provides relatively superficial and often subjective data	• Experts • Managers/supervisors • Customers • Targeted performers • Groups outside the organization facing similar issues • Benchmark organizations
Observation	• Provides directly acquired data at the source • Is credible • Is relatively easy to tabulate and report	• Requires observer training • Is costly and time consuming • Is not always feasible • Prompts people to act differently • Unless sampled broadly and at different times, may not reflect the general situation	• Targeted performers • Supervisors • Customer reactions • Work transactions • Meetings
Structured interview	• Is generally easy to construct • Permits delving deeply	• Is costly and time consuming to conduct	• Management • Experts • Customers

Technique/Tool	Advantages	Disadvantages	Sources/Targets
Structured interview (continued)	• Is detailed and rich • Allows for probing • Adds context and color	• Requires some interviewer training and practice • Bias and subjectivity can intrude in questioning and responding • Is difficult to analyze and synthesize	• Supervisors • Targeted performers • Peers of targeted performers • Former performers • New hires prior to job entry • Performers quitting the job or organization
Focus group	• Is efficient, compared with interviews • Permits delving deeply • Generates synergy among participants	• Requires scheduling of 7 to 10 participants simultaneously • Subjectivity may intrude in questioning and responding • Group think (effect of a strong leader) • Difficult to analyze, synthesize, and report results of several groups	• Management • Customers • Targeted performers • Supervisors • Experts • Former performers
Performance testing	• Provides hard data • Gathered under controlled conditions • Reflects actual performance; is credible	• Can create test anxiety • Demands test validity • Can be costly and time consuming • Could incite worker negative reactions	• Targeted performers • Potential job hires

2. Score each intervention against each of the four selection criteria, using the following scoring system:

    - 4 = Perfect fit. No problem.
    - 3 = Good fit. We can make it work.
    - 2 = Okay fit, but not a great choice here. We will have to stretch.
    - 1 = Poor fit. This will require a lot of effort, and we probably should not do it.
    - 0 = Cannot be done. Eliminate this intervention.

3. When you've scored all interventions for all four criteria, total the scores across and rank-order the interventions. Retain the higher-ranking interventions, placing a checkmark in the last column of the retained row(s). The cutoff point will depend on resources, politics, and other practicalities. If there are no zeroes in an intervention, don't lose it even if it gets eliminated. You may wish to return to it later if necessary and feasible.

Involve stakeholders in making your scoring decisions. The more they participate, the greater their buy-in. Exhibit 5-2 shows an example of a completed Performance Intervention Selection Matrix.

Worksheet 5-1: Performance Gap Analysis

Question	Findings	Gap Factor	Recommended Actions
Information			

1. Are expectations clearly communicated?
— Clearly sent
— Clearly received
		☐ Lack of clarity
		  ☐ In transmission
		  ☐ In reception
			☐ Clarify communication of expectations

2. Is there any conflict over expectations? — Conflicting expectations — Conflicting priorities		☐ Conflicting expectations ☐ Conflicting priorities	☐ Resolve/eliminate expectation conflicts
3. Are expectations achievable given capabilities, resources, and constraints? — Acceptable — Attainable		☐ Expectations unacceptable ☐ Expectations unattainable	☐ Modify expectations
4. Are there adequate role models of desired performance? — Appropriate/ credible models — Accessible models		☐ Lack of appropriate models ☐ Inaccessible role models	☐ Provide role models

5. Are there performance standards?
— Clear and measurable
— Reasonable and attainable
		☐ Lack of clear, measurable performance standards
		  ☐ Unmeasurable standards
		  ☐ Unreasonable standards
			☐ Specify/modify performance standards

6. Do workers receive feedback?
— Timely
— Specific
— Confirming/corrective
— Work-related, not personal
		☐ Lack of feedback that is
		  ☐ Timely
		  ☐ Specific
		  ☐ Confirming/ corrective
		  ☐ Task-focused
			☐ Develop a feedback system

7. Do workers have access to required information?
— Easy to access
— Timely
— Accurate and up to date
— Clear and comprehensible
		☐ Lack of access to required information
		  ☐ Hard to access
		  ☐ Not timely
		  ☐ Inaccurate/out of date
		  ☐ Unclear
			☐ Provide access to required information

Question	Findings	Gap Factor	Recommended Actions
Tools and Resources			
1. Are required equipment and tools readily available? — Reliable — Efficient — Safe		☐ Equipment and/or tools unavailable ☐ Unreliable ☐ Inefficient ☐ Unsafe	☐ Provide adequate equipment and/or tools
2. Are materials and supplies available? — Quantity — Quality		☐ Lack of materials and/or supplies ☐ Quantity ☐ Quality	☐ Provide adequate materials and/or supplies
3. Is there time to perform correctly? — Amount — Timing		☐ Lack of sufficient time ☐ Amount ☐ Timing	☐ Provide sufficient time and/or scheduling
4. Are there adequate job aids, performance-support tools, and/or reference materials to facilitate performance?		☐ Lack of support materials to facilitate performance	☐ Provide job aids, performance-support systems, and/or reference materials
5. Is the environment supportive of desired performance? — Physical — Administrative — Emotional		☐ Lack of supportive environment ☐ Physical ☐ Administrative ☐ Emotional	☐ Redesign the environment
6. Is there adequate human support to monitor and encourage desired performance? — Management/ supervisory — Specialists — Co-workers		☐ Lack of human support ☐ Management/ supervisory ☐ Specialists ☐ Co-workers	☐ Provide human support
7. Are policies, processes, and/or procedures supportive of desired performance? — Available — Based on sound logic and efficient — Clear and comprehensible		☐ Lack of supportive policies, processes, and/or procedures ☐ Not available ☐ Not sound ☐ Not clear	☐ Provide/redesign supportive policies, processes, and/or procedures

(continued on page 52)

Worksheet 5-1: Performance Gap Analysis (continued)

Question	Findings	Gap Factor	Recommended Actions
Incentives/Consequences			

1. Is compensation adequate for desired performance?
— Competitive
— Fair
		☐ Inadequate compensation
		   ☐ Not competitive
		   ☐ Perceived as unfair
			☐ Adjust compensation

2. Are there appropriate financial rewards for desired performance?
— Perceived as fair
— Perceived as fairly distributed
— Efficiently administered
		☐ Lack of appropriate financial rewards
		   ☐ Unfair
		   ☐ Unfairly distributed
		   ☐ Poorly administered
			☐ Provide appropriate financial rewards

3. Are there meaningful non-pay incentives or recognition for desired performance?
— Valued by recipients
— Perceived as fair
		☐ Lack of meaningful non-pay incentives
		   ☐ Insufficient or nonexistent
		   ☐ Not valued
		   ☐ Unfair
			☐ Provide meaningful non-pay incentives or recognition

4. Do workers see a relationship between superior performance and career advancement?
— Perceived as adequate
— Perceived as fair
		☐ Lack of relationship between performance and career advancement
		   ☐ Inadequate
		   ☐ Unfair
			☐ Link career-advancement opportunities with performance

5. Are incentives and rewards scheduled appropriately?		☐ Poor timing of incentives and rewards	☐ Redesign timing of incentives and/or rewards

6. Are workers punished for performing correctly?
— By management/ supervisors
— By co-workers
— By customers
		☐ Punishment for desirable performance
		   ☐ By management
		   ☐ By co-workers
		   ☐ By customers
			☐ Eliminate punishments for desired performance

7. Are workers rewarded for performing incorrectly?
— By management
— By co-workers
— By customers
		☐ Rewards for undesirable performance
		   ☐ By management
		   ☐ By co-workers
		   ☐ By customers
			☐ Eliminate rewards for poor performance

Question	Findings	Gap Factor	Recommended Actions
Knowledge and Skills			

1. Do workers possess the essential skills and knowledge to perform adequately?
— Basic skills/knowledge
— Advanced or technical skills/ knowledge
— Skills/knowledge for specific tasks
		☐ Lack of essential skills/knowledge
		   ☐ Basic
		   ☐ Advanced/technical
		   ☐ Task-specific
			☐ Provide training

2. Are workers able to discriminate between good and poor performance?
— In others
— In themselves
		☐ Lack of discrimination between good and poor performance
		   ☐ Others
		   ☐ Self
			☐ Provide performance discrimination training with feedback

3. Are workers "fluent" and smooth in their performance?
— Speed
— Smoothness
		☐ Lack of performance fluency
		   ☐ Slow
		   ☐ Hesitant
			☐ Provide practice with feedback

4. Do workers have sufficient opportunities to apply skills and knowledge to maintain proficiency?
— Frequency
— Variety
		☐ Lack of opportunity to maintain proficiency
		   ☐ Lack of frequency
		   ☐ Lack of variety
			☐ Provide periodic practice with feedback

Capacity			

1. Do workers have the required capacity to perform correctly?
— Personal characteristics and values
— Intellectual
— Emotional
— Interpersonal
— Management/ organizational
— Physical/perceptual/ psychomotor
		☐ Lack of capacity to perform
		   ☐ Personal traits
		   ☐ Intellectual
		   ☐ Emotional
		   ☐ Interpersonal
		   ☐ Management
		   ☐ Physical
			☐ Revise selection criteria and procedures; shift personnel and/or tasks to match capacity with job requirements

(continued on page 54)

Worksheet 5-1: Performance Gap Analysis (continued)

Question	Findings	Gap Factor	Recommended Actions
Capacity (continued)			

2. Do workers possess required prerequisites to perform correctly?
— Education/training
— Technical
— Experience
		☐ Lack of prerequisites
		  ☐ Educational
		  ☐ Technical
		  ☐ Experiential
			☐ Select for prerequisites; train or provide seasoning experience

3. Do workers possess appropriate political/cultural/linguistic capacity to perform correctly?		☐ Lack of political, cultural, and/or linguistic capacity	☐ Select for appropriate political, cultural, and/or linguistic requirements

4. Do workers have personal limitations that prevent them from performing as desired?
— Family
— Health or disabilities
— Education
— Other
		☐ Personal limitations that inhibit desired performance
		  ☐ Family
		  ☐ Health or disabilities
		  ☐ Education
		  ☐ Other
			☐ Provide accommodation or resources to overcome limitations

Motivation			

1. Do workers value the required performance?
— Initially
— Over time
		☐ Lack of value for desired performance
		  ☐ Initially
		  ☐ Over time
			☐ Demonstrate value

2. Are workers confident they can perform as desired?
— Underconfident
— Overconfident
		☐ Lack of appropriate level of confidence
		  ☐ Underconfident
		  ☐ Overconfident
			☐ Provide credible models and support; provide examples of consequences arising from overconfidence

3. Do workers feel threatened in their work?
— By management/supervisors
— By co-workers
— By their work environment
		☐ Threatening work conditions
		  ☐ Management
		  ☐ Co-workers
		  ☐ Environment
			☐ Eliminate threats and threatening conditions

Question	Findings	Gap Factor	Recommended Actions
Motivation **_(continued)_**			

4. Do workers perceive that they are treated fairly?
— In work assignments
— In career advancement
— In compensation
— In hiring practices
		☐ Perceived lack of fairness
		  ☐ Work assignments
		  ☐ Career advancement
		  ☐ Equity
			☐ Eliminate discriminatory practices; demonstrate fairness and equity practices

Task Interferences			

1. Do workers perform tasks that interfere with desired performance?
— Tasks interfere
— Conditions interfere
		☐ Interferences
		  ☐ Tasks
		  ☐ Conditions
			☐ Eliminate interfering conditions; eliminate or reassign interfering tasks

External Forces			

1. Are there factors outside the workplace that affect attainment of desired performance?
— Economic
— Cultural/political/ social
— Physical
— Health-related
		☐ External factors that inhibit desired performance
		  ☐ Economic
		  ☐ Cultural/political/ social
		  ☐ Physical
		  ☐ Health-related
			☐ Counter or accommodate for external factors

2. Are there competitive factors that affect attainment of desired performance?		☐ Competitive factors	☐ Counter or accommodate for competitive factors
3. Are there events occurring that affect attainment of desired results?		☐ External events	☐ Exploit or accommodate for external events

An Activity for You

Engineering effective performance begins with a sound front-end analysis. Chapter 5 of _Training Ain't Performance_ presents a model for doing this, as well as detailed explanations and tools. What we have included in this chapter of the _Fieldbook_ adds tools to your front-end analysis repertoire. Now it's time for you to go into action. Here is what we suggest:

1. _Select a small project on which to conduct a front-end analysis._ We recommend that you select the project based on these three criteria:

   • It is relatively small and self-contained. You can readily collect information and data.

Worksheet 5-2: Performance Intervention Selection Matrix

Interventions	Selection Criteria				Total	Rank	Retain (✓)
	Appropriateness	Economics	Feasibility	Acceptability			

- It is somewhat "rich." In other words, it's not something that very obviously requires mostly training (for example, a new system no one has ever seen).
- It's for a compliant client. The client should be someone friendly, open, and cooperative. Stack the deck in favor of attaining front-end analysis success. A secondary benefit here is that you can later use the client to help sell the value of conducting FEAs to other clients.

2. *Identify the desired outcome.* Using Harless' job aid, determine whether this is a new performance FEA or a diagnostic one. If this is a first for you, we suggest starting with a diagnostic FEA.

3. *Complete the first seven steps* of the Engineering Effective Performance Model (the front-end analysis) using the tools provided in *Training Ain't Performance* and in this chapter. Be systematic and thorough. Involve your client and appropriate team members in the process and activities.

4. *Assess what works for you and where you experience difficulties.* Debrief the process and results with your client.

An Activity for Your WLP Team

Bring your team together. Share your FEA experience from the individual activity above with all team members and, if possible, with your manager. Review the process, show the tools you used, and present your findings and recommended performance interventions. Identify problems you encountered. Share the lessons you learned. Then encourage team members to undertake their own FEAs. Act as a mentor to them. This will not only provide support to your colleagues; it also will strengthen your own knowledge and skills. Make sure everything is well documented for sharing, learning, and establishing a precedent for others.

Exhibit 5-2: Sample Completed Performance Intervention Selection Matrix: Customer Service Improvement

Interventions	Selection Criteria				Total	Rank	Retain (✓)
	Appropriateness	Economics	Feasibility	Acceptability			
Elimination of task interferences	4	3	2	3	12	3	✓
Job redesign	3	1	1	3	8	4	
Environmental redesign	3	0	0	2	5	5	
Process redesign	4	4	3	3	14	2	✓
Provision of resources	4	3	4	4	15	1	✓

Chapter Summary

This chapter reviewed the Engineering Effective Performance Model from chapter 5 of *Training Ain't Performance*. It focused particularly on the first seven steps, which are the most important ones for performance consulting—the front-end analysis. In this chapter

- you reestablished the link between business needs and human performance improvement interventions.
- you stepped through a job aid that guides you to conduct thorough FEAs.
- you encountered exhibits and worksheets that guide you during the FEA process, help organize your findings and thinking, assist in decision making, and ensure documentation of what has been done.
- you undertook your own FEA with a willing client.
- you shared your FEA experience with your team.

This chapter has been a most crucial one for you as a performance professional. By conducting successful, rigorous FEAs, you set the stage for developing interventions with a high probability of success. In the next few chapters, we'll explore a number of these interventions.

Developing Learning Interventions— Systems and Models

This chapter

- ◆ reviews the definition of *intervention* and its cousins: *solutions* and *performance enhancements*
- ◆ examines some effective learning systems models from a performance perspective
- ◆ presents an information chart for each learning intervention system, which guides you in selecting and applying it
- ◆ gives you the chance to try out one (or more if you wish) of these learning intervention systems and then to help your WLP team do the same thing.

Tools in this chapter include

- ◆ information charts and job aids for developing five types of performance-based learning systems.

Interventions and Means to Eliminate Barriers

Up to this point, our focus has been on analysis—determining where the performance gaps lie, how they relate to business needs, how important it is to eliminate (or at least decrease) them, what factors affect them, and what to do about those factors. Please don't fear that the only thing you get to do is analyze, or that your clients will complain about analysis paralysis. The fact is that the front-end analysis—the diagnosis of the malady— is critical. A sloppy or hurried analysis can result in commitment to costly and not necessarily appropriate actions.

But now the call is to **action!** It's time to select and develop suitable interventions to address the performance problem. First, however, what is an intervention? In *Training Ain't Performance* (p. 110), we defined an *intervention* as "something specifically designed to bridge the gap between current and desired performance states. It can be complete unto itself or part of a basket of interventions. It is a deliberately conceived act or system that is strategically applied to produce intended performance results." The definition also included the following important point: "An intervention can also include removal of an obstacle that prevents performance from occurring."

So, for your purposes as a performance professional, you not only have to figure out what to create, but you also have to pinpoint practices, conditions, or barriers that require undoing. In some ways, eliminating time-honored practices, silo-mentalities, or "sacred cows" (usually the boss's favorite things) can be much more difficult than adding something new. Your analysis may point to the right solution (what should be done), but office politics can make the execution brutally difficult.

Speaking of *solutions*, that's a softer, friendlier way of saying *interventions* or *barrier eliminations*. If necessary, use the term *solution* or even *performance enhancement* to decrease the jargon threat. In your heart, however, know that *intervention* is what you do.

Worksheet 6-1 offers a brief list of intervention examples. To encourage your perusing them, we ask you to place a "C" beside those interventions that require you and/or others to create something and an "E" beside those that demand elimination of a performance obstacle.

Worksheet 6-1: Performance Intervention Examples—Add or Subtract?

Instructions: Place a "C" beside those interventions that require creating something and an "E" beside those that demand you eliminate something.

Performance Intervention	Create or Eliminate?
1. Training for the new salesforce	
2. Developing a job aid to identify "accredited" customers	
3. Simplifying an existing procedure	
4. Decreasing the number of steps in a procedure	
5. Removing trivial tasks	
6. Establishing selection criteria for a position	
7. Dismantling physical barriers to permit easier traffic flow	

Here are our answers: 1-C, 2-C, 3-E, 4-E, 5-E, 6-C, 7-E. In some instances, elimination of obstacles may require creation/development activities. For example, simplifying an existing procedure may require both an elimination of some wasteful elements and a rewriting of the procedure in its simplified state. The main point here is that both creating and eliminating are simply two aspects of the performance professional's intervention strategies.

Learning Interventions

In both *Training Ain't Performance* and this *Fieldbook,* we make the strong argument that there is a critical difference between training and performance. *Training* is a costly activity. *Performance* is a desired result—it's means (training) versus end (desired behavior and accomplishment). Having made our position clear, we now have to affirm that there are links between training and performance. Training is one of the many ways (that is, interventions) you can use to produce performance. It's appropriate if the main reason for lack of performance (either actual or planned) is skill or knowledge that is missing or insufficient.

Robert Mager, one of the most important pioneers in the performance field, has developed this test: "If you put a gun to their heads and they can't do it, then this is a skill and/or knowledge deficit and perhaps training is appropriate." It's not a very pretty or friendly way to discern the problem and solution, but it's highly effective! If the performer truly doesn't know how to perform, then some kind of learning intervention may be necessary.

Training Versus Learning

There is a huge difference between training and learning. Simply put, training is a stimulus—something done to trigger a desired response (that is, learning). Training is always a cost. It requires an expenditure of effort and resources. Learning is a benefit (although some learning can be viewed as a detriment if you learn the wrong things). It is the gain that results from training.

But what if we could obtain learning without training? Wouldn't it be great to get the benefit without incurring the training cost? Do you think it can be done?

☐ Yes
☐ No

The answer is overwhelmingly "yes." Training is only one of the means for triggering learning. In fact, most of what you have learned didn't result from some carefully designed program of deliberate activities administered to produce specific learning outcomes. By far, the human learner acquires most of his or her learning from life events that result in experiences. Even highly trained craftspeople reach expert levels of learned performance through practice, trial and error, reflection, experimentation, and informal feedback from many sources (for example, colleagues, managers, customers, the environment in which the process or product either works or doesn't, and most importantly from self-evaluation). Training certainly can help, as can other means for acquiring learning.

Table 6-1 lists and describes some effective and frequently used means for triggering and supporting learning beyond the classroom. We present them in overview.

Table 6-1. Learning Interventions

Intervention	Description	Examples
Learning labs	Environments equipped with a variety of resources, specifically designed to foster learning through application and practice. Learning labs usually contain computers and other audio and visual equipment, equipment needed to do a job, materials and supplies for practice, and practice exercises and cases for learners. The learning labs may be staffed with proctors to assist learners and provide feedback. Learning labs are best used for practice and for building fluency of performance. They foster a great deal of self-learning.	• Language labs for practicing conversation • Technician labs for diagnosing equipment failures and practicing repairs • Scientific labs for conducting experiments under supervised or controlled conditions • Simulation labs that mimic a wide range of actions so that learners can test principles and hypotheses, and then witness results • Computer labs in which programs on many different subjects are installed and learners operate the programs to acquire and practice skills
Simulations/simulators	Simulations are representations of real or hypothetical systems. They enable learners to acquire knowledge of the system being simulated (its elements, interactions, and rules) and skills to diagnose system problems, manipulate systems, and observe/evaluate results. Simulators are constructed pieces of equipment that resemble the real or hypothetical system and operate like the real thing. Their advantage is that they generally cost much less than real equipment and they present less risk to the learner and equipment. Simulations and simulators can be almost exact replicas in appearance and/or functioning (high fidelity) or abstract and highly simplified representations (low fidelity) of the real thing.	• Flight simulator • Supermarket simulation • Stock market simulation • Ecosystem simulation • Mock United Nations • War games • Mechanical (or computer software) simulation of the movement of planetary bodies based on Kepler's laws
Self-instruction	Structured learning on your own. Some self-instruction, whether paper based or computer based, is carefully designed. It takes the learner through a lesson step by step and provides careful, targeted practice as well as confirming or remedial feedback. Other forms of self-instruction can be more loosely constructed with only objectives to attain, resources from which to learn, instructions on what to do, and evaluation checklists. Self-instruction is effective, but not for all learners. It requires self-discipline and a willingness to take charge of the learning for it to be effective. By building in a control system to monitor learning activities, progress, and outcomes, self-instruction is an inexpensive means for achieving a certain level of learning results.	• A how-to program for hobbyist woodworkers • A continuing education program on new changes to laws for lawyers • A cookbook on making pasta dishes • A computer-based statistics course • A self-instructional program on a new line of products
Webinars	Webinars are seminars run via the Internet. Sophisticated software products and services (for example, Webex, Centra, and Interwise) make conducting classes through computer use easy and effective. Well-designed Webinars of 20 to 40 learners (sometimes many more, although this can diminish effectiveness), all in different locations, are highly interactive and participative. Webinars allow people and organizations to avoid costly, time-consuming travel. A Webinar can include print materials (sent in advance via email), still and animated visuals, complete audio (telephone or voice-over Internet protocol), whiteboards, quizzes, teamwork, and virtually anything that can be done in a classroom.	• Accounting class • Webinar on front-end analysis with case and teamwork • Management course • Problem-solving, decision-making, and planning Webinar workshop

Intervention	Description	Examples
Webcasts	This is essentially a broadcast of an event that generally has relatively high production quality. It often resembles a television show, but is delivered via the Internet. It can be viewed at the same time as the Webcast is taking place or later (recorded). In their real-time-viewing versions, Webcasts often include interaction with the geographically dispersed viewers/participants observing the Webcast on their own computer screens. A variation has groups of learners meeting in various locations for local discussion/interaction, sometimes with a facilitator on site.	• New product launch • Major initiative of an organization • Townhall meeting • Newscast format to bring everyone up to date • Panel discussion on major issues
Conferences	Conferences generally bring together large numbers of people whose interests cluster around some clearly defined central themes. Experts generally present the latest information about major points of interest for attendees. Many sessions are designed as workshops to foster learning and practice. Some include sessions aimed at building knowledge and mastery of something specific, and offer testing and certification. Most of the learning at conferences occurs informally between sessions, at social events, or in personal exchanges. The key values of a conference are the cross-pollination of ideas from diverse sectors of a specialty and the building of relationships that maintain collaborative learning exchanges after the conference event.	• Medical specialist conference • Professional conference • Trade conference • Sales conference • Parent-teacher conference • International conferences on human rights, global warming, reproductive health, poverty, or ecology
External educational programs	Beyond the organization for which one works is an endless array of learning programs. Some focus on specific themes (for example, leadership, security); colleges and universities offer educational programs on various topics; and the Learning Annex has an ever-changing catalog of nearly 8,000 adult learning opportunities. Certification programs abound in high-tech, aviation, medicine, and cookery. Many of these external educational offerings are filled with innovative designs and offer experiences that can benefit an organization. (*Note:* We took a Learning Annex course on museum displays and spent a day with display designers and taxidermists. The result: many ideas and techniques for designing multisensory learning that we've used in corporate learning programs.)	• University degree programs • Adult education programs • Specialist center education programs • Hobbyist clubs and associations • Commercially available learning opportunities • Certification programs • Organized excursions and visits • Professional/trade organization learning programs
Internet exploration	The Internet has brought a virtually limitless cornucopia of learning opportunities to anyone with access to a computer. This multi-dimensional audio-video library requires careful navigation to systematically mine its benefits. Guided exploration of themes, communities of interest, blogs, access to all the major newspapers of the world, a plethora of specialized journals (often for a fee), specialist chat rooms, museums, technology centers, online courses (even in universities halfway around the globe)—all enhance learning opportunities.	• System engineering chat room • Tours of the Louvre Museum • Exploration of technology themes • Academic investigations and sharing • Benchmark services • Online universities

The learning interventions in Table 6-1 are far from a complete listing of possibilities. They are an indicative sampling of the many options to which you as a performance professional can turn to "intervene" when knowledge and/or skills are lacking. Many of the alternatives listed are less expensive than designing, developing, and delivering a training program live or in an e-learning version. They can be selected and adapted rapidly in many cases. Others, such as simulations/simulators or Webcasts are often costly and take a long time to implement. However, there are times when these learning options are worth the investment, especially in areas of high risk or major corporate change. For example, a number of subway systems (Paris, New York, Montreal) have highly sophisticated simulators for their subway train operators. These simulators can reproduce a wide range of emergency situations and are necessary to build and maintain emergency-handling skills. The front-end analysis and return-on-investment (ROI) calculations (chapter 10 in *Training Ain't Performance*) will help you decide whether to make the investment.

An Activity for You

Select a training program in your organization with which you are familiar. Conduct an informal after-the-fact front-end analysis on the performance gap that generated this training program. Given that there was a skill/knowledge gap and that new knowledge and/or skills had to be acquired, scan the menu of entries in Table 6-1 and select one of these as an attractive alternative to whatever actually was done. Compare the existing training choice with the learning option you selected along the dimensions listed in Worksheet 6-2, Comparing Learning Interventions. For each dimension, informally decide which one is the better of the two. (*Note:* In judging individual and organizational acceptability, think not only of short-term resistance to change, but also of long-term acceptability if the intervention produces the desired results.)

Worksheet 6-2: Comparing Learning Interventions

Instructions: Check off the better choice for each dimension.

Dimension	Original Intervention	Alternative Intervention
1. Fit with the true gap between desired and current states	☐	☐
2. Cost to design, develop, implement, and deliver	☐	☐
3. Time, resources, capabilities, and overall feasibility to design, develop, implement, and deliver	☐	☐
4. Acceptability to the individual performer	☐	☐
5. Acceptability to the organization	☐	☐
6. Probable long-term benefit	☐	☐

Better choice, overall

Reasons: _____

_____

_____

_____

An Activity for Your WLP Team

With your team, conduct a discussion not only of the alternative learning interventions in Table 6-1, but also of others that your colleagues suggest. Then have the team break into subgroups (if there are enough people), choose an existing training program, and do the following:

1. Backtrack to conduct a rapid, informal front-end analysis to determine whether the original performance gap resulted from a lack of skills/knowledge.
2. If so, instruct each team to select an attractive alternative from the Table 6-1 list, augmented by their contributions.
3. Have each team use Worksheet 6-2 to compare the actual (original) training programs with their selected alternative choices.
4. Debrief the exercise, first one team at a time, then all together. Draw conclusions and suggest actions going forward.

Some Effective Learning Systems Models

Now we "up the ante," as they say in betting games. We raise the learning intervention stakes by turning our attention to whole learning systems, some of which are rarely used although they have demonstrated effectiveness. We're not certain why some beneficial systems aren't used more frequently, but our experience tells us that many people in the learning and performance world either don't know about them, don't know how to develop and implement them, or simply are fearful of rocking the boat.

The fact that you are reading this *Fieldbook* (and, we hope, doing the activities) sets you apart. You're not fearful and, with the right assistance, you are willing to try something if it appears to have a high probability of success.

Here are five (of many) learning systems that have stood the test of time and have demonstrated effectiveness. Several of these were briefly introduced in *Training Ain't Performance* (pp. 113-116): natural experience, experiential learning, and structured on-the-job training (SOJT). The other two, learner-controlled instruction and individual developmental plans, are new additions. For each of these learning systems models, we have created an information chart that can familiarize you with them and help you try them out.

Natural Experience

What is it?

- As its name suggests, this "system" is as close to the way we naturally learn as possible. The twist is that the placement and general set of natural experiences the learner will acquire are, to a large extent, planned.
- The individual learner or group of learners is placed in the natural environment. Learners become part of the work or usual participant group (for

example, railway office staff who normally process purchase requisitions from the operations workers are given hardhats, steel-tipped boots, and appropriate clothing and are placed in the "yard" or on the line to work with the regular work shifts; police are placed in shelters for the homeless for two weeks as shelter employees).

- Learning takes place in the real environment.
- The learner learns through real-life, trial-and-error events and is treated as much as possible like the real worker, inmate, victim, counterperson, or whatever role she or he is assigned—no privileges.
- To the extent possible, learners share the same conditions as the "real people" for the duration of the natural experience.

With whom can it be used?

- It is best used with people who will have to deal with those whose jobs, conditions, or backgrounds are considerably different from their own. Generally this includes managers or professionals whose work requires them to understand people with whom they'll be working or whom they'll be serving or managing.
- It is also effective for preparing personnel who will be expected to function well in new contexts or cultures.
- This can be effective as a prior step to full hiring and/or training. By spending several days or a week working in the district compound of a natural gas company, a few days in a call center, or a month in a shelter for battered victims, the learners acquire mental models of the job, conditions, and context. They decide whether the job fits them. It also provides an experiential base that makes subsequent training more meaningful.
- Natural experience is appropriate in crosstraining situations: sales personnel spend time working in the distribution center and distribution personnel spend time working with the sales group, experiencing customer interface and competitive pressures.
- Natural experience is also appropriate for management personnel who have not spent time "in the ranks" doing the front-line jobs.

For what type of content can it be used?

- It is best used to acquire "life" experiences, as opposed to technical or specialized content knowledge.
- Natural experience, as a learning intervention strategy, is best applied for acquiring knowledge of and ability to perform within unfamiliar contexts; under conditions dramatically different from those with which the learner is familiar; and frequently with people whose backgrounds, habits, and culture are very different from the known.

- This is a learning system that offers emotional dimensions. It is particularly effective where attitudes require re-examination and realignment with respect to a group of people or a work/social/cultural/linguistic/geographic context.
- The focus should be on social/cultural learning more than technical knowledge and skills acquisition although these may be acquired through natural experience (for example, learning how to adjust locomotive airbrakes while working in the railway yard; serving customers in a restaurant while learning what it is to be "in the hospitality business").
- Learners can become familiar with the language and rudiments of a job if the natural experience is an initial exposure to a position.

What are the components?

- Because natural experience is *natural*, there are few "components" required. The main component is the natural setting.
- Appropriate clothing, tools, and materials for the setting are needed.
- Adequate time is needed to enable the learner to become used to the setting and able to function at a survival level within it, and to begin performing in some useful way.
- A daily journal to record events, learning, and reflections can be helpful.

How does it work?

- The learner is assessed to ensure that he or she possesses sufficient capability (physical, mental, emotional) to benefit from the natural experience.
- The learner is provided with a set of general objectives—a purpose—for participating in the experience. This includes some form of anticipated outcomes, such as a general mental model of the environment and people operating within it, an appreciation of the realities of the environment and people, a basic set of coping skills, a set of new concepts and vocabulary terms, and possibly an enthusiasm for making a positive contribution to improve the context or for functioning positively within it.
- The environment for the natural experience is prepared to receive the learner. Co-workers and supervisors should know the primary reason why the learner is being placed in their environment.
- If necessary, the learner is briefed prior to the experience.
- The learner enters the environment and tries to function within it.
- During the experience, the learner not only acts to survive and contribute in a "natural manner," but also reflects on her or his experience there.
- At the end of the specified time period, the learner leaves the natural experience environment to return to his or her usual position, or is given additional training and returns to the natural experience setting for ongoing seasoning.

What are the advantages?

- Natural experience is the real thing and, as such, it gives learners an opportunity to deal with the world as it is.
- A dose of reality has a dramatic impact on learners. It can markedly alter attitudes and perceptions.
- This type of experience can create a clear portrait of a job or work situation for learners and thus increase the meaningfulness and effect of subsequent training.
- Natural experience requires the learner to act naturally. This permits the learner to assess whether this is the right job for her or him. It also permits the organization (or an educational institution) to determine whether a person possesses the right stuff for the work.
- The cost of designing natural experience is generally very low.

What are the disadvantages?

- It is a time-consuming means of learning. Given that a learner has to have sufficient time to orient himself or herself to new surroundings and people, adapt to these, and then try to act in a useful manner, adequate time must be allocated to make the experience worthwhile.
- If the natural experience is very different from the world that the learner knows, she or he can be traumatized by the experience, with consequent negative results.
- Both learner and receiving environment require some preparation, and this may decrease the naturalness of the experience.
- If not exploited soon afterward, the value of the natural experience fades.
- *Natural* means that there is a lack of predictability in outcomes. Negative learning may result (for example, unsafe ways of doing things, ways to get around the system, inefficient behaviors, or unproductive attitudes).

What resources are required?

- *Personnel:*
  - a performance consultant, managers and specialists to determine what the natural experience should be, its objectives, length of time, and how the experience and learner should be assessed
  - an administrative person to set up the mechanics of the experience
  - a training professional to monitor and track progress
  - a host to welcome and orient the learners.
- *Time:*
  - time to design and develop the objectives, process, and procedures for the natural experience
  - time to prepare all parties involved

- administrative and trainer time to prepare, run, and monitor the experience and the learners
- learner time
- debriefing time.

◆ *Costs:*
- minimal costs because this is a natural experience
- personnel and, in some cases, lost opportunity costs.

What are some examples?

- ◆ Internships
- ◆ Field placements
- ◆ Practica
- ◆ Assignment to a team or task force
- ◆ Temporary job placement
- ◆ Duty rotation
- ◆ Field placement prior to new-hire training.

Experiential Learning

What is it?

- ◆ This is a method or system for building learning through doing and reflection.
- ◆ Experiential learning is very similar to natural experience. However, the individual or group also participates in structured debriefing sessions.
- ◆ Not only do learners experience either the real thing or a psychologically realistic simulation, but they then reflect on the experience encountered in a structured manner, drawing conclusions or planning new courses of action.

With whom can it be used?

- ◆ Although it can be used with any learner, including young children, it is best applied in the workplace with learners who have not experienced certain events or situations, but who require such experience to better perform in their jobs (for example, new supervisors, managers who will be negotiating contracts, new instructors).
- ◆ People who know the theory of complex interactions (physical, social, or social-physical) but have never experienced the real thing can benefit from this system of learning.

For what type of content can it be used?

- ◆ It is most suited for content that involves complex interactions—mostly of a social nature (although operating equipment in an emergency context would also qualify).

- Defined content is best. Unlike natural experience in which the learner may encounter a variety of events, sometimes in random fashion, experiential learning usually works best with specified content (for example, handling an awkward negotiation or experiencing how it feels to be a disabled person traveling on a subway).
- This works well for content that fits into a professional course of study (for example, an internship or structured practicum in a hospital for a social worker) and requires real or realistic activity as well as structured reflection.

What are the components?

- Essentially there are two main components: the experiential activity and the structured debriefing.
- The experiential activity is one that is planned and designed to enable learners to engage in real-world or real-world-like situations. It can be of any duration, but usually has a defined time limit. During the activity the person gets to do what is required in real life and to feel the same emotions that the real thing would generate (for example, going to a subway station in a wheelchair and navigating from a starting point to a distant destination; preparing and delivering a lesson on a specified content topic to a group of learners).
- The structured debriefing and reflection phase is conducted by a trained and proficient facilitator who elicits from the learner what occurred, why events transpired, what the implications are, how this affects performers and performance in the real world, what conclusions can be drawn, and what changes or actions the learner will take going forward.
- Other components include journals, printed questions for reflection, and equipment/materials that are typically required for the activity.

How does it work?

- Generally a job or work requirement analysis is conducted to determine those experiences that are essential to a person's functioning well in the job. Examples of these might be counseling a poor performer, hiring the right person for a key job, presenting the organization's position at a press conference, or making critical decisions and resolving issues under high pressure or emergency conditions.
- For each identified experience, a situation is designed or is identified in the real-world context.
- The learner is placed in the activity and acts naturally.
- There may be a number of activities of variable lengths and conditions, depending on the nature of the job and/or expectation.
- At the conclusion of the activity, the learner is drawn through a structured debriefing designed to help build her or his understanding of what

occurred during the activity and what courses of action are best suited to the circumstances.

- The learner draws conclusions about his or her experiences, makes decisions about future conduct, and either continues with new experiential activities or repeats the experience for practice and additional insights.

What are the advantages?

- Compared to natural experience, the main advantages of experiential learning are shorter time requirements for each activity; greater control over process and outcomes; lower risk/threat; guided discussion and reflection on experiences, including drawing out of principles and conclusions; and ability to re-experience under controlled conditions.
- Compared with more traditional learning systems, experiential learning requires actual doing under real or realistic conditions. The affective dimension is much greater than in conventional systems. Reflection and conclusions are based on actual rather than imagined experience.
- Learning can build through a series of experiences and structured thought.
- The system is a highly engaging approach to learning and, when integrated with other systems, adds depth to the learning process.

What are the disadvantages?

- Experiential learning is not as "real" as natural experience. It's more deliberate and thought out.
- Experiential learning consumes time and resources.
- This is not a strong method for acquiring technical or other forms of declarative knowledge.
- As with natural experience, despite structured debriefings there is some uncertainty about learning outcomes.

What resources are required?
- *Personnel:*
  - an instructional designer to identify appropriate experiences and design the activities and debriefings
  - a content/subject matter expert to ensure that the activities are valid and authentic
  - an expert facilitator for the structured reflection-debriefing (this person also may be the content expert).
- *Time:*
  - experiential activities development time
  - administrative time to organize activities
  - subject matter expert and facilitator time to validate the activities and develop the debriefing questions

- learner time
- debriefing time.
- *Costs:*
  - activity and debriefing development costs
  - personnel costs for administrating and monitoring experiential learning activities.

What are some examples?

- Structured practica with debriefing sessions
- Structured and mentored internships
- Field placement with coaching
- On-the-job practice and work sessions with debriefings
- Supervised transitional work settings following training
- Practice teaching with observation/recording and debriefing.

Structured On-the-Job Training

What is it?

- SOJT is traditional on-the-job training (OJT) (apprenticeship, tutoring, mentoring) with structure built in to increase efficiency and effectiveness.
- It is a means of organizing and assisting personnel who provide OJT to help them train according to a prescribed plan.
- It is a method to ensure consistency in receiving OJT experiences, regardless of where or with whom the trainee is placed. This is a key characteristic of SOJT.
- SOJT provides a system with generic models for OJT for various positions, but it allows for adaptation to individual locations and trainees—structure plus flexibility.
- SOJT gives employee-trainees an overall view of the job as defined by the tasks that compose it. In this respect, SOJT is both organized and comprehensive.
- SOJT includes a means not only for structuring OJT experiences, but also for evaluating trainee progress and trainer effectiveness. A well-planned SOJT system includes trainee self-evaluations, trainer evaluations of trainee performance, and more formal mechanisms for certifying performance capability.

With whom can it be used?

- It is applicable to any training population.
- It is most frequently used with nonmanagement and lower-level supervisory personnel and specialists (for example, cashiers, counterpeople, salespeople, account representatives, and plant workers).

- SOJT is often used with entry-level positions where volume and/or turnover is high or where only one person or very few people require training at the same time.

For what type of content can it be used?

- It is typically used for well-designed procedural and technical tasks, and not for tasks at higher decision-making, problem-solving levels.
- It is particularly useful with skills/knowledge that can be easily demonstrated by master performer employees (for example, filling out orders, taking inventory, tracking shipments, or handling cash).

What are the components?

- SOJT requires a series of task listings for each position, organized by major area of responsibility, usually in the form of checklists.
- Frequently there is a manager's guide explaining how to organize an SOJT plan (including how to make local adaptations), monitor its implementation, and evaluate progress.
- There is always a trainer's manual containing guidelines on effective SOJT techniques, instruction on how to use the task lists as a training mechanism, and methods for guiding and evaluating the trainee. The model used most often is one based on "teach-prompt-release."
- There is also always a trainee manual that defines the job in terms of responsibilities and tasks and helps monitor personal progress. This guide also explains the role and responsibilities of the trainee as a learner. Usually this trainee's guide contains a progress map or chart.

How does it work?

- The manager, with trainee assistance, creates a training plan based on job needs and trainee background and experience, using the generic task lists for the job. The manager customizes these task lists to meet local needs. A performance professional and/or instructional designer can be very helpful here.
- The manager assigns specific experienced employees to act as structured on-the-job trainers for the various parts of the plan. Generally the selected experienced employees receive some form of training to prepare them to deliver the structured training.
- The manager distributes manuals and appropriate task lists to trainers.
- The manager orients the trainee to the training system, introduces him or her to the trainers, and explains both the trainee's role in the process and the manager's expectations. The manager also gives the trainee a structured OJT learning guide and progress checklist.

- The trainee follows the training plan, moving from trainer to trainer until she or he demonstrates competency in all SOJT tasks. The trainee self-evaluates. The SOJT trainers also evaluate trainee performance using evaluation checklists, and they provide feedback to the trainee.
- The trainee and manager meet to review training experiences and evaluate readiness for permanent job assignment. This step may include a formal certifying of performance capability.

What are the advantages?

- SOJT is extremely flexible and is easily adapted to local circumstances.
- This training can be implemented at any time with any number of employees.
- This system is similar enough to traditional OJT to be easily accepted by managers, experienced employees, and trainees.
- The structure increases consistency of OJT from trainee to trainee.
- The system makes OJT more efficient.
- The trainee remains on the job during training, thus reducing costs.
- The generic task lists help managers create basic plans that allow for adaptation.
- Training in this system is the job itself.
- Trainees interact and work with a number of employees who serve as role models.
- Trainees obtain an overall sense of the job in a structured manner.
- The system enables the manager to assess trainee strengths and weaknesses in a structured fashion.
- Design and production costs of training materials are relatively low, compared with most other training methods.

What are the disadvantages?

- It requires thorough job analyses for all SOJT positions.
- It requires careful and systematic pilot-testing prior to implementation.
- It requires involving a number of personnel to perform training and management tasks, thus causing a bit of a personnel drain.
- Because it is entirely local in its administration, it is difficult to track and control. (In some instances, however, the WLP group can become involved and build in tracking mechanisms.)
- Its application is limited to situations in which master performers are on location and available to train.

What resources are required?

- *Personnel:*
  - competent SOJT designers
  - managers to help with job analyses and monitor trainee progress
  - master performer employees to act as SOJT trainers.

- *Time:*
  - lengthy job analysis time
  - adequate lead time to validate each SOJT "package"
  - manager and trainer-employee time
  - trainee learning time.
- *Costs:*
  - heavy analysis and validation costs
  - minimal production costs
  - minimal delivery costs
  - manager, trainer, and trainee salaries, plus lost opportunity costs for SOJT trainers whose work may suffer as a result of trainee-guidance responsibilities.

What are some examples?

- Training in a manufacturing setting that receives only a few new hires each year
- Call centers that continuously receive new hires
- Supermarkets that continuously receive part-time employees
- Distribution center workers who are occasionally brought onboard
- Fast-food operations.

Learner-Controlled Instruction

What is it?

- Learner-controlled instruction (LCI) is a learning system and a strategy that shifts power from instructor to learner. In contrast to traditional training systems where the instructor establishes the content, controls the sequences, selects the media and presentation mechanisms, and assumes responsibility for evaluating learning achievement, in LCI the power and control over these factors and the responsibility for learning are delegated to the learner.
- This is a system in which the individual learner/trainee selects from a variety of resources to acquire skills/knowledge and to demonstrate competence.
- Although learners control the pacing, sequencing, and choice of learning resources, delegation of instructional control is constrained by three factors:

  1. the variety of content and informational sources made available
  2. a designer, with expert input, who states the objectives that the learner must achieve
  3. tools for measuring knowledge/skill acquisition that are created by people experienced in the content areas with the assistance of learning, performance, or evaluation professionals.

With whom can it be used?

- LCI is best applied to professional, supervisory, and management positions (for example, retail store managers, sales and insurance representatives, general managers).
- It works best with autonomous learners who have some measure of control over decision making in their jobs (it's not good for training infantry foot soldiers or performers of repetitive tasks).
- It is particularly useful for geographically dispersed populations.
- LCI has advantages with heterogeneous populations—people who come into a job position with very diverse mastery levels.
- One of the major virtues of LCI is that it accommodates trainees entering at any time—no groups or classes are required (although classes on a particular relevant topic can be included as resources for learning).
- It is often used with learners who will be assigned to a location other than where they are learning the job.

For what type of content can it be used?

- LCI is best used for higher-level skills, particularly those in which decision making plays a major role.
- It is very appropriate for management and professional practice content.

What are the components?

- LCI requires a set of overall objectives.
- A set of detailed specific performance objectives for which the learner must demonstrate mastery at the end of training is also needed. Often there is a "review board" that verifies this mastery.
- For each specific objective, LCI provides one or more learning experiences consisting of
  - the objective
  - a description of the activity
  - a measurement device for assessing proficiency (both by the learner and by a qualified third party)
  - a standard of acceptable performance
  - a description of learning resources
  - a time plan for accomplishing the learning.
- An administrative manual for the trainee is needed to explain how the system works.
- A "box" of resources (for example, training booklets, procedural write-ups, articles, videos, audiotapes, online courses, Websites to visit, a case database) should be provided.

- A real-world environment (for example, a training electronics dealership) in which the learner completes the learning activities and demonstrates competencies should be provided. In many cases, certain locations are identified as exemplary or training locations. The manager and key staff in those locations are trained to facilitate LCI and to act as mentors or guides.
- A management system is required for tracking and monitoring learner progress and environmental constraints.
- There should be a system for providing assistance and reinforcement contact to trainees.
- An evaluation system is required for certifying that the learner has mastered all the tasks and can either assume the assigned role or receive further seasoning prior to final assignment.

How does LCI work?

- Trainees go through a preassessment to determine their learning needs.
- Based on individual learning needs, the trainee selects specific learning objectives to complete and schedules their completion.
- The trainee consults with a training administrator to verify and adjust the training plan. In some cases there is a local mentor who assists.
- The learner completes each appropriate learning experience related to the objective, accessing appropriate resources, demonstrating and assessing his or her skill, and accessing additional resources for remediation as appropriate.
- Skill levels are determined through self-assessment, environmental feedback, and/or expert verification, often via a local mentor. Learners collect evidence of results.
- Periodically the training administrator meets with the learner to monitor progress and deal with environmental constraints or identify additional learning resources.
- The learner, usually with the help of a mentor, determines when she or he is ready to be a "candidate for graduation" based on her or his assessment of learning progress and the assessment of the mentor. The training administrator consults with the learner and others on readiness.
- A team of appropriate people capable of assessing the learner's competency is assembled and drills the candidate, using prepared guidelines. The purpose of this drill is to determine whether the learner is ready to move to an operational position.
- Successful candidates graduate and become available for the job for which they have trained.
- Unsuccessful candidates or those requiring more seasoning are required to engage in further learning activities until ready for re-examination.

What are the advantages?

- The LCI system is extremely efficient because the focus is on results rather than learning activities. Learners can progress very rapidly (for example, one company reduced learning time from 52 weeks of OJT to, on average, 6 weeks of LCI).
- There is no waiting for classes because the learner operates independently and can begin training at any time.
- Learning can be conducted anywhere there is access to a real-world environment. Learning activities can include taking field trips, analyzing competitive practices, reading, practicing, attending courses, or even performing operational tasks.
- Training focuses only on what is needed for each individual.
- Training is very close to the job itself.
- The system does not drain personnel resources because these are tapped only as needed.
- The trainee learns to select his or her own resources, manage time, evaluate personal results through concrete evidence, and determine readiness to terminate training (often with consultation)—all of which leads to developing an autonomous self-starter. The process of LCI, in addition to the content, helps build independent managers and professionals.
- The training environment benefits from what the trainee learns about it and what she or he can contribute to improve it.

What are the disadvantages?

- A well-functioning LCI program requires people skilled at designing such a system, and lengthy design time.
- It requires a broad variety of resources.
- It demands careful and systematic testing and validation of the system.
- There must be total buy-in by all levels of management. Independent learners, even when placed in a planned environment, can cause some fear among those not used to "learner control."
- LCI often results in nonautonomous candidates washing out early (which may also be an advantage).

What resources are required?

- *Personnel:*
  - competent LCI designer
  - training administrators who track learner progress
  - people within the training environment to act as resources and evaluators
  - additional people to constitute evaluation teams.
- *Time:*
  - lengthy job analysis and considerable design time

- adequate lead time to validate the system
- learner time, during which learners are removed from their own immediate work environments and job responsibilities to pursue training (an average LCI program runs 6 to 12 weeks, but usually is shorter than traditional learning systems).
- *Costs:*
  - heavy analysis, design, and validation costs
  - minimal production and delivery costs
  - costs for resources and materials
  - personnel salaries and lost opportunity costs.

What are some examples?

- Supermarket manager program
- Mega-bookstore manager program
- Buyer training program for a fashion store chain
- Patent analyst program for a government agency
- Project manager development program to transform high-tech specialists into project managers.

Individual Development Plan

What is it?

- An individual development plan (IDP) is an organized and detailed training and learning plan.
- There are two major types of IDPs, each one very different from the other:
  - In a person-oriented IDP, an individual is assessed in terms of his or her career potential, diagnosed for training and development needs, and prescribed a customized plan generally containing two or three areas for development per year. The purpose is to build performance capability continuously in a person deemed able to steadily increase her or his value to the organization.
  - A position-oriented IDP is based on an analysis of the skills, knowledge, experiences, and attitudes required for a specific position. People selected for the position are provided with an array of competencies they should acquire, activities they should participate in, and resources that are available. The IDP is adjusted to the background and characteristics of the individual. The purpose in this instance is to enhance performance capabilities until each person in the targeted position is fully functional and capable of peak performance.
- With an IDP created for a specific person, that person is almost entirely accountable for executing the plan, although there is some sharing of responsibility with the supervisor and, in some cases, a performance professional.

- In the person-oriented IDP, planning generally covers a period equal to a full performance appraisal cycle (for example, one year). In the position-oriented case, timelines are negotiated.
- In all cases the IDP is a carefully conceived and documented plan that guides the individual through a series of learning experiences that result in increased competencies and confidence to perform.

With whom can it be used?

- Although it can be used with any population, it is generally used for training and development of management or key professional personnel.
- It is especially useful for one-of-a-kind positions (such as chief executive officer, vice president of advertising, general manager, senior project director, or performance consultant).

For what type of content can it be used?

- IDP can include content for any aspect of a job for which resources (including people, documents, and events) can be identified and accessed by the individual (for example, creating displays, analyzing turnover, and handling employee grievances).
- In the person-oriented IDP, management topics (such as time and stress management or making presentations) or personal growth skill areas (such as leadership or interpersonal skills) are likely to be included.
- The position-oriented IDP tends to focus more on training content (for example, front-end analysis, evaluation); the person-oriented one essentially leans toward development topics that lead to directly applicable performance.

What are the components?

- *Person-oriented IDP:*
  - a manager's guide explaining her or his role in creating IDPs for employees and how to do it
  - an employee's guide explaining his or her role and responsibility in developing and carrying out the IDP
  - a set of IDP forms or worksheets for documenting the plan
  - resource lists (such as company course catalog, organization charts)
  - a means for verifying performance capability.
- *Position-oriented IDP:*
  - a manager's guide explaining her or his role in adapting a generic IDP model to individual needs/characteristics and organizational requirements
  - an employee's guide that explains his or her role and responsibilities in adapting the generic IDP and in carrying it out

- generic IDP models for specific job positions that include
  — areas of responsibility
  — learning experiences that relate to each area of responsibility
  — resources that relate to each area of responsibility
  — recommended/average learning time for each area of responsibility
  — spaces for making adaptations, entering specific timelines, and adding additional relevant resources
  — some means for verifying or demonstrating performance capability.

How does it work?

- *Person-oriented IDP:*
  - During the appraisal or assessment process, specific development areas are identified jointly by manager and employee.
  - Following procedures from the manager's guide, the manager creates an IDP for the employee with the employee's input and agreement. Performance professionals can assist here.
  - Specific checkpoints or milestones are established.
  - The employee executes the plan with the manager's support.
  - At established checkpoints, the manager and employee meet to evaluate progress and make needed adaptations.
  - At the end of the appraisal or some other specific period, both the employee and manager critique the end result and determine if development in prescribed areas is sufficient or if further work is required. It is useful to have data or artifacts that provide evidence of performance capability.
  - A new IDP is developed for the individual, which may or may not contain elements of the previous plan.
- *Position-oriented IDP:*
  - Upon appointment to the position (or when promotion to a position has been decided), the manager and employee meet to discuss the IDP strategy, adapt the generic plan, establish timelines, and add resources.
  - The employee executes the plan and issues periodic (for example, monthly) progress reports to the manager. These include evidence of performance capability.
  - The employee and manager meet as needed to adapt the plan, make other required resources available, and interact as trainee and resource person/subject matter expert. This process continues until all areas of responsibility in the plan have been accomplished and performance capability concretely documented.
  - At completion of the IDP, the employee and manager meet to debrief and evaluate performance to date. An outcome of this meeting may be a prescription for additional development in particular areas.

What are the advantages?

- Both types of the IDPs focus specifically on individual development needs. There is very little extraneous activity in the plan. It is a tailored, customized plan.
- Manager and employee monitor progress closely. They have opportunities to interact productively, which helps develop their relationship.
- Activities and resources are job related and rarely involve travel, except for specifically selected events (such as a seminar or conference, an off-site visit, or lunch with a specialist).
- The employee learns while performing on the job.
- There is room for adjustment along the way.
- In the person-oriented IDP, every employee reporting to a manager can be working simultaneously on his or her own IDP.
- In the position-oriented IDP, there is no lag time between job entry and training, so unproductive startup time is reduced.
- Because the IDP is created with both the individual's characteristics and the organization's needs in mind, all activities are relevant.
- Other than occasional consultation and assistance from a performance professional or human resource specialist, the training and development of the individual resides essentially with the employee and manager.
- The IDP is performance based and evidence driven.

What are the disadvantages?

- Because it is individualized, some of the peer sharing that occurs in group training is not present.
- It is a long-term training and development strategy, and does not respond to immediate skill/knowledge needs when something urgent occurs.
- The content and activities of the IDP components are not as structured as in a usual training program. Self-selection of experiences can lead to omissions.
- It does not work well with employees who are not self-starters or who are constantly overworked.
- It is demanding of a manager's time—particularly with the position-oriented IDP.
- Because employees perform on the job while carrying out their IDPs, task interference can occur and prevent on-time plan completion.
- There are no formal testing components to measure true competency attainment. The bottom line is the performance outcome.

What resources are required?
- *Personnel:*
  - competent IDP developers and job analysts (for position-oriented IDPs) to define the key behaviors and accomplishments required of the position

- manager or, in the case of senior managers or executives, a personal coach or counselor
- learner-employee
- some human resource department or performance professional assistance.
- *Time:*
  - fairly heavy IDP system development time
  - heavy job analysis, and activity and resource identification time
  - manager and trainee time—a commitment to a predetermined number of employee days is essential.
- *Costs:*
  - relatively high IDP system development costs
  - relatively high job analysis, and activity and resource identification costs
  - manager, coach, counselor, and employee-trainee salary costs
  - resource costs (for example, attendance at seminars, off-site visits, book purchases).

What are some examples?

- An IDP for the new head of the legal department who has not had industry experience
- An IDP for a new Supreme Court justice who has never been a judge
- IDPs for performance consultants transitioning from essentially training-driven environments
- A highly individualized plan for a marketing executive promoted to the senior management team
- IDPs for business consultants coming from industry into a government agency.

Summarizing Learning Systems

All of the preceding learning systems have their place in the ever-expanding toolkit of the performance professional. We have found variations of all of these in many of the workplace settings we've visited over the years. Only rarely, however, have we found enlightened WLP teams with repertoires of learning systems from which they systematically make appropriate selections to match a given performance need.

To close this discussion of learning systems, Table 6-2, A Comparison of Learning Systems, synthesizes what we have presented. Review it and use the table when you select and implement an appropriate, effective learning system for your next project.

An Activity for You

Select one of the learning systems and deepen your knowledge of it. We provide some relevant resources as a starting point at the back of this *Fieldbook*. Hunt for others on your own. Also try to find people and organizations that have applied the system you've

Table 6-2. A Comparison of Learning Systems

Learning System	Used with Individuals	Used with Groups	Expertise Required for Design	Expertise Required for Delivery	Cost	Time Requirement for Learner	Short- or Long-Term Performance Outcomes
Natural experience	X	X	Moderate	Low	Low	Long	Long-term
Experiential learning	X	X	High	Moderate	Moderate	Medium	Long-term (some short-term)
Structured on-the-job training	X		Moderate	Moderate	Moderate	Integrated into job	Short-term (immediate application)
Learner-controlled instruction	X		High	Moderate	High	Medium to long (depending on job complexity)	Short- and long-term
Individual development plan	X		Moderate to high	Moderate	Moderate to high (depending on selected experiences)	Long	Long-term

selected. Write to www.astd.org or www.ispi.org (the International Society for Performance Improvement's Website) and ask if anyone can provide assistance based on their experiences. Gather information and, if possible, examples of the learning system's application. Build up a file of information and resources pertinent to this system.

An Activity for Your WLP Team

Share with your team the information you have gathered about your chosen learning system. Discuss its applicability to your organization. Together, develop a plan to implement and monitor this learning system. Ask team members to choose the specific roles they will assume in the project. Collect process and outcome data about the learning system and its utility within your environment.

Appendix B in this *Fieldbook* provides a brief description of an SOJT project one of the authors helped conduct at a brewery in a developing nation. Not only does it describe the project in overview, but it also presents solid evidence of its usefulness in the work context.

Chapter Summary

This was a lengthy chapter because it provided you and your WLP team with many learning interventions, all aimed at improving human performance by helping build required skills, knowledge, experience, and productive attitudes. Look at everything you did:

- You learned to discriminate between two types of performance interventions—one in which you create something and one in which you eliminate a barrier.
- You gathered more detail on a number of learning interventions, the purpose of which is to increase the individual's skill, knowledge, and experience base to promote greater performance capability. During this process you differentiated between training (the stimulus) and learning (the response).
- You and your team were encouraged to conduct an after-the-fact front-end analysis of a performance gap already addressed in your organization. You selected an alternative, attractive intervention and compared it with what was actually done.
- You studied five learning systems that are effective, but less frequently applied as performance interventions.
- After exploring these learning systems, you were encouraged to research one and, with your WLP team, create a project and monitor an example of it in your organization.

You have crossed a huge amount of learning intervention terrain. Now, you're ready to step beyond learning. The next chapter opens up an in-depth examination of an often-used non-learning intervention: performance or job aids.

Nonlearning Interventions:
Job Aids

This chapter

- has you step right into the first—and probably the most common—nonlearning intervention for the performance consultant: job aids
- introduces you to seven types of job aids
- provides you with building instructions and at least one example of each job aid
- encourages you and your WLP team to create and try out some of these aids.

Tools in this chapter include

- an overall information chart on job aids
- a job aid for building each type of job aid.

In *Training Ain't Performance* (p. 117) we defined *nonlearning intervention* as "actions or events designed to change conditions that facilitate attainment of performance. Anything that removes an obstacle [for example, eliminates an inefficient procedure, removes a physical obstacle to facilitate flow of goods, or reduces a level of supervision that hampers rapid decision making] or adds a facilitative element to the performance system [for example, provides more efficient, safer tools; introduces a new procedure that speeds up order processing; or adds speedbumps to reduce accidents] qualifies as a nonlearning intervention." This includes but is not limited to information systems, feedback systems, task interference, selection, work redesign, and others. This chapter focuses on one category of nonlearning interventions, job aids.

What Are Job Aids?

The easiest way to define job aids is as "external memory aids." Here's an apt analogy. Your computer has an internal memory that you can draw on at any time to do your work, but CD-ROMs, flash drives, backup tapes, DVDs, and other add-on devices are elements of *external* memory that you attach when you need the help they offer. When you don't need them, you disconnect and set them aside. It's the same with job aids—you use them when you need them and store them when you don't.

There are two types of job aids: *simple job aids* and *performance-support tools and systems*. Simple job aids are usually tangible—either in paper and print form or made into relatively easy-to-use devices that can be manipulated (such as a PDA or a wooden slide rule). They are usually inexpensive and help you do the job—that is, obtain a desired result easily and readily.

Performance-support tools and systems range from the simple and static (such as a pop-up screen in a fill-in-the-blanks format with questions that help you accomplish some task, like placing an order for window shades) to the highly dynamic and complex (for example, an electronic GPS system that guides you on a trip, a tool that helps you diagnose a trauma victim, or one that predicts the paths of weather systems). Almost all of the more advanced performance-support tools and systems in the latter category are computer based. They guide and prompt your actions toward desired ends.

What the simpler job aids and the more complex performance-support tools and systems have in common are two characteristics: both are external to you and both give you information and lay out a set of actions that you don't have to commit to memory. When you need to perform some task, you turn to the job aid and do what you're told. Voilà! You obtain the desired result (for example, arrive at your destination, bake a cherry pie, or identify the exact path of the thunderstorm). All you have to know is how to use the job aid that's right for your intended outcome.

In this *Fieldbook* we emphasize the simpler job aid for several reasons. First, you can develop job aids that boost performance dramatically for a relatively small investment in time and effort. In terms of payoff, the time and resource costs are small, so job aids offer a high ROI. Second, most evolving performance professionals are very capable of developing job aids, which are natural extensions of the training and coaching you already know. Third, electronic performance-support tools and systems generally require a degree of knowledge and skill considerably beyond that of the performance professional. As a WLP team member, you may spot the need for such a system and recommend one, but experienced specialists become involved when things get moving. Your role then is to make sure that the right ends will be achieved by the performance-support mechanism you recommend.

Job Aids

Let's look more closely at job aids and examine their critical dimensions.

What are they?

- When added to the work situation, job aids are anything that improves job performance by guiding, facilitating, or reminding performers what to do in accomplishing job tasks.

- Job aids commonly have the following characteristics:
  - They give information that enables the user to know what actions and decisions are called for in a specific task.
  - They reduce training time by minimizing the amount of knowledge or the skills the user must remember to perform the task.
  - They assume the user has prerequisite skills/knowledge to carry out specified actions and to interpret information.
  - They are used during actual performance of the task.

With whom can they be used?

- Use job aids with any and all populations. Even if your performers are illiterate, you can guide performance using symbols, icons, illustrations, and actual photographs.

For what type of content can they be used?

- All content areas are appropriate, but only those parts of the content that involve multiple-step or complex tasks (for example, a mechanic can use a job aid that describes specific evaluations of engine valve wear and the adjustments required for a particular car model). Job aids are also good for tasks that are infrequently performed or that require consideration of a number of factors to make a decision or initiate an action.
- Job aids can only be used in work settings that permit their use. For example, a car salesperson in a showroom can use product sheets to complete a pricing offer, but a pitcher can't use a job aid to throw a curve ball during a baseball game.
- Job aids are especially helpful in procedural tasks (such as setting the alarm on a watch) or in making decisions that require taking several if-then considerations into account (such as determining if an applicant qualifies for a $50,000 loan).

What are the components?

- Instructions on how to use the job aid (if necessary)
- One or more of the following:
  - step-by-step procedures that specify all the actions and decisions required to complete a given task
  - mnemonic devices or word lists
  - illustrated lists—diagrams, drawings, photographs, or symbols
  - decision trees or tables that guide one through choices to be made relative to a task
  - flowcharts, which usually present steps and decision points in a procedure (also known as *algorithms*)
  - checklists, forms, or worksheets that guide the recording of task outputs

- models or samples of acceptable task outputs that can be used to guide the desired job performance (such as samples of contracts for legal secretaries and filled-out receipts for counter personnel, or model reports for specialists or managers).

How do you create them?

1. Conduct a task analysis to determine all the elements required in the task and the sequence of actions and decisions to be followed.
2. Select the most appropriate format for the job aid (for example, list, decision table, flowchart, form, checklist, or model).
3. Create a prototype job aid and instructions for its use.
4. Test the job aid and instructions with sample performers, and then revise as required.
5. Distribute the job aid and monitor its use to verify its applicability and results.

Job Aid Rules

Here are a few simple rules for constructing job aids.

- No matter what type of job aid you're creating, always consult expert performers as you conduct an analysis of the targeted task or decision process. Verify and validate accuracy, completeness, and currency (that is, is this the latest, most up-to-date information and procedure?).
- Think visually in laying out information. Use tables. Illustrate lists if necessary. Create clear samples and models. Use color. Make the job aid durable, as well as easy to see and manipulate.
- Make the job aid and accompanying instructions as simple as you can. The fewer the words and elements, the easier it is to use.
- Test and retest the job aid to ensure that results match work process and output specifications (for example, efficient, safe, timely, effective, and/or error-free output).

Seven Types of Job Aids

Job aids abound, and they come in such a vast variety that performance professionals require some ways of classifying them. Based on a number of books and articles we've come across, we feel these seven categories are useful: step-by-step procedure, worksheet, directory display, decision tree and table, algorithm flowchart, checklist, and sample/ensampler. None of these are difficult to create, although doing them well requires both experience and a sense of visual logic. In the descriptions below, we'll show you a sample of each type.

Step-by-Step Procedure

What is it?

- This is probably the most common type of job aid. Essentially, it lists a series of steps to achieve a desired result. Often, step-by-step procedures are incorporated into user guides and help systems. It specifies both behaviors and accomplishments. It's a "how-to" type of job aid. Often it also specifies "when to" simply by the sequence of actions. Step-by-step job aids usually specify actions and show expected results. What is wonderful about this type of job aid is that you don't have to remember how to/when to/in what sequence to do something. The job aid is your external memory.

What is it best used for?

- Procedures that are important to perform without error, either because of the task's critical nature or outcome or because a simple error ruins the result (for example, if we don't include the yeast, the bread won't rise)
- Procedures that you do infrequently (such as resetting the time on a digital clock when the power goes off), or ones that are similar to several other procedures you do only occasionally (like changing the brightness, contrast, image size, or color palette on a computer monitor).

How do you develop one?

- You always begin by observing a master performer in action. If there is documentation, verify it with expert performers. Break the procedures into a correct sequence of steps, each of approximately equal size and complexity. It is extremely important to take into account the characteristics of the people who will use the job aid: physical-manipulative capabilities, age (if relevant), education/reading level, background, and experience. Eliminate unnecessary wording (which slows down the actions) or jargon. For success, your watchwords are *concise, precise*, and *correct.*
- Use visual cues as practical. Lay out the job aid visually for ease of viewing, mental processing, and application. Test and retest it with sample tryout subjects who authentically represent the end users. Produce it in a durable, easy-to-use format.

Examples include the one depicted in Figure 7-1. Some other examples include cookbooks, how-to-fix-it guides, equipment maintenance manuals, and illustrated fitness routines.

Worksheet

What is it?

- The worksheet is similar in many ways to the step-by-step procedure job aid but, whether paper based or electronic, it requires the user to enter information to complete the task. Worksheets often are used for calculating something, such as total cost of repair, amount of tax to be paid, or alternative bottom-line results of different investments. This *Fieldbook* and *Training Ain't Performance* contain numerous worksheets. They involve the user in actions right on the page and produce an accomplishment.

Figure 7-1. A Step-by-Step Procedure Job Aid

Frozen Royal Blush

Strawberry ——

Whipped —— cream

Strawberry syrup, frozen strawberries, and vanilla —— yogurt

Ice to top ——

Do	
1. Fill ice to top of 16 oz. glass.	
2. Add strawberry syrup 4/5 of the way up.	
3. Pour cup contents into a blender.	
4. Add syrup, frozen strawberries, and 1/2 cup of vanilla yogurt.	
5. Blend until smooth.	
6. Pour blended mixture back into cup.	
7. Top with whipped cream and a strawberry.	

What is it best used for?

- As its name suggests, it is best used for guiding work activities to deliver a desired result (think income tax form). You don't have to remember what needs to be done. You simply follow the worksheet cues and fill in the blanks. One of our favorites is a four-page worksheet that an energy-conservation consultant (usually a certified plumber or air conditioning technician) fills in while examining a building—typically an apartment building or residence. It guides the consultant on where to look, what to measure, what to test, and what to calculate. At the end of page four, alternatives appear along with estimated costs, payback in energy savings over time, and ROI.

How do you develop one?

- Your starting point is accurate documentation, if available, and a master performer. You function like an instructional designer to record what has to be done. You select the most efficient layout. Then, step-by-step you cue the actions to be performed and the calculations that accompany each one.

You include space to enter interim answers and final results. This type of job aid requires a great deal of tryout-testing with a wide variety of divergent examples. Pay most attention to its ease of use.

There are many examples of worksheets. Figure 7-2, Training Session Scripting Sheet, is one we included in our book *Telling Ain't Training*. It's one of two worksheets used to design a training session. Notice that the worksheet includes prompting instructions wherever the user will enter information. Exhibit 7-1 shows the worksheet filled in by a trainer.

Worksheet 7-1, Calculating Value, Worth, and ROI, is from another of our publications, *Front-End Analysis and Return on Investment Toolkit* (pp. 100-101). The worksheet requires calculations based on figures, some of which have been obtained and calculated in previous worksheets. Exhibit 7-2 shows the same worksheet filled in with data from an actual project.

Other examples of worksheets are federal tax forms, electronic software for calculating your taxes, and forms that tailors use when measuring a customer for a new suit.

Directory Display

What is it?

- You probably encounter directory displays (sometimes called *arrays*) almost every day of your life. You enter a new building and want to locate Dr. Pringle, but there's no one to point the way. Do you wander from floor to floor and door to door? Of course not. You check the directory—*Dr. Pringle, 518.* The information is displayed alphabetically and in columns. The *518* gives you the floor and room number. This is standard and familiar code, just like the alphabet. Directories may be on cards, on wallcharts, in PDAs, in elevators, or attached to a telephone. In a sense, highway signs showing upcoming cities, roads, highways, distances, and distances with arrows are forms of displays.

What is it best used for?

- The name says it all: to *display directions* to a person, place, phone number, code, or resource. There is no point in memorizing everyone's name, location, office number, or phone number. Use the directory display to find out what action to take (go to the fifth floor, room 518) to achieve the desired result (meet with Dr. Pringle).

How do you develop one?

- The first, and probably most important step is to select the directory's content. Then determine the best organizational display mode. Originality is far less important than familiarity and ease of use. The more familiar the cues used in the display (for example, an alphabetical listing), the less foreknowledge or learning required to use the job aid.

Figure 7-2. Training Session Scripting Sheet with Prompting Instructions

Session title: _Taken from the training session planning sheet_

Target audience: _Taken from the training session planning sheet_

Time allotted: _Taken from the training session planning sheet_

Objectives: _Taken from the training session planning sheet. If there is an overall objective, state this first. Then include the specific objectives._

Do	Say	Resources	Time
This resembles stage directions in a play. List in order what both trainer and learners actually do—what can be observed.	_This is like the script of a play. You provide the trainer with actual words or speaking suggestions. If the trainer requires content help, detail the content points. If the trainer requires instructional methods guidance, detail instructional messages he or she is to state._	_This is like the prop specifications for a play. For each instructional activity or event, list the media or resource requirements._	_For each instructional activity or event, list the exact time allotment._

Exhibit 7-1: Sample Training Session Scripting Sheet, Completed

Session title: Selling tickets, collecting money, and giving change

Target audience: State fair ticket sellers [15 participants per session]

Time allotted: Two hours, 30 minutes

Objectives:

Overall objective:

Participants will be able to sell the exact number and type of tickets, collect the exact amount of money, and give the correct change for any customer without error and at an average time of 20 seconds per transaction (maximum eight people per transaction).

Specific objectives:

- Identify the exact numbers and types of admission tickets the customer requests.
- Calculate the exact total cost in 10 seconds with no errors.
- Collect the correct total amount with no errors.
- Give the customer the exact change with no errors.

Do	Say	Resources	Time
• Smile warmly. Pose questions to group.	• Ask: "As you face this new job as ticket sellers, what concerns, even fears, do you have right now?"		• Eight minutes
• Write responses on flipchart (F/C).	• State: "As I point to each item you have given me, raise your hands if you feel this. I'll write down the numbers."	• F/C and felt-tip markers.	
• Point to each item on the F/C, count raised hands, and jot down number.	• State: "As you can see, quite a few of you share the same fears and concerns. Let me assure you that this is normal. Everyone is a bit scared of the unknown. What is great for you is that this session will lay a lot of those concerns and fears to rest. Let's see why."	• F/C and felt-tip markers.	

(continued on page 96)

Exhibit 7-1: Sample Training Session Scripting Sheet, Completed (continued)

Do	Say	Resources	Time
• Show key points from rationale.	• Explain how this session prepares the learners to serve the customers despite all the noise and pressures. • Stress the benefits and fun the learners will derive from the practice exercises in this session, and that they possibly will win prizes.	• Prepared F/C sheet with session benefits for learners.	
• Show prepared F/C with objectives. • Read, explain, and discuss overall and specific objectives. Move briskly. If there are concerns, put these on a separate sheet for handling later.	• State: "Here are the objectives for this session. Let's read the overall one first and discuss it. Then I'll briefly explain each of the specific objectives you will achieve by the end of this session.	• Prepared F/C sheet with objectives.	• Three minutes

Worksheet 7-1: Calculating Value, Worth, and ROI

Instructions: The following are guidelines for calculating the value of a given set of interventions, the worth of these interventions compared with costs, and the ROI for the entire project.

1. State lowest individual deficiency/improvement cost; state highest individual deficiency/improvement cost. If this is an estimate, you must work with client specialists to obtain these.

   lowest = _____   highest = _____

2. State lowest and highest number of deficiencies/improvements per worker per year (or other suitable time period). If this is an estimate, you must work with client specialists to obtain these.

   lowest frequency = _____   highest frequency = _____

3. Multiply lowest and highest frequencies per individual worker by the number of workers to obtain total deficiencies/improvements per year (or specified time period).

   lowest frequency x number of workers = _____

   highest frequency x number of workers = _____

4. Multiply lowest individual cost by lowest frequency and highest individual cost by highest frequency to establish range of annual value.

_____		_____		_____
lowest individual cost	x	lowest total frequency	=	lowest value

_____		_____		_____
highest individual cost	x	highest total frequency	=	highest value

5. Multiply number of expected years of life of the recommended interventions by the lowest and highest values.

_____		_____		_____
number of years	x	lowest value	=	lowest total value

_____		_____		_____
number of years	x	highest value	=	highest total value

6. Multiply lowest total value by the lowest percentage of anticipated impact from recommended interventions and highest total value by highest percentage of anticipated impact to establish range of estimated values obtained from the recommendations. It is essential to work with client experts to determine the percentages.

_____		_____		_____
lowest percentage	x	lowest total value	=	lowest estimated value

_____		_____		_____
highest percentage	x	highest total value	=	highest estimated value

7. To calculate worth, divide lowest and highest estimated values over the expected years of life of the interventions by the estimated total cost.

   $$W_L = \frac{V_L}{C} \qquad W_H = \frac{V_H}{C}$$

   $$= \qquad\qquad =$$

(continued on page 98)

Worksheet 7-1: Calculating Value, Worth, and ROI (continued)

8. Express the results as a ratio.

W_L = _____:1 W_H = _____:1

9. To calculate ROI, enter the estimated value and cost figures (potential ROI) or true figures (actual ROI). Divide lowest and highest values minus total cost by total costs, and multiply by 100.

$$ROI_L = \frac{V_L - C}{C} \times 100 \qquad\qquad ROI_H = \frac{V_H - C}{C} \times 100$$

=   =

10. Express the results as a percentage.

ROI_L = _____% ROI_H = _____%

- For large amounts of information (such as all the telephone numbers in a city or a complete code listing for ordinary auto parts), use either easy-to-access manuals or electronic directory software (like the kind found in personal address books).
- If you have several format possibilities, try them all to see which one takes the least amount of effort and time (behavior) to achieve the most accurate result (accomplishment). Try testing both the effectiveness and the efficiency. Produce the display directory in the most usable and durable format.

  Examples include two of the figures here. Figure 7-3 shows a display directory that sticks to the hand-held receiver of a telephone. Figure 7-4 combines visual and verbal cues for navigating a college campus.

  Display directories are ubiquitous: airport gate directories, personal pocket directories, hazardous materials manuals, traffic direction panels, subway maps, and lots, lots more.

Decision Tree or Decision Table

What is it?

- Decisions to be made range from the simple (for example, what do I do if the machine jams?) to the very complex (for example, should we invest in the development of this new product?). For certain types of routine decision making or for decisions that are made infrequently, decision trees and tables are helpful. They are physical representations of the considerations and choices you must go through to reach a "final" decision.
- A decision tree looks just like a tree. It's graphic and it spreads out branches each time a choice has to be made. The three parts of a decision tree are its "nodes" in which a question is raised, its "branches" that pose conditions or

Exhibit 7-2: Value, Worth, and ROI: Voice Messaging Example

Instructions: The following are guidelines for calculating the value of a given set of interventions, the worth of these interventions compared with costs, and the ROI for the entire project.

1. State lowest individual deficiency/improvement cost; state highest individual deficiency/improvement cost. If this is an estimate, you must work with client specialists to obtain these.

   lowest = _____$10_____   highest = _____$20_____

2. State lowest and highest number of deficiencies/improvements per worker per year (or other suitable time period). If this is an estimate, you must work with client specialists to obtain these.

   lowest frequency = _____110/year_____   highest frequency = _____220/year_____

3. Multiply lowest and highest frequencies per individual worker by the number of workers to obtain total deficiencies/improvements per year (or specified time period).

   lowest frequency x number of workers = _____110 x 300 = 33,000_____
   highest frequency x number of workers = _____220 x 300 = 66,000_____

4. Multiply lowest individual cost by lowest frequency and highest individual cost by highest frequency to establish range of annual value.

$10		33,000		$330,000
lowest individual cost	x	lowest total frequency	=	lowest value
$20		66,000		$1,320,000
highest individual cost	x	highest total frequency	=	highest value

5. Multiply number of expected years of life of the recommended interventions by the lowest and highest values.

3		$330,000		$990,000
number of years	x	lowest value	=	lowest total value
3		$1,320,000		$3,960,000
number of years	x	highest value	=	highest total value

Existing data show that the:

- Average cost of handling customer complaints   = $48
- Average number of complaints handled annually   =   8,000
- Average annual cost of complaint handling   =   8,000 x $48
                                                                                        $384,000

- Average cost of fines plus associated legal and administrative fees   = $870,000

Therefore:

- Lowest total value (deficiencies, complaint handling, and fines)   = $990,000 + 3 ($384,000 + $870,000)
                                                                                                                = $4,752,000

- Highest total value (deficiencies, complaint handling, and fines)   = $3,960,000 + 3 ($384,000 + $870,000)
                                                                                                                = $7,722,000

(continued on page 100)

Exhibit 7-2: Value, Worth, and ROI: Voice Messaging Example (continued)

6. Multiply lowest total value by the lowest percentage of anticipated impact from recommended interventions and highest total value by highest percentage of anticipated impact to establish range of estimated values obtained from the recommendations. It is essential to work with client experts to determine the percentages.

40%		$4,752,000		$1,900,800
lowest percentage	x	lowest total value	=	lowest estimated value
60%		$7,722,000		$4,633,200
highest percentage	x	highest total value	=	highest estimated value

7. To calculate worth, divide lowest and highest estimated values over the expected years of life of the interventions by the estimated total cost.

$$W_L = \frac{V_L}{C} \qquad W_H = \frac{V_H}{C}$$

$$= \frac{\$1,900,000}{\$683,491^*} \qquad = \frac{\$4,633,200}{\$683,491}$$

$$= 2.78 \qquad = 6.78$$

*estimated total cost previously calculated

8. Express the results as a ratio.

$$W_L = 2.78:1 \qquad W_H = 6.78:1$$

9. To calculate ROI, enter the estimated value and cost figures (potential ROI) or true figures (actual ROI). Divide lowest and highest values minus total cost by total costs, and multiply by 100.

$$ROI_L = \frac{V_L - C}{C} \times 100 \qquad ROI_H = \frac{V_H - C}{C} \times 100$$

$$= \frac{\$1,900,000 - \$683,491}{\$683,491} \times 100 \qquad = \frac{\$4,633,200 - \$683,491}{\$683,491} \times 100$$

$$= 178.1 \qquad = 577.9$$

10. Express the results as a percentage.

$$ROI_L = 178.1\% \qquad ROI_H = 577.9\%$$

state considerations, and the "decisions" that logically derive from the path you take as you respond to the node questions and select the appropriate consideration/condition branches.

- A decision table operates in much the same way, but it is laid out as a table. It helps you take multiple factors into account in making your decision.
- Selecting a tree or a table is mainly a usability issue. If there is a long list of considerations, decision tables are more difficult to navigate.

What is it best used for?

- Decision trees and tables are used to guide you in making decisions. If a person is uncertain how to act or if specific rules must be applied to take action, these two aids are extremely useful. They produce fast expert-like

Figure 7-3. Emergency Response Directory

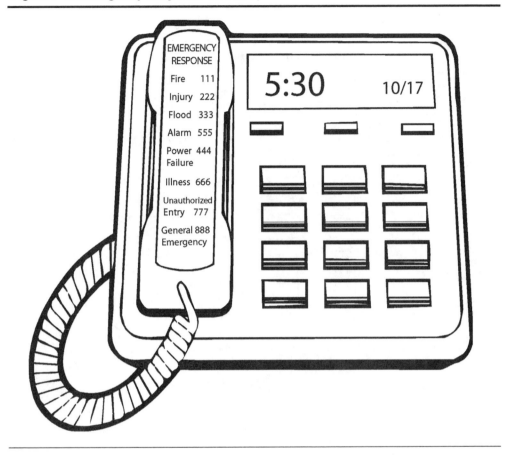

decisions with very high probability of accuracy and success. They don't work well in situations where the decision maker must use his or her judgment (although one option is to include "turn this over to a supervisor" or "... to an XYZ specialist" as a decision choice. Both decision trees and tables can be used with practically any content, although decision software is generally used for very complex decision making.

How do you develop one?

- To develop a decision tree or table, you require true decision-making experts and all legal or policy documentation. You list in sequence all of the steps and pertinent considerations/conditions. As in logic, you have if-then rules and/or considerations/conditions.
- When all of the steps, conditions, rules, and decision options have been documented, one-by-one, you lay them out graphically in a tree or tabular format, depending on complexity. You may even try it out both ways.
- It's critical that you test your representation with numerous scenarios and have experts verify decision outcomes each time. When you obtain consistently correct results, test the decision tree or table with end users. Modify for usability and user-friendliness. Monitor use and decision results.

Figure 7-4. Campus Map

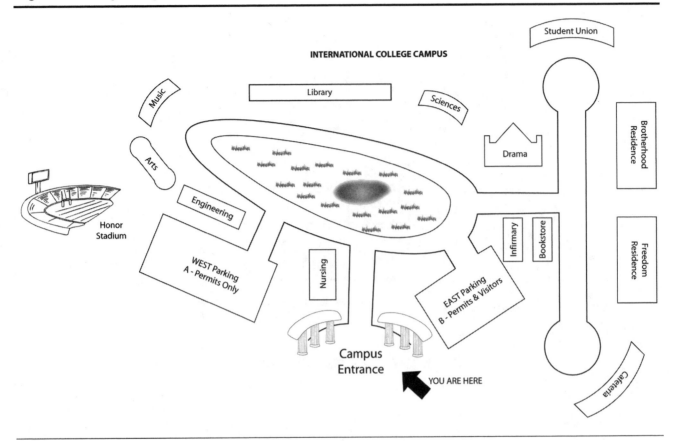

Examples include Figure 7-5 and Exhibit 7-3. Figure 7-5 shows a decision tree for approving a loan of $2,000 or less. Exhibit 7-3 is a relatively simple decision table. More complex tables often require commercially available programming and decision software.

Decision trees and tables are used by consumers to make bank account decisions, by technicians for troubleshooting and maintenance, and even by physicians when there are several factors to consider before prescribing medication.

Algorithm Flowchart

What is it?

- This is one of our favorite types of job aids. Much like a decision tree, it leads you along a path that requires actions and decisions that result in a final outcome. The word *algorithm* basically refers to a step-by-step procedure that guides you to produce a solution to a problem. If you follow the steps in the pathway with the same information, you will always arrive at the same result.

- Algorithms in the form of flowcharts are very useful in guiding relative novices to achieve near-expert results. Their most common work-related uses, beyond solving mathematics problems, are diagnosing and troubleshooting equipment failures.

Figure 7-5. Decision Tree: To Lend or Not to Lend?

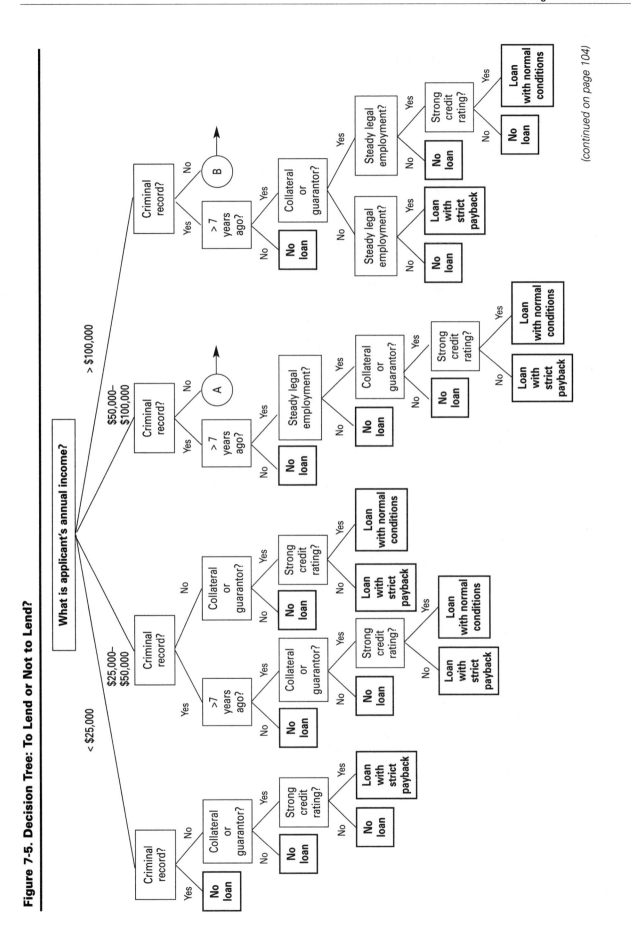

(continued on page 104)

Figure 7-5. Decision Tree: To Lend or Not to Lend? (continued)

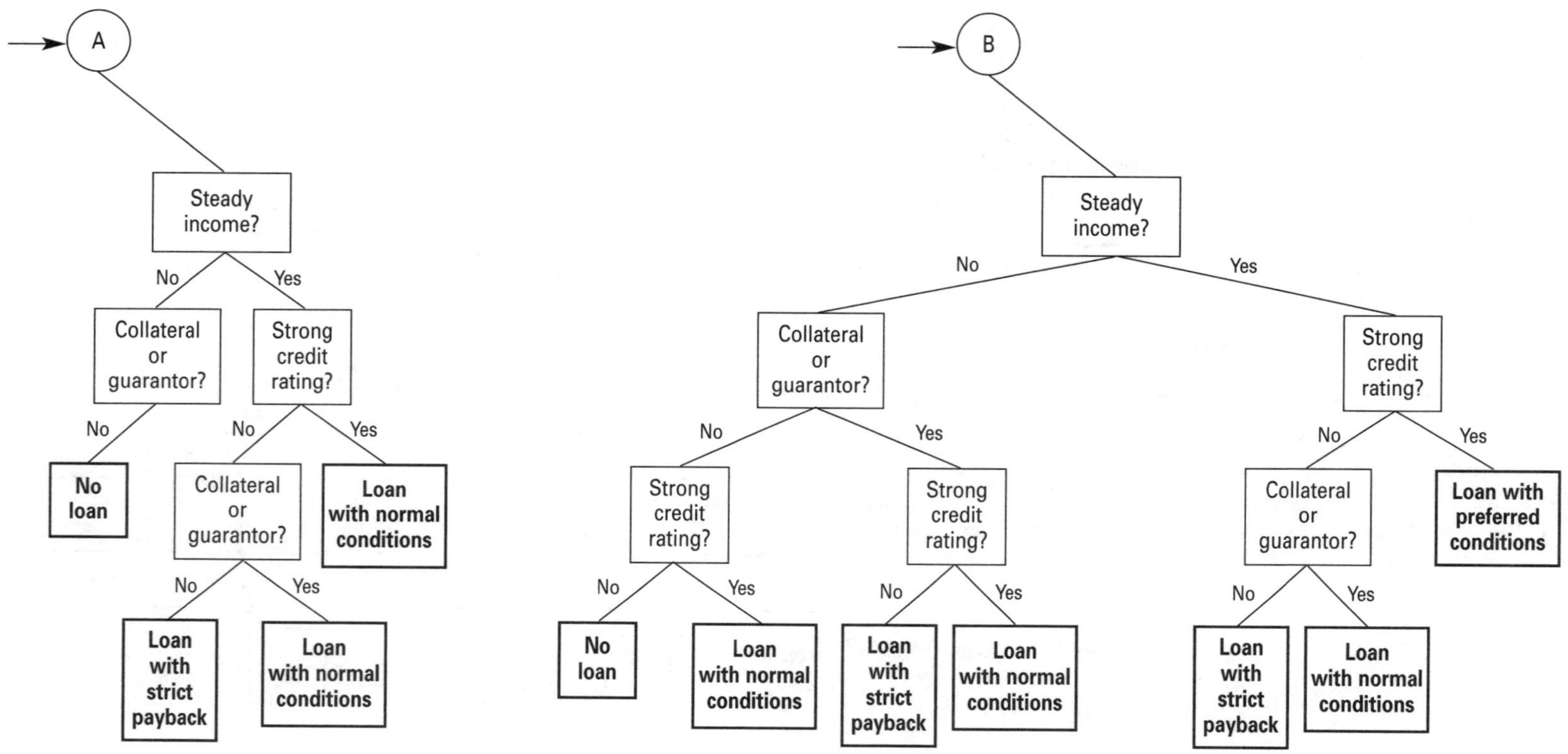

Exhibit 7-3: Decision Table: How to Handle Frozen Foods After a Power Failure

If the food is...	And is...	Then...
Partially thawed (some ice crystals remain)	• Meat, poultry, fish, shellfish • Produce • Dairy • Juice • Baked goods	Refreeze.
	• Organ meat • Stews, casseroles, other cooked combinations	Do not refreeze. Cook and serve. (Refreeze only after cooking.)
Thawed, but cold (below 40 ºF)	• Meat, poultry, fish, shellfish • Produce • Organ meat	Cook and serve. (Refreeze only after cooking.)
	• Juice • Dairy • Baked goods	Refreeze.
Thawed, and warm (above 40 ºF)	• Any food except baked goods	Discard.
	• Baked goods	Serve.

Adapted from "Keeping Food Safe During Emergencies," available at http://www.fsis.usda.gov/Fact_Sheets/Keeping_Food_Safe_During_an_Emergency/index.asp.

Note: We've adapted this decision table without expert verification, so before you even think of using it, go to the Website listed or check with a food expert.

What is it best used for?

- Algorithm flowcharts are best used for any type of procedure that requires action steps with decision-making points that lead you to a wide variety of appropriate results. One of the most elaborate ones we've ever seen was for part-time Internal Revenue Service employees who assisted taxpayers who called in for help. By following their algorithm flowcharts, the part-time customer service agents first asked questions (for example, "Was your total income for the past 12 months more than $5,000?"). Then, based on yes-no responses, they suggested actions before moving on to more questions. Occasionally a customer response led to a box (an action) in the flowchart that read, "Hold please while I connect you with a supervisor"—an action recommended when the agent could not make an informed decision for the caller.

How do you develop one?

- Select a procedure that includes both actions and decisions that a person must perform with 100 percent accuracy while not necessarily possessing expertise in the work or content area.

- Adopt the point of view that the desired task to be accomplished is made up of simpler steps arranged in a sequence.

- If all of the steps in the sequence are observable (for example, starting up a piece of equipment, filling out a tax form), then watch an expert do it. Ask what is happening and why the expert is doing each action. Ask what decisions she or he is making. Then, from your notes, attempt the procedure yourself, if feasible and safe. Observe your own performance, and if there are gaps in your understanding of the sequence, get additional information from the expert performer.

- If the sequence in the steps is intellectual, with steps that cannot be observed, or if demonstration of performance is not feasible because the equipment is unavailable or the software is still under development, question experts or master performers as they rehearse the procedure (actions and decisions) for you. If possible, try out or simulate the procedural steps while an expert or master performer verifies your performance.

- If any of the actions or decisions in the procedure appear to be the result of an unconscious effort, infer what steps or decisions were made or are necessary. Test to verify accuracy.

- Represent the procedure as a flowchart. Use ⬭ to start or stop, ▽ for inputs, ▭ for actions or mental operations, ◇ for yes-no decisions, and ○ (with an alphabet letter in it) to go to another part of the flowchart where you will find a →○ with the matching alphabet letter.

- The flowchart should show the sequence of actions and decisions in a way that clearly includes simultaneous and alternative sequences. The final action should lead to successful completion of the desired task. Try out and revise the algorithm flowchart with likely end users. Make it as simple and easy to use as you can.

As an example, Figure 7-6 shows how to check for phone messages in a particular organization with a quirky phone system.

Algorithm flowcharts are frequently used for equipment or service installations, repair manuals, complex work procedures, even telephone sales call scripts.

Checklist
What is it?

- A checklist is probably the most usual type of job aid we create for ourselves and others. It's like a "to-do" list on an external memory device that triggers actions. You check off each one as you accomplish it.

- Another way to view a checklist job aid is as a thought/action prompter. It may contain only the tasks themselves, or it may also include what to consider or incorporate before, during, or after the task.

- In some cases, it may list the characteristics of tasks being done (for example, in a checklist for writing a proposal, there may be an enumeration of

Figure 7-6. Algorithm Flowchart: How to Check for Telephone Messages

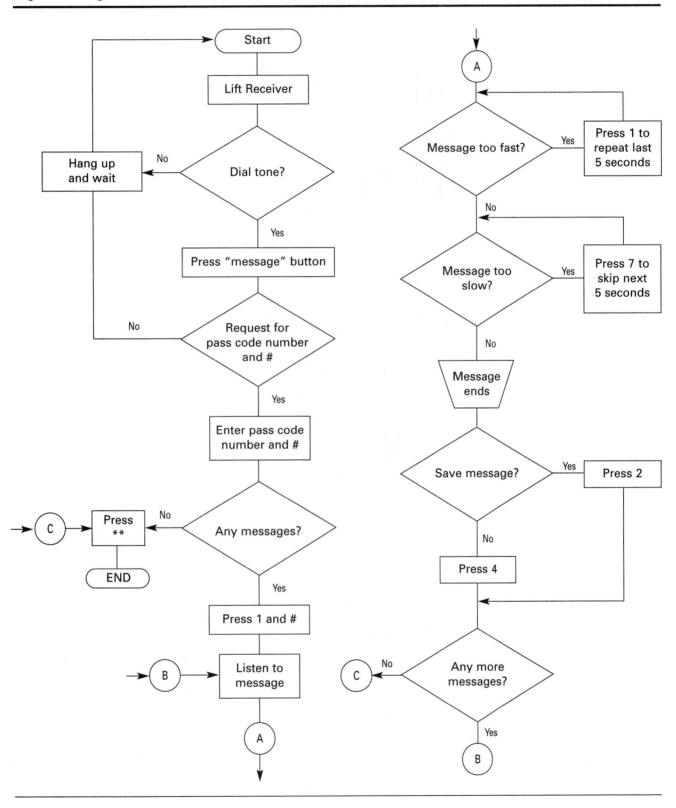

the items to include in the proposal and a list of guidelines or caveats for *how* to present the items—"don't use the passive voice, write sentences with no more than 25 words, use only company examples, and so forth).

What is it best used for?

- There are four main uses for a checklist: to trigger an action, to include an item, to prompt an idea or a resource, and to verify either that something has been done or is included/excluded.

How do you develop one?

- Analyze very thoroughly what must be done, included/excluded, or verified. If it is a prompting checklist, include as many ideas or items as possible (for example, all food and household items that might be considered each week for shopping).
- List all of the identified items in a logical sequence, and lay out the checklist in a user-friendly manner.
- Verify the list with experts and then test it with end users in a variety of scenarios.

Examples are presented in Exhibits 7-4 and 7-5. Exhibit 7-4 is one of our favorites—we use it every time we travel. Feel free to use it yourself, with whatever modifications you require or want.

Exhibit 7-5 is a checklist example from *Telling Ain't Training*. This one helps you verify the content and characteristics of test items.

Other examples are pilot checklists for verifying an aircraft's readiness prior to takeoff; a laundry checklist with items for washing, dry cleaning, or pressing; a quality checklist to verify that a product conforms to quality standards.

Sample or Ensampler
What is it?

- Sometimes the best way to achieve expert performance from nonexperts is by providing them with an item representative of what you want them to produce. The samples—usually several to help the nonexpert "get it"—are very clear. All the performer does is replace the sample content with his or her own content. The finished product looks exactly like the samples.
- An ensampler is a collection of samples. It acts as a resource and contains a broad array of samples organized by logical categories or alphabetically. The most common ensamplers are style guides for citing references and producing correctly formatted bibliographies; manuals of different types of business letters; contract collections organized by type of contract; and printers' templates for invitations, menus, letterheads, and other print materials.

Exhibit 7-4: Travel Checklist

HOME ARRANGEMENTS

Three days prior to travel:

- ☐ Order limousine for transport to airport
- ☐ Arrange for mail pick-up
- ☐ Arrange for plants to be watered
- ☐ Cancel newspaper for duration of trip
- ☐ Leave itinerary with both family and office (dates, phone, hotel, and so forth)

Day of travel (or night before if early morning travel):

- ☐ Check all appliances (off?)
- ☐ Throw out foods that spoil
- ☐ Run dishwasher
- ☐ Turn down heat in winter and air conditioning in summer
- ☐ Set back-up alarm for early morning travel
- ☐ Take garbage out
- ☐ Turn off faucets in laundry room
- ☐ Water plants and move plants to get light
- ☐ Tidy home
- ☐ Set television for recording
- ☐ Check for telephone messages
- ☐ Check all windows and patio doors (closed and locked?)
- ☐ Set security system (xxxx)

PACKING REQUIREMENTS

To carry on:

- ☐ Laptop computer
- ☐ PDA
- ☐ Cell phone, extra battery and charger
- ☐ Mirror, makeup, contact lenses, spare eyeglasses, sunglasses, and so forth
- ☐ Work materials, business cards, and pens
- ☐ Currency (US and/or foreign) and blank checks (business and personal)
- ☐ Umbrella
- ☐ Medications
- ☐ Passports, airplane tickets, car and hotel confirmations, discounts, and so forth
- ☐ Keys
- ☐ Books, reading materials, and the like
- ☐ Letters to be mailed
- ☐ Credit cards (worldwide and local)
- ☐ Camera, film, and binoculars

To send through:

- ☐ Clothing (suits, shirts, pants, dresses, sweaters, coat, and so forth)
- ☐ Clothing accessories (shoes, purses, ties, belts, hosiery, gloves)
- ☐ Exercise bag with correct and sufficient gear and journal
- ☐ Spare tote bag for items acquired on trip
- ☐ Underwear and nightwear
- ☐ Exercise clothing, shoes, heart monitor, sport watch
- ☐ Toiletries, hair dryer, and so forth

Exhibit 7-5: Test Item Verification Checklist

Test Item Verification

Instructions: Apply this checklist to each test item, whether it is oral or written or a performance measure. Line up each test item with its corresponding objective. For each test item, answer each question.

	Yes	No
1. Does the item require exactly the same performance and standards as stated in the objective?	☐	☐
2. Is the learner performance in the item verifiable?	☐	☐
3. Is the type of item selected the most appropriate one for verifying objective attainment?	☐	☐
4. Is there an answer key, a correction checklist, or a verification instrument for the item?	☐	☐
5. Are all resources required to respond to the item available to the learner?	☐	☐

If you checked off even one "no," the item does not match the objective perfectly. Rework the item until you can check off every "yes" for it.

What is it best used for?

- Use this for any type of content that results in a tangible output, is difficult to explain in words, and is easy to show by example. The samples, alone or in an ensampler collection, are models. The user looks at the sample and substitutes her or his content for the model content. Visual layouts, legal and literary formats, floral arrangements, clothing or furniture ensembles, even verbal scripts to use for specific social occasions all provide excellent opportunities for creating samples or ensamplers.

How do you develop one?

- Identify the topic you want to exemplify.
- Either collect excellent existing samples (such as letters, logos, or room layouts) or have experts produce models.
- Organize each grouping in a logical manner.
- Bind each grouping in separate collections with a table of contents and/or an index if there are many items. You may also bind multiple collections that are related and then create a comprehensive table of contents and index.
- Verify all sample entries with experts.
- Try out the samples/ensamplers with end users. Watch how they produce their own products based on the samples. If necessary, add guiding comments or suggestions. A verification checklist may prove helpful in some cases.

Exhibit 7-6 shows samples of entries in a reference list done according to the publication style required by the American Psychological Association (APA). A writer preparing a manuscript for the APA would present his or her source information in these sequences. Figure 7-7 shows sample sets of commercial stationery with logos and appropriate information. A printer would insert customer-specific information into the chosen template.

Samples and ensamplers are very common in how-to books and manuals, depicting such a diverse group of topics as birdhouse designs, garden layouts, table settings, and holiday hors d'oeuvre tray displays.

An Activity for You

Because job aids can be so effective and efficient, you must be itching to develop one yourself. Great! That's exactly what we encourage you to do right now. Select an area in which performance can be enhanced by the use of a job aid. Determine

---

Exhibit 7-6: Ensampler: Rules for Listing References in APA Style

Single author, book

Applesmith, J. G. (2006). The reign of the dinosaurs. New York: Crunch Publishing Co.

Dolittle, K. (2004). Cooking with flair: Recipes that let you show off your skills to best advantage. Los Angeles: Kitchen Press.

Multiple authors, book

Greenhill, S., & Papineau, G. (2005). Creating online newsletters: Guidelines and Samples. Montreal: Professional Products Press.

Bellweather, B. D., Happenstance, G., Morganstein, A.R.B., & Jacoppi, M. (2001). Family, kinship and clans: The social impact of blood relationships. Cambridge, UK: Academic Publishers.

Figure 7-7. Samples: Commercial Stationery Sets with Logos

which of the seven types of job aids described above best fits the need. Create a prototype. Obtain whatever expert assistance you require. Try it out with sample users, and then revise it until it produces satisfactory results.

An Activity for Your WLP Team

Report to your team about the job aid you developed and tested. Describe the need/opportunity that prompted its development, and show them the prototype. Explain how you designed and developed it and how you tried it out. Share your observations and your test findings, and then display the final product. Have the team try it out, if feasible.

Review all of the job aid types as a group. If there are enough people, form small groups. Ask teams to identify opportunities for applying a job aid and then select an appropriate type. Set a time at which all groups will return to the WLP team as a whole to present their job aids and the test results. When that has occurred, debrief findings and draw conclusions.

Chapter Summary

This chapter presented you with the most natural step to take in moving from a training to a performance perspective. Job aids are first cousins to training. The major difference is that they do not require any learning beyond how to apply them. In this chapter

- you acquired definitions for *nonlearning intervention, job aid,* and *performance-support tools and systems*
- you reviewed the relationship between the terms *performance aid* and *job aid*
- You studied seven types of job aids with information about their use and creation, along with examples
- you and your WLP team got to develop your own performance aids and try them out.

In the next chapter, we turn the performance requirements up a notch. We examine some of the major environmental dimensions of the workplace that affect performance and we engage in developing more performance enhancement interventions.

Nonlearning Interventions: Environmental

This chapter

- ◆ opens with an introduction to the range of environmental factors that affect human performance at work
- ◆ focuses on three of the most influential environmental interventions and describes how you can create and implement them
- ◆ guides you and your WLP team in identifying those gaps within your organization for which each intervention would be appropriate.

Tools in this chapter include

- ◆ information charts for three types of environmental interventions: expectation setting, feedback systems, and task interference elimination.

The Environment and Its Impact on Human Performance at Work

In the discussion of Gilbert's Behavior Engineering Model, which we presented in *Training Ain't Performance* (pp. 38-41) and revisited in chapter 4 of this *Fieldbook*, you learned that approximately 70 to 80 percent of the factors affecting people's performance at work were environmentally based, rather than individually based. The logical conclusion to draw is that you have to begin with the environmental factors if you are going to change or improve performance.

As a performance professional, you can apply Gilbert's, Harless', or Rummler and Brache's model to identify influential environmental factors. No matter what their classification scheme—or anyone else's for that matter—you will have to consider the following five dimensions of the workplace environment: physical, social-cultural, work systems and processes, management, and psychological.

The Physical Dimension

In the 19th century most industrial workplaces were dismal and dangerous. Work sites were designed to accommodate the new machines of the industrial revolution, not the people. Machine productivity was the overriding concern, so workers and their managers had to perform under dreadful conditions and for long hours—as many as 75 hours weekly. The atmosphere in these environments was often foul and unhealthy. As a consequence there were frequent illnesses, injuries, and deaths from unshielded machinery and contaminated material.

Our modern work settings are far from that hideous past. With the steady increase in the valuing of human capital and the major achievements being derived from knowledge work as opposed to physical labor, the new work environment has been redesigned to foster mental output. This has given rise to the fields of ergonomics, industrial architecture, and environmental design that not only make for pleasant working conditions but also foster greater human productivity. Although as a performance professional you are not a workplace designer, you still can intervene at the physical environmental level to improve performance. Table 8-1 lists some physical environmental factors that affect workplace performance and suggests some ways in which you may intervene.

The entries in Table 8-1 are only indicative of some of the possible physical factors that can affect performance and the appropriate potential interventions. Numerous physical factors abound. Be on the lookout for these as sources of inadequate—or potentially insufficient—performance.

The Social-Cultural Dimension

One of the most dangerous things a performance professional can do is rely on her or his own sense of what it right or wrong when dealing with new workplace environments. Our personal perceptions can be quite misleading with respect to what is occurring. Here is an illustration from an actual case.

Supervisory Abuse

Jessica had recently graduated from the university in her country's capital and was delighted to obtain a position with a pharmaceutical firm upcountry, several hundred miles from the university and her home. The child of a prosperous, educated, and well-traveled family, Jessica was proud that she would be financially independent and on the path to a career as a human resources/ training professional.

At the plant to which she was assigned, her job was to ensure adequate training and performance support for manufacturing personnel. She soon noticed that supervisors frequently shouted at assembly-line workers and packers. She was horrified and determined to eliminate this vile practice.

Fortunately, a mentor interceded before her outraged enthusiasm drove her too far. He encouraged her to go into the plant and spend a week working on the line. Wonderful advice, as Jessica soon discovered that in this unfamiliar cultural climate, things were not quite as they appeared to her. True, supervisors shouted at the workers as they strutted about very seriously noting inadequacies and errors. However, as the workers pointed out to Jessica, this was to show that the supervisors were taking their jobs seriously. The shouting demonstrated conscientiousness and authority. The workers paid absolutely no attention to the supervisors and their noisy displays. Everything was fine.

Table 8-1. Physical Environmental Factors and Potential Interventions for the Performance Professional

Physical Environmental Factor	Potential Interventions
Uncomfortable work space or physical surroundings	• Analyze surroundings to determine points of discomfort and eliminate or overcome them • Analyze work requirements and redesign space to facilitate efficient, comfortable work environment
Noise and visual distractions	• Create sound and visual barriers • Introduce "white noise" • Add sound-absorption materials to ceilings and walls • Move work surfaces and furniture away from line-of-sight distractions
Inadequate lighting	• Change lighting to provide clear, non-harsh illumination • Mix indirect lighting to reduce glare with directly targeted lighting to illuminate points of focus • Add antiglare filters to computer screens
Inadequate access to required resources or materials	• Relocate resources and tools closer to work stations • Eliminate unnecessary barriers (physical or administrative) to obtaining required resources and materials
Poorly adapted tools and equipment	• Analyze defects in tools and equipment, and build a business case for improving or replacing improper items
Environmental threats to safety	• Assign specialists to identify causes and points of risk, and have those causes and risks eliminated
Difficulties getting to the work site on time (for example, distance, barriers, traffic)	• Examine ways to stagger work shifts to off-peak working hours • Analyze possibilities for telecommuting • Build a business case for providing transportation
Health and wellness issues	• Have specialists verify health hazards and institute measures to eliminate them • Verify foods that are available at the work sites and work with a nutritionist to adjust menus and offerings • Build a business case for fitness facilities/classes at the work site

In a study in which one of this *Fieldbook*'s authors participated, a structured on-the-job performance improvement program was developed for new brewery workers in Cameroon, West Africa. The program was based on successful practices and models developed in the United States. What soon became evident was that the social-cultural assumptions and understandings in the United States are not the same as those in Cameroon, and a great deal of program adaptation was necessary. Table 8-2 provides some examples of major social-cultural differences between the two nations.

What Table 8-2 illustrates is that the performance professional must carefully observe and gather a great deal of social-cultural information in unfamiliar settings. Our advice is to observe, gather information from credible sources, create hypotheses, and then verify and reverify your perceptions and understandings before making

Table 8-2. Sample Social-Cultural Differences in Setting Up an SOJT Program: Cameroon Contrasted with the United States

United States	Cameroon
• Trainers are selected on the basis of technical competence and ability to communicate.	• Trainers are selected on the basis of ability to do the job, their tribal origin, and their social status.
• Feedback focuses on performance.	• Feedback is based on performance, but it is important not to humiliate a trainee and to take into account his or her social status.
• The best performers demonstrate the correct performance.	• The person demonstrating must be male if the learners are all male, older than the learners, and of the appropriate cultural background.
• The manager judges learners based on performance.	• The manager is a father-figure who protects the learners, in return for their respect and obedience.
• Learners are expected to be on the job on time.	• Time is rather fluid, and family or clan responsibilities often are of greater priority than work requirements.
• Selection of trainers is based on objective criteria.	• Selection of trainers is highly subjective and often based on family ties or clan obligations.

recommendations or taking actions. To ignore the social-cultural dimensions of a work environment is to decrease the likelihood of achieving performance improvement success.

The Work Systems and Process Dimension

There is a huge body of literature on the design of work systems and even more on work processes. The complexities of the two areas are beyond the scope of this *Fieldbook*, but it is essential that you understand the nature of your clients' work systems—how they operate, interconnect, and are monitored. Asking for nontechnical descriptions of how the work gets done in a work unit can help you understand the operation, whether it is as simple as selling coffee or as complex as monitoring a nuclear power plant. As you form a mental model of the work system, investigate and test your understanding. The more closely your vision of how the work gets done matches reality, the more likely it is that you will be able to spot inhibiting factors or weak spots and then identify means for overcoming them.

What is true of work systems is equally true of work processes. Finding out how the work gets done often enables you to identify blockages, points of disconnection, or inefficiencies. In one of our projects to decrease billing errors in a railway company, we tracked the entire process of transporting goods by train. In analyzing and detailing the process, we uncovered numerous points at which errors could be (and were) made. Based on the findings, the process by which goods are transported, tracked, and charged for underwent a dramatic redesign.

On a lighter note, here is a description of an actual project for improving performance in the distribution center of a national retailer:

Look! I'm a Piece of Merchandise

Note: The following is a true story. We strongly recommend that you not follow Shirley's example, although it does give a new meaning to the performance professional becoming intimately familiar with the client's process.

A woman we'll call Shirley is an eager and enthusiastic performance consultant. She wants to understand at a deep level what her clients do and how they do it. Her new assignment was to help improve performance in a highly automated retail distribution center where items are stored until needed and then shipped off to several hundred stores.

With the silent collaboration of a team of distribution center workers, Shirley decided that the best way for her to understand the entire process was to experience it as an item of merchandise. So one morning, dressed in overalls and a hard-hat, she was picked up at a supplier site, loaded into the trailer of an 18-wheeler, delivered to the distribution center, and then unloaded onto a pallet. She was wrapped in plastic and sent off on an automated path to be labeled with a bar code. Firmly attached to her automated pallet, she was moved to an assigned storage location, automatically hoisted into the air with grapples, and shunted into a storage bin 40 feet above the ground. A short time later she and her pallet were lifted out of the bin, lowered to the ground, and sent to a loading dock where they were raised by forklift onto a truck and eventually delivered to a store several miles away.

The eight-hour episode was immensely dramatic for Shirley. As she put it, "I now understand the distribution process in a far more meaningful and personal way than before I undertook this adventure."

The Management Dimension

Geary Rummler and Alan Brache (1995) certainly knew with whom they were dealing when they wrote about managing the white space in the organization chart. So much of what goes on in organizations does not appear in the neat boxes displaying the management hierarchy and formal reporting relationships. Here are some examples:

- ◆ *"The way we do things around here."* This is a useful definition for cultural norms. The performance professional must quickly figure out who is really allowed to speak to whom, what constitutes the informal pecking order, who facilitates and who blocks whether something is done. Not all apparently equal managers are equal in fact.
- ◆ *Informal leadership.* Someone may have the official title of decision maker, but often desired performance changes hang in limbo until influential individuals give their unofficial signal that these are acceptable. The person signaling may possess no formal title but wield a great deal of informal decision power.

- *Organizational language.* In many organizations management signals its true level of commitment through coded words that everyone implicitly understands. Is a message sent to please regulators or shareholders, or because the desired performance is really one that people are expected to implement? As a performance professional, you must discover and sort through these environmental codes to determine how serious management is about a performance issue and its resolution. Table 8-3 provides a few examples of code.

- *Management sponsorship/championing.* The person who sponsors or champions an initiative makes a huge difference in the level of support it receives as well as the probable success of its implementation. Here are three rules of thumb with respect to sponsorship/championing:

  1. If there is no senior sponsor or champion, there is a low probability of adoption.
  2. The more senior line support an initiative receives, the greater the probability of its success.
  3. A performance improvement initiative that involves multiple levels of management from the start has a higher probability of success than one championed solely by senior management.

The Psychological Dimension

Improving human performance in the workplace ultimately means change. Change often engenders resistance, especially if those directly affected by the

Table 8-3. Senior Management Statements and Their Meanings

They Say . . .	They Mean . . .
"It is expected that all personnel will adhere to regulations as prescribed in Section 3.4 of the Operating Rules."	"We're getting pressure from inspectors. We have to make this statement to appease them and look as though we're doing something."
"Based on complaints we have been receiving from customers, all customer service agents are henceforth expected to demonstrate empathy and caring service in their interface with customers in order to ensure both efficiency and satisfaction."	"Be nice within the 300 seconds you are allotted per customer call."
"Product knowledge and effective demonstration are keys to successful sales. We will be monitoring enrollments and test scores in the product knowledge and demo workshops. If you have not participated in a training workshop and/or you do not achieve a 90 percent test result, you will be called in for counseling and a note will be placed in your file."	"We're serious about this one. It's important. Don't ignore this message. We mean business."

change perceive it to be burdensome, difficult, disruptive, not in their best interests, a threat, a flavor of the month, or quite simply a nuisance that disturbs the status quo. This is why the performance professional must be aware of the psychological factors involved in change and, from the start, take actions to decrease the potential for apathy or active resistance. Table 8-4 offers some concrete suggestions for dealing with several of the psychological factors associated with performance improvement/change initiatives.

Table 8-4. Negative Perceptions about a Performance Improvement or Change Initiative and Ways to Counteract Them

Negative Perception	Potential Action
"This is bothersome. Who needs it? I've got a lot to do without more changes."	• Create early dialogue with end users. Identify their issues, concerns, and tasks. Verify where they experience bothersome problems and interruptions. Develop counter strategies and actions for overcoming these and inform users and performers that their issues are being addressed. • Keep your interventions/interactions with users and performers low key. Avoid interfering with their current work. Don't be a pest.
"Oh my! Whatever they're trying to do means more work for me."	• Verify current performer and manager workloads. Look for means to reduce effort. Inform direct stakeholders of this. • Keep in mind that your main task is to improve performance while reducing unproductive effort.
"This is going to be hard. I'm not sure I'll be able to do it."	• Analyze performer's current capability levels. Identify gaps with respect to potential new job demands. Build prerequisite training and performance-support systems. • Eliminate new jargon. Keep the language and terminology as familiar as possible. • Break new performances into digestible chunks. Build competence by degree with a great deal of reinforcement along the way. • Select a credible small sample of the performers and help them achieve success. Have them show others how "easy" it is to perform in the new way.
"This change is not in my best interest. It may mean losing my job, losing fellow workers, or hurting my income and career."	• Examine changes to identify whether threats are real. Work to reduce these. Stress personal, meaningful benefits to performers, customers, colleagues, and managers. • Meet with performers to identify fears. Build interventions and communications to minimize these.
"Another flavor-of-the-month! If I keep my head down and stick to the old ways, this too shall pass."	• Separate enthusiastic management beliefs and slogans from fundamental performance improvement requirements. • Collect solid evidence to support the need for improvement and the personal benefits for all concerned. • Avoid flavor-of-the-month labels (such as management by objective, empowerment, management by walking around) and speak in terms of specific, local issues. Also avoid fanfare. Focus on key, meaningful performances and adopt a task-oriented approach (for example, reduce waste by 10 percent, rather than total quality management, reengineering, quality process, or any other cliché).

Putting It All Together

Although this seems like so much to consider and do, it is really not that difficult. As a performance professional you are an agent of change. Professionally speaking, you must be in tune with your surroundings. Considering all of the workplace environmental dimensions described above becomes natural over time. To help you progress in this direction, we propose some activities for you and your team.

An Activity for You

Select a project that you have already completed, are in the process of doing, or with which you are very familiar. Using your knowledge of the project, check off in Worksheet 8-1 the environmental factors that might affect performance. We've left spaces in each environmental dimension for you to add items not included in the worksheet. We're not asking you to do a data-based environmental analysis, but your diligent reflections should identify a few red-flag items and make you more observant of factors that many performance professionals miss.

Now carefully review your worksheet entries. Consider the overall impact on the desired performance improvement initiative if the relevant factors were dealt with.

An Activity for Your WLP Team

Make copies of Worksheet 8-1 on which you wrote your findings and about which you reflected. Distribute them to your team members for discussion. Draw out their observations about the case and then have them work in small groups to examine other projects, using blank copies of Worksheet 8-1. After 30-40 minutes, bring the entire team together to share their observations on the various projects and, more important, to determine what steps the team should take going forward. Add to your growing repertoire of tools a list of potential environmental factors to which WLP team members should pay attention, and some recommended interventions.

Three Major Environmental Interventions

Over the years we have regularly encountered three environmental factors that appear to recur in almost all performance improvement cases. These are (1) lack of clear, specific, and meaningful expectations; (2) lack of timely, useful, and specific feedback; and (3) disruptive task interferences. It's amazing how frequently these performance-killers appear in different settings, individually or in combination. So we'd like to close this chapter with advice for overcoming each of these performance inhibitors.

Setting Clear Expectations

What are they?

- ◆ Clear expectations are expressions of anticipated behaviors and/or accomplishments to be generated by the performers.
- ◆ They are a set of clearly defined performances that the performer knows are desired by the organization.

Worksheet 8-1: Analysis of Environmental Factors Affecting Performance

Environmental Dimension	Has a Potentially Significant Impact on Performance	Reason(s) and/or Evidence	Recommended Intervention
Physical			
• Uncomfortable work space	☐		
• Noise or visual distraction	☐		
• Inadequate lighting	☐		
• Inadequate access to required resources or materials	☐		
• Poorly adapted tools/equipment	☐		
• Threats to safety	☐		
• Difficulty getting to the work site	☐		
• Health and wellness issues	☐		
• Other:	☐		
• Other:	☐		
Social-cultural			
• Language	☐		
• Culture	☐		
• Ethnicity	☐		
• Gender	☐		
• Status	☐		
• Corporate culture	☐		
• Geographic differences	☐		
• Work styles	☐		

(continued on page 122)

Worksheet 8-1: Analysis of Environmental Factors Affecting Performance (continued)

Environmental Dimension	Has a Potentially Significant Impact on Performance	Reason(s) and/or Evidence	Recommended Intervention
Social-cultural (continued) • History/background	☐		
• Education	☐		
• Other:	☐		
• Other:	☐		
Work Systems/Processes • Incompatibilities	☐		
• Site operations	☐		
• Disconnects	☐		
• Inefficiencies	☐		
• Competing	☐		
• Inconsistencies	☐		
• Other:	☐		
• Other:	☐		
Management • Informal leadership	☐		
• Management style	☐		
• Management systems	☐		
• Levels of hierarchy	☐		
• Inconsistencies	☐		
• Lack of committed sponsorship or champion(s)	☐		
• Recognition/reward practices	☐		

Environmental Dimension	Has a Potentially Significant Impact on Performance	Reason(s) and/or Evidence	Recommended Intervention
Management (continued) • Credibility	☐		
• Communication style	☐		
• Other:	☐		
• Other:	☐		
Psychological • Change is perceived as bothersome or as a nuisance	☐		
• Change is perceived as burden-some (more work)	☐		
• Change is perceived as difficult	☐		
• Change is perceived as not in the performer's best interest	☐		
• Change is perceived as a job/career threat	☐		
• Change is perceived as a flavor-of-the-month	☐		
• Other:	☐		
• Other:	☐		

- It is understood that the expectations are both achievable, given the skills/ knowledge of the performer and resources/constraints of the environment.
- The anticipated behaviors and/or accomplishments are verifiable.

With whom can this intervention be used?

- It can be used with populations whose behaviors and/or accomplishments you wish to trigger, improve, or maintain.
- It applies to any individual or group. Generally, the more routine and repetitive the job, the more specific and detailed the expectations should be.

What are the components?

- The components of clear performance expectations are straightforward. They include
  - clearly defined behaviors and/or accomplishments, including performance standards.
  - a defined set of rules and/or procedures for communicating performance expectations to the performer. This contains what to communicate, when to communicate, how the communication is conveyed, and who does the communicating.
  - a means for verifying that performers comprehend and accept the expectations, or for identifying their concerns.
  - a system for monitoring the appropriateness and feasibility of expectations, and a means for adjusting them to organizational conditions.
  - a system for verifying attainment of expectations.

How does the intervention work?

- Establish performance requirements and standards that are meaningful to the performer and desired by the organization.
- Convert performance requirements and standards to statements of expectation.
- With sample performers, verify the clarity and lack of ambiguity in the statements of expectation. Revise as appropriate.
- Identify who will communicate the expectations and where and when this will occur.
- Monitor expectations for appropriateness and feasibility, and revise as necessary.
- Verify attainment of expectations.

What rules should be followed in setting performance expectations?

- Less is more. Create succinct statements of expectation.
- Express expectations in terms and language performers understand.
- Provide written copies of the statements of expectation to which performers can refer.
- Avoid vague or ambiguous language. Be specific and precise. Define all technical terms and concepts to make sure that everyone is working with a common set of understandings.
- To clarify, provide samples or models of desired behaviors and/or accomplishments.
- If there are dangers of misinterpretations, provide close-in (that is, almost, but not quite right) non-examples to help performers discriminate between acceptable and unacceptable performance. Make sure that all value-based

terms are defined in verifiable ways so that there are organizational meanings attributed to these terms rather than varied individual ones.

- Select the most appropriate person and means for communicating expectations. In most cases the immediate supervisor is the best source for communication and clarification of work-related expectations.
- Continuously monitor expectations for relevance, feasibility, and certainty that they are not in conflict with other work priorities.
- Monitor performance to verify that it conforms to expectations.

Developing Feedback Systems

What are they?

- Feedback systems are organized means for providing information about behavior or its effects to an individual or group, with the intention of influencing future performance.
- The information provided is deliberate and purposeful and is aimed at influencing behaviors and outcomes in desirable ways.
- Appropriately designed, implemented, and delivered feedback increases the probability of having the intended effect on future performance.
- Feedback systems have two purposes with respect to influencing future performance: maintain current performance through confirmation (confirming feedback) and change current performance toward desired directions (corrective feedback).

With whom can feedback be used?

- You can develop a feedback system for any population whose behaviors and/or accomplishments you wish to maintain or improve.
- Feedback systems are appropriate for all individuals and groups at all levels of an organization.

For what type of content can it be used?

- All types of content
- All types of performance.

What are the components?

- Feedback systems contain
  - clearly specified behaviors and/or accomplishments, including standards.
  - metrics or other defined means or tools for verifying behaviors and/or accomplishments.
  - a defined set of rules and/or procedures for communicating feedback on performance to the performer. This includes what to communicate, when to communicate, how the communication is conveyed, and who does the communicating.

How does a feedback system work?

- Establish and communicate specific performance objectives and standards that are meaningful to the performer so that the performer knows what is required (clear expectations).
- Create means for verifying performance, either through observations, performance monitoring systems, or results checks.
- Establish suitable metrics that are quantitative and/or qualitative, as appropriate.
- Observe, monitor, and/or verify performance.
- Provide unambiguous and timely feedback on performance.

What rules should you follow in developing a feedback system?

- Focus the feedback system on the performance, never on the person. (For example, "Notice the angle of the knife as it slices the bread. It's tipped to the right. For correct slicing, it must be perpendicular to the cutting board," rather than, "You are cutting at too much of an angle. You should hold your knife straighter.")
- Ensure that the feedback system gives confirming feedback to influence the performer to maintain performance.
- The feedback system also must provide corrective feedback to influence the performer to change performance in a desired direction.
- When providing confirming feedback, avoid corrective feedback and vice-versa. Simultaneous reception of confirming and corrective feedback confuses the performer and decreases performance.
- The feedback system must provide specific feedback, but it should not be so detailed that it overloads the performer's ability to process the information.
- The system can provide confirming feedback either publicly or privately, but must provide corrective feedback only privately.
- The feedback system should provide confirming feedback after successful behaviors and/or accomplishments.
- It also should provide corrective feedback after behavior and/or accomplishment. However, this form of feedback is particularly effective if also given just prior to the *next* performance attempt.
- For simple tasks the system should give feedback immediately.
- For complex tasks, however, it should allow for some time delay before giving feedback so the performer is in a mental state that helps reception and consideration of the feedback.
- It may be most useful to establish logical checkpoints from which performers engaged in a complex task can benefit from feedback. Don't wait until the entire task has been completed to provide feedback.

- Feedback systems must adjust the amount and nature of the feedback to match the level of performance difficulty.
- As part of developing a feedback system, identify opportunities for feedback to occur naturally from the environment, in addition to or as a replacement for human-generated feedback.
- Provide models from which performers can draw correction or confirmation without having to rely on human intervention.

Eliminating Task Interferences

Unlike the two previous forms of performance intervention whereby you develop something, in this case you are taking something away.

What is task interference?

- Task interference is anything that presents an obstacle or barrier to performing a required action.
- Task interferences come in a wide variety of guises. They can be physical objects or barriers that interfere with the accomplishment of a task (for example, locked doors that must be unlocked repeatedly, poorly designed work spaces that require additional effort to do the job, or phones that ring constantly), administrative delays or requirements (for example, filling out a form time after time, or demanding unnecessary authorizing signatures), low priority (often trivial) must-do tasks (for example, writing long reports after each customer visit, or restocking items before helping the next customer), continuously shifting priorities, co-workers asking for assistance, and many more.
- True task interferences genuinely decrease desired performance and are generally a drain on achieving valued accomplishments.

With whom can task interference elimination be used?

- It is appropriate for all jobs and all performers.
- It is especially important in key jobs. Examples include reducing public relations activities for researchers in a cutting-edge biotechnology firm, assigning administrative tasks to assistants for major decision makers, providing bussing assistance to waitstaff in a busy restaurant, and eliminating nonpriority tasks that interfere with sales visits to potential customers.

What are the components?

- Because eliminating interferences is not a system per se, there are no specific components. Generally, however, there are four phases: (1) identifying priority tasks, (2) identifying interferences, (3) eliminating interferences or reassigning lower-priority interfering tasks to others, and (4) monitoring performance change.

How does it work?

- When conducting a front-end analysis, identify priority tasks and accomplishments for the performers.
- Identify obstacles and interferences to achieving priority accomplishments.
- Determine if obstacles and interferences can be eliminated or reassigned.
- Eliminate interferences; reassign low-priority tasks to others.
- Monitor performance changes.

What rules should you follow in eliminating task interferences?

- It is essential to be ruthless in identifying and eliminating interferences. This may require destroying "sacred cows" (like the CEO's weekly staff meetings) or not sharing accomplishments with team members each day. It may also require re-examining policies and procedures to eliminate traditional practices that don't provide benefit.
- Make sure that the interferences you plan to eliminate are truly interferences and will not create future problems (for example, doing away with certain paperwork may create serious legal or audit issues).
- Apply the "least-cost-competent" rule for reassigning lower-priority tasks. This means giving reassigned tasks to capable but less costly or critical players (for example, reassign the typing of senior-level management memos to less costly administrative personnel who may do the reassigned task as well as or even better than the manager).
- Implement task interference elimination carefully and systematically. Explain changes and provide meaningful rationales. Emphasize benefits to performers (for example, additional discretionary time for professional development).
- Monitor performance and communicate improvements to all stakeholders.

An Activity for You

Expectations, feedback, task interferences...these are so important to workplace performance that they should always remain close to the surface of your thoughts in performance improvement projects. Look for opportunities to implement these interventions as early as possible. Review your current projects. Examine your front-end analyses. Focus sharply on one or all three of these performance interventions. The payoffs are quick and dramatic.

An Activity for Your WLP Team

We strongly recommend reviewing the three major performance improvement interventions with your team. Have them hunt for opportunities to clarify expectations, develop a feedback system, and eliminate or reassign interfering tasks. Monitor results and share them with the entire team and appropriate stakeholders. Individually or together, these three constitute the interventions that generally require relatively little effort to develop, incur the least cost, and generate the highest ROI.

Chapter Summary

This chapter addressed nonlearning, environmental interventions to attain desired performance. In it

- ◆ you examined the environment and its effect on human performance in the workplace.
- ◆ you encountered a variety of environmental dimensions that influence the behaviors and accomplishments of performers in the work setting: physical, social-cultural, work systems and processes, management, and psychological.
- ◆ you and your WLP team selected projects to examine or re-examine for potential environmental factors that affected performance, and you used a worksheet to help you in your analysis.
- ◆ you studied what we believe to be the Big Three performance improvement interventions. They are not necessarily the most important, but the lack of clear expectations, the lack of timely and usable feedback, and the presence of task interferences seem to crop up in a great many places. Clearing these up is relatively quick and inexpensive, and often produces spectacular results.
- ◆ you examined a front-end analysis that indicated one, two, or all three of these environmental interventions were appropriate, and we recommended that you apply the interventions and monitor results.

This was a very important chapter for you as a performance professional. If you are used to creating learning interventions whenever the organization is faced with a performance improvement or change requirement, this chapter content offered new perspectives and tools.

The next chapter continues exploring nonlearning interventions. In it you will encounter the emotional dimensions of workplace performance. Turn the page to enter this intriguing new territory.

Nonlearning Interventions: Emotional

This chapter

- presents you with a category of performance interventions that is less familiar to training and performance professionals than are learning and environmental interventions—emotional interventions
- introduces a model that serves as both a diagnostic and a prescriptive tool for selecting and implementing a major form of emotional intervention—incentive systems
- provides a "recipe" for creating an incentive system intervention, and offers an example
- includes guidance on initiating workplace motivation interventions
- suggests activities for you and your WLP team to build competency in this less-well-traveled region of human performance improvement.

Tools in this chapter include

- the Performance Improvement by Incentives Model
- a set of guidelines for applying the model
- prescriptive guidelines for enhancing workplace motivation.

Incentives, Motivation, and Workplace Performance

The "emotional" dimensions of the workplace setting are somewhat murky and vague for most performance professionals. There are two reasons for this. The first is that most of you have come into your training and performance-support roles via previous, unrelated subject-matter expertise. Perhaps, for example, you were an excellent salesman, technician, accountant, or call center agent. Your proficiency at doing the job plus your personal characteristics and interests made you a desirable candidate for your current training/performance-support position. You may have been a training professional with appropriate academic qualifications and experience and been placed in your current post because you know about learning. Whatever your situation, it is highly unlikely that you are a motivation or incentive specialist. In our studies of training and WLP organizations, we have met very few incumbents with that form of expertise.

The second reason that the area of emotional intervention is relatively uncharted for us is that a great deal of belief, opinion, and myth inhabit this territory. When performance is not as it should be, a manager can quickly jump to the conclusion that "my people aren't motivated," and respond to that conclusion with an order to "get me a motivational speaker to fire them up." Other managers may interpret lack of performance when workers know how to do a job as a sign that they need some form of incentive to "get them going." Intuition appears to prevail here, based on subjective decision making.

We spent more than a year as members of a research team studying incentives and motivation and their relationship to workplace performance. We reviewed all of the existing published research we could find and delved in depth into more than 140 companies, questioning developers and administrators of incentive systems, recipients of incentives, and recipients' supervisors about their incentive practices and results. In this chapter we share our findings with you, translating them into actionable guidelines that you may apply as a performance professional.

The Performance Improvement by Incentives Model

Business and industry in the United States spend more than $60 billion annually on formal, identifiable training programs, activities, and infrastructure. That's an impressive sum. But the amount pales in comparison with the estimated $117 billion in annual expenditures for tangible incentive programs aimed at encouraging workers of every variety to perform well—or at least better. The interesting (and frightening) aspect of this is that almost all of the decisions about which incentives to use, for whom, and how they should be applied are made with very little or no reference to research on incentive use. Furthermore, most decisions regarding incentives are made unsystematically, rarely on the basis of data from previous incentive ventures. The bad news is that enormous quantities of money are spent inefficiently to attain desired results from employees and third-party partners. The good news is that this state of affairs offers wonderful opportunities for you, the performance professional, to clean things up.

So to help you prepare for this opportunity, let's take a look at the Performance Improvement by Incentives (PIBI) Model. Derived from research on motivation and incentives, this model has been validated through an examination of best practices in an array of workplace organizations.[1]

---

1. All of the preceding information and the PIBI Model itself have been derived from a study funded by SITE Foundation and sponsored by the International Society for Performance Improvement. Results of the study have been published in Stolovitch, Clark, and Condly 2002.

Overview of the PIBI Model

You can use the PIBI Model for both *diagnostic* and *prescriptive* purposes. It helps you determine whether an incentive-type intervention is appropriate, guides you step-by-step to develop and implement a relevant incentive system with a high probability of success, and points out where and how to troubleshoot your incentive system intervention if difficulties arise. Figure 9-1 illustrates the eight major "events" for selecting, implementing, monitoring, and troubleshooting incentive system interventions.

In Table 9-1 there is a brief description of what happens in each of the model's eight events.

Creating Your Own Incentive System

The PIBI Model helps you systemically view how all the events of an incentive system intervention fit together, from initial findings in the front-end analysis to

Figure 9-1. The Eight Events That Make Up the Performance Improvement by Incentives Model

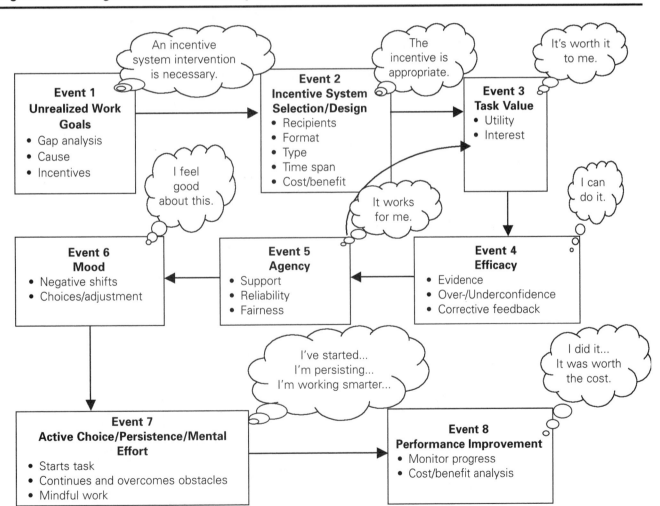

Table 9-1. PIBI Model—Descriptions of the Eight Events

Event	What Happens

Event 1: Unrealized work goals	• The front-end analysis indicates a performance gap.
	• People possess the skills and knowledge to perform as desired, but are either avoiding achieving targeted results or don't wish to try.
	• Through further analysis, you may discover
	  —Performers are distracted by less-important or competing goals that are easier to achieve or more rewarding
	  —Desired performance goals are perceived as either not challenging enough to bother with or too challenging (out of reach)
	  —Desired performance goals are unclear, vague, abstract, purposeless, uninteresting, or even considered degrading.
	• An incentive system intervention is deemed appropriate.

Event 2: Incentive system selection/design	• Desired performance goals are clearly defined and endorsed by credible leaders.
	• Introduction of an incentive system intervention is approved.
	• The appropriate recipients of the incentives are identified.
	• The format of incentive approach is selected:
	  —Quota system—incentives for exceeding current performance levels or a pre-set base; the more one succeeds, the higher the reward
	  —Piece-rate system—incentives for producing more
	  —Contest system—top performers get the reward.
	  Of all the systems, quota works best..
	• The type of incentive is selected (it is essential to confer with the recipients in making the choice):
	  —Money—research shows this has the most powerful effect if viewed as significant by recipients.
	  —Travel or gifts—generally effective, and typically less costly than monetary incentives. Implementation is key.
	  —Recognition—generally the least expensive form of incentive (for example, employee-of-the-month designation, performance awards). Research is unclear on the impact of recognition alone, but it indicates greater effect if coupled with tangible incentives.
	• The length of the incentive system intervention is determined. In general, longer programs (one year or more) have greater impact than do shorter ones.
	• A cost/benefit analysis is conducted to determine the most cost-effective incentive system and the expected ROI.

Event 3: Task value	• For the selected incentive system to be of value, it must more than overcome the effort of working longer, harder, or smarter.
	  —Utility value—if achieving the performance goal is not considered valuable to the performers, the incentive must be strong enough to build commitment to the goal.
	  —Interest value—the greater the interest (intrinsic value) performers have in achieving the goal in and for itself, the less powerful or costly the incentives have to be.
	  —Skill/Importance value—if performers see that achieving the performance goal will help build personally meaningful skills or contribute to advancement, the incentives need not be as costly as if the contrary were true.

Event 4: Efficacy	• When the value of the task and incentive has been accepted as adequate, performers try to determine whether they can do it—efficacy (self and team). • The more evidence (through examples, explanations, results) performers receive that they can achieve desired results, the greater their commitment. • Performers who are under- or overconfident ("I can't do it," or "This is so easy I don't need to expend effort") become detached. • The more timely and meaningful corrective feedback performers receive to help them succeed, the greater their sense of efficacy.

Event	What Happens
Event 5: Agency	• Agency has to do with performer belief about how much support the organization will provide to achieve desired performance. Proper implementation of the incentive system intervention is critical. • Agency increases when the following are provided: training, frequent supportive feedback, models for coping with difficulties, appropriate tools and time, fairness, ownership of results, and an environment in which there is a high probability of success. • As agency declines ("The organization doesn't support me"), task value and efficacy also decline.
Event 6: Mood	• Workers' emotional states strongly affect performance. • A negative work atmosphere can powerfully harm a well-designed and -supported incentive system. • Positive environments and emotions foster commitment and improve results.
Event 7: Active choice/ persistence/mental effort	• To verify that the incentive system intervention is working in the initial stages of implementation, monitor three types of behaviors: —Starting the task—performers are actually beginning to engage in the right behaviors, ones they either previously resisted or were unwilling to do. —Continuing the task and overcoming obstacles—performers are doing more of what they initiated and are doing it better. They are persisting and overcoming obstacles more than before the incentive system was implemented. —Carrying on the task mindfully—performers are thinking about how to achieve performance success. They are innovating and developing novel success strategies.
Event 8: Performance improvement	• The desired performance goals are being achieved and the gap is decreasing. Making this determination requires monitoring and measurement. • Cost/benefit analysis and ROI calculations are performed to verify the effect of the incentive system intervention.

verification of improved performance. What follows here is a "recipe" for creating an incentive system of your own. The recipe is laid out as an outline of prescriptive task steps that very closely match the PIBI Model, event by event. (Some of the words are different from those used in the model. This is to make doing—that is, creating an incentive system intervention—a bit easier.) We recommend you read through this recipe as you would in cooking or baking to obtain a sense of the flow and sequence of steps. Picture what is happening at each step. Note that we divide each event of the PIBI Model into three phases: *implementation* (what you do), *monitoring* (what you check), and *repair* (what you fix or cause to have happen to make things work). Each event also contains principles for you to apply as you proceed. Following this recipe is an example of its application.

An Incentive System Intervention Recipe

Event 1: Unrealized Work Goals

1.1 Implementation

    1.1.1 Identify unrealized work goals based on an analysis of the gap between current and desired performance.

    1.1.2 Specify performance goals that are concrete and challenging, but feasible.

1.2 Monitoring

    1.2.1 Determine if gap is the result of skills/knowledge deficiency.

    1.2.2 Determine if gap is caused by environmental obstacles or deficiencies.

    1.2.3 Determine if gap is motivation based.

1.3 Repair

    1.3.1 For a gap based on skills/knowledge deficiency, provide training and/or job aids.

    1.3.2 For a gap based on environmental obstacles or deficiencies, remove obstacles or correct deficiencies.

    1.3.3 For a gap based on motivational deficiencies, consider using an incentive system.

Principles:

It is rare for a single intervention to be sufficient for achieving workplace results. Even if the major cause for the gap between desired and actual performance is motivation based, and incentives are appropriate, always verify that skills/knowledge and environmental conditions also are sufficient to achieve goals.

The more challenging the goal, the greater the effort individuals or teams must exert. However, they must perceive the goal as possible to achieve with maximum effort.

Event 2: Incentive System Selection/Design

2.1 Implementation

    2.1.1 Specify the target recipients of the incentives. (When feasible, teams are the preferred target.)

    2.1.2 Involve management and (as culturally appropriate) targeted recipients of the incentives in the incentive system selection/design process.

    2.1.3 Select incentives that are workable and acceptable to the organization and attractive to the targeted recipients. The possible incentive types are monetary, gift/travel, and recognition. Monetary is often the preferred choice. Verify this for your setting.

    2.1.4 Select from the three incentive system formats: quota, piece-rate, contest. When feasible, quota is the preferred choice.

    2.1.5 Specify the time span: long term (greater than one year), intermediate term (six months to one year), or short term (less than six months). When possible, a long-term time span is preferred.

2.2 Monitoring

    2.2.1 Verify to ensure that targeted recipients, supervisors, and organizational management understand the details of the incentive system.

2.3 Repair

    2.3.1 Re-communicate incentive system specifics to individuals or units that demonstrate a lack of understanding about the incentive system.

Principles:

Although the participation of the targeted recipients generally is desirable in selecting incentives and/or designing the incentive system, the level, nature, and process of participation must be appropriate to cultural, national, and organizational norms. For multicultural and global organizations, verify to determine the appropriate level of participation for the various affected groups.

An incentive system may be composed of more than one type of incentive. It may include a combination of monetary, gift/travel, and recognition elements.

Event 3: Task Value

3.1 Implementation

    3.1.1 Communicate to target recipients, their supervisors, and all other concerned parties the nature of the incentive system and its mechanics so that the link between the incentive(s) and the desired improved performance is clear and unambiguous.

    3.1.2 Explain that the incentive offered is intended to create "utility" value for achieving beyond current levels of performance.

3.2 Monitoring

    3.2.1 Verify that utility value has been established. Verify that targeted recipients value the incentive enough to increase their performance and maintain it in the face of distractions and other priorities.

    3.2.2 Check to find if interest is waning.

3.3 Repair

    3.3.1 Revise details of the incentive system to increase utility.

Principle:

The less the inherent interest in the task to be performed, the more there is a need for a valued incentive to be linked to it to drive performance. The incentive serves a utility purpose—it replaces interest in the task with interest in money or gifts. Communicate a clear and strong relationship between the two.

Event 4: Efficacy

4.1 Implementation

    4.1.1 Provide evidence from the past performance of the targeted individuals and teams that they are capable of achieving at the desired level, and/or describe the success of other individuals and teams similar to the targeted recipients.

4.2 Monitoring

    4.2.1 Monitor team and individual confidence that they can achieve the desired performance levels and earn the incentives. Watch for evidence of underconfidence or overconfidence.

    4.2.2.1 Determine if there is evidence of underconfidence in the form of errors in performing the task, a gradual withdrawal from performing the task, and/or a negative mood shift when talking about the performance goals or incentives.

    4.2.2.2 Determine if there is evidence of overconfidence in the form of errors—and when confronted with such errors or poor performance, there is a refusal to accept responsibility or the worker's mood shifts to anger when talking about the task or the incentive program.

4.3 Repair

    4.3.1 Focus on task performance and specify what is necessary to increase performance. Do not focus negatively on the person or team.

    4.3.2 For underconfidence, break the task into smaller, more manageable components, and provide help.

    4.3.3 For overconfidence, provide convincing evidence that the strategy performers are using is flawed, and demonstrate that another approach will succeed.

Principles:

The greater the confidence of the individuals and teams to achieve desired performance improvement goals, the higher the probability of their achieving success, especially with respect to challenging goals. But overconfidence is a performance stopper. Overconfident people often apply the wrong strategy (or maintain inappropriate beliefs) and do not take responsibility for their failure to achieve the performance goal.

The less confidence the individuals and teams have that they can achieve desired performance improvement goals, the greater the need to provide support by breaking the feared task into smaller tasks and offering help. This strategy often raises the confidence level.

Event 5: Agency

Note: The greatest number of incentive system breakdowns generally occur in this event.

5.1 *Implementation*

5.1.1 Provide management support for task performance in the form of clear communication about the incentive system, fair and equitable management of the system, effective work processes, adequate resources, and assistance as required and feasible.

5.1.2 Use a transparent administrative system for tracking achievements and rewards.

5.1.3 Communicate individual and team progress on a regular and frequent schedule.

5.2 *Monitoring*

5.2.1 Develop an effective system in which targeted recipients are encouraged to report concerns and problems associated with organizational support of employee performance and its management of the incentive system.

5.2.2 Do not punish people for reporting problems, even if the problems turn out not to be substantive.

5.3 *Repair*

5.3.1 Thank the people who report problems and investigate them.

5.3.2 Report the results of your problem analysis to the person or team who reported it.

5.3.3 Make a plan to remove barriers to performance or provide convincing evidence that perceived barriers do not exist.

Principle:

Perceived implementation breakdowns result in targeted recipients reassessing task value downward. This has a negative effect on task performance and defeats the purpose of the incentive system.

Event 6: Mood

6.1 *Implementation—none*

6.2 *Monitoring*

6.2.1 Monitor workplace climate for negative mood changes (anger, negativity).

6.3 *Repair*

6.3.1 Let people decide how to do their jobs and decorate their work space (within reason and if they do not intrude on others).

6.3.2 Adjust environment to improve workplace climate (for example, permit listening privately to music while working, if possible).

6.3.3 Provide positive, energetic, and fair managers and work models.

Principle:

Workplace climate and individual mood can have an effect on motivation and performance. Mood is often a strong indicator of performance shifts and motivation. When mood becomes sufficiently negative, performance slows or stops. Strong positive mood is not essential, but strong negative emotion must be avoided.

Event 7: Active Choice/Persistence/Mental Effort

7.1 *Implementation—none*

7.2 *Monitoring*

7.2.1 Verify that targeted recipients are

- choosing to perform the targeted tasks in the desired manner
- persisting at the targeted tasks
- mentally engaged ("using their heads") to achieve desired results.

7.3 Repair
    7.3.1 Cycle back through the events of the PIBI Model to identify the cause(s) for failure of active choice/persistent behavior/exertion of mental effort.

Principles:
Tasks for which incentives have been provided may lead to neglect of other essential tasks that carry no incentives. Monitor to ensure that targeted recipients perform all necessary tasks related to the job. Make receipt of incentives contingent on this accomplishment.

    A decline in active choice, persistence, and/or mental effort signals a need to repair the value, the agency, and/or the efficacy (see Events 3, 4, and 5).

Event 8: Performance Improvement

8.1 Implementation—none
8.2 Monitoring
    8.2.1 Monitor progress continually.
    8.2.2 Monitor the cost/benefit analysis of the incentive system.
8.3 Repair
    8.3.1 Review Events 1 and 2 when performance does not increase. It is possible that the gap analysis was incorrect and that people lack adequate knowledge and skills to perform or that the work processes or materials are missing or inadequate. It is also possible that the incentive is not creating value for the task, and so requires adjustment.

Principle:
The success of the incentive system is judged by the attainment of performance goals at a cost that is less than the value of the results. For example, you wouldn't want to put in place an incentive system that costs $500,000 when the value of anticipated results fell short of that figure. Ongoing monitoring of progress toward goals and communication of successes to targeted recipients and other affected groups are necessary to sustain incentive system momentum.

An Incentive System in Action

Although the PIBI Model recipe is sound and it works, it may be difficult to imagine it in action. The scenario that follows brings to life an application of the steps you just reviewed. As you read through the Lightning Sales scenario, mentally place yourself in the context and imagine that this is your project.

The Scenario: Lightning Sales
Organization: Lightning Electronics
Situation: Lightning produces a superior line of products at very reasonable prices (20-30 percent less than the big-name manufacturers). It also has a very good reputation for technical support. Given the current economic conditions in which everyone is trying to reduce equipment costs, and based on various market studies it has conducted, Lightning's management believes that there is a huge opportunity to increase sales of its peripheral products (such as printers, plotters, scanners, keyboards, hard drives, and monitors) through independent vendors. Lightning knows that customers tend to go for well-known brands, and that those popular manufacturers often provide special incentives to sales reps in the form of prizes, meals, and merchandise.
Desired performance improvement: Increase sales of Lightning peripheral equipment through authorized vendors. Increase sales by 200 percent.

Means: Launch an effective incentive system to encourage sales reps to push Lightning products.

Targeted incentive recipients: Sales representatives for outside vendors who sell a broad variety of peripheral equipment from multiple manufacturers, many of which have far greater name-brand recognition than Lightning has.

Prescriptive Steps
Event 1: Unrealized Work Goals

1.1 Implementation

    1.1.1 There is a gap of 200 percent between actual and possible sales volumes.

    1.1.2 The desired performance goal is concrete and specific (a 200 percent increase in sales), challenging (a rather large annual increase in sales), but feasible (according to market analysis).

1.2 Monitoring

    1.2.1 The sales gap is not the result of skill or knowledge deficiencies because there is no evidence that the sales staff is poorly trained or is skillfully inadequate.

    1.2.2 There are no environmental obstacles keeping the sales reps of the outside vendors from selling Lightning products.

    1.2.3 The gap is motivation based. The sales reps are aware of the high quality and low cost of Lightning's products, but they receive incentives from competing manufacturers to sell their products.

1.3 Repair

    1.3.1 No additional training is required.

    1.3.2 No environmental obstacles must be removed.

    1.3.3 The use of an incentive system is warranted because the performance deficit is motivation based and because other manufacturers offer incentives for the sale of their products.

Event 2: Incentive System Selection/Design

2.1 Implementation

    2.1.1 Incentives will be offered to all outside vendor sales reps individually. Lightning is convinced that sales will increase because the sales reps can earn the same incentives as with other manufacturers, and they can market more aggressively to consumers a product of higher quality at a lower cost—features that will boost sales.

    2.1.2 Lightning management does not involve outside vendor sales reps in the design of the incentive system because they are located in retail outlets throughout the United States. Lightning surveys them regarding their openness to an incentive system. Survey results reveal a widely positive response.

    2.1.3 Lightning does not want to spend more in incentives for a given volume of sales than do competing manufacturers, so the chosen incentives will match (in cost and kind) the various gift and travel incentives offered by the competing manufacturers.

    2.1.4 The format will be a quota system. All sales reps who sell Lightning products at rates greater than the "average" sales rep (as determined by an examination of sales data) will be eligible for gifts of their choosing that increase in quality and cost as their volume of sales increases.

    2.1.5 Because Lightning's incentive system is a match for the incentive systems of other manufacturers, the system will last indefinitely.

2.2 Monitoring

    2.2.1 Formal letters are to be mailed to each sales rep explaining the particulars of Lightning's new incentive system. Additional letters will be sent to each store's sales manager to distribute to newly hired sales personnel. Lightning Electronics will verify receipt of the letters and encourage the sharing of information among sales reps and managers. Lightning also will verify that there is interest in and approval of what is being proffered.

2.3 Repair

    2.3.1 A follow-up letter is mailed to each sales manager to verify that sales reps have received letters from Lightning. If there are any concerns about appropriateness of the incentive system, Lightning will make suitable modifications based on sales rep and manager input.

Event 3: Task Value

3.1 Implementation

    3.1.1 Formal letters are mailed to each sales rep, explaining the particulars of Lightning's new incentive system. Additional letters are sent to each store's sales manager to distribute to newly hired sales personnel.

    3.1.2 A feature of the letters is mention of how the incentives are intended to motivate the sales reps to make extra effort to market Lightning products. Also stressed are Lightning's high quality and excellent service reputation, which create high consumer value.

3.2 Monitoring

    3.2.1 A return-requested survey form asking for questions or comments is included with the letter sent to sales reps and sales managers. Lightning uses the survey results as an indicator of how well the reps understand the utility value of the incentives offered. The interest that sales reps have in selling computer products for a living is not one of Lightning's concerns. Their only concern is with the utility value the sales reps have for Lightning's products.

3.3 Repair

    3.3.1 If future sales data indicate that there are stores that have not shown any marked increase in sales, or that have not made any claims on incentive gifts, Lightning will verify that those sales reps have been properly informed of the incentive system.

Event 4: Efficacy

4.1 Implementation

    4.1.1 Lightning mails copies of trade journal articles that demonstrate how effective incentives can be in greatly boosting sales. Additionally, Lightning asks sales managers to scour their own sales records to see how sales of competing manufacturers' products increased when incentives were first offered.

4.2 Monitoring

    4.2.1 Lightning will ask vendor sales managers to determine if sales reps doubt they can increase sales of Lightning products.

    4.2.1.1 Sales managers will be asked to report to Lightning if there are reps who display signs of underconfidence about selling Lightning products, such as reductions in sales efforts, or sour talk about Lightning's products and its incentive system.

4.2.1.2 Sales managers will be asked to report to Lightning if there are representatives who are displaying signs of overconfidence about selling Lightning products, such as expecting to receive very expensive incentive gifts, bragging about how much they can sell, and blaming their failures on Lightning's "lousy" product quality.

4.3 Repair

4.3.1 A few weeks into the program, Lightning will send a general troubleshooting letter to sales reps and their managers. The letter will address various difficulties that sales reps may be encountering in increasing sales.

4.3.2 Part of the letter will address underconfident reps and will seek to provide sales remediation information.

4.3.3 The other part of the letter will seek to reduce levels of overconfidence by explaining how reasonable increases in sales can be accomplished.

Event 5: Agency

5.1 Implementation

5.1.1 A select number of Lightning's customer service personnel are made available to the sales representatives to assist them with any questions or concerns they might have about the operation of the incentive system.

5.1.2 Because Lightning knows that if its recordkeeping is inaccurate, sales representatives will reassess the value of its incentive system and probably focus their attention on selling competing products, management will devote a specific number of accountants to tracking and monitoring sales, revenues, and the earning and awarding of gift incentives.

5.1.3 Monthly progress reports will be mailed to all vendor sales managers, enumerating the year-to-date sales of Lightning products for each sales rep.

5.2 Monitoring

5.2.1 Lightning's customer service personnel, as well as its Website and email address, can be used by sales reps to get answers to questions or express concerns about the incentive system.

5.2.2 It is Lightning's policy to investigate all concerns raised, and to report to the complainant the results of the investigation without prejudice.

5.3 Repair

5.3.1 Lightning sends out small notes or cards thanking sales representatives (who have identified themselves) for their interest in the incentive program.

5.3.2 Results are reported to sales representatives who made the original complaint.

5.3.3 Lightning's management is cataloging complaints and concerns to determine if there is a pattern to them. From the catalogued complaints and concerns, management will develop a plan to correct the problems.

Event 6: Mood

6.1 Implementation—none

6.2 Monitoring

6.2.1 It is not possible for Lightning to monitor the mood of sales reps directly. Therefore, it is relying on sales managers to report mood changes, and on reps to send in complaints via email, Internet, phone, or fax.

6.3 Repair

6.3.1 Lightning is not telling the outside vendor sales reps how to sell Lightning's products. The sales reps are free to use whatever marketing or sales strategy they wish to meet their sales objectives. Lightning does, however, provide excellent sales and technical documentation, as well as efficient sales aids.

6.3.2 Lightning does not involve itself in details of the reps' physical work environments.

6.3.3 Lightning encourages the sales managers to speak with their sales reps to stimulate participation in the new incentive system.

Event 7: Active Choice/Persistence/Mental Effort

7.1 Implementation—none

7.2 Monitoring

7.2.1 Via the monthly reports with aggregated and individual data, each sales manager and sales rep is made aware of his or her total sales, the kinds of gifts that could be earned, and how much progress needs to be made to reach particular desired incentives.

7.3 Repair

7.3.1 If failures to raise sales persist, then Lightning will reassess the details of the entire incentive system and take appropriate corrective measures.

Event 8: Performance Improvement

8.1 Implementation—none

8.2 Monitoring

8.2.1 Through its accounting system and monthly reports, Lightning will track sales data and deliver those data to its vendors' sales reps.

8.2.2 Lightning will perform a quarterly cost/benefit analysis to determine if sales have increased, how much has been spent on incentives, and if maintenance of the incentive system is warranted.

8.3 Repair

8.3.1 If progress is not being made toward meeting the work goal, or if the system fails the cost/benefit analysis, then Lightning will reassess the system and its stated work goals.

An Activity for You

Creating and implementing a complete incentive system intervention is very desirable, but it's most likely beyond the realm of feasibility for you at this point. What you can do, however, is review past and current projects to determine if any of them might have fared better if an incentive system had been devised. What indicators were present to suggest this to you? Imagine that you had a mandate to develop an incentive system to meet the desired performance goals of the project. Apply the PIBI Model recipe to it and mentally walk through each of the events. Decide what would have to be done, concretely, to achieve success.

An Activity for Your WLP Team

Bring your team together to examine the PIBI Model, the recipe, and the Lightning Sales example. Discuss the roles that team members might play in helping develop and implement an incentive system intervention. Then as a team find out if there is a current incentive program within your organization. As investigators, discover as much about it as you can. Here are some questions for which you should obtain responses:

1. In what part of the organization has the incentive system been implemented?
2. Why was an incentive system selected?

3. What is the desired performance outcome?

4. Who selected the incentives? Were recipients involved in any way in the selection?

5. On what basis was the incentive system selected (for example, previous success, collected data, or vendor recommendation)?

6. How was the incentive system introduced?

7. What attempts were made to ensure the appropriate levels of task value, efficacy, and agency?

8. Is the incentive system working well? What are the process and results indicators?

9. Has a cost/benefit analysis been conducted? What is the ROI?

10. Based on all the information you have gathered, what is working and what is not?

As a team, apply the PIBI Model and determine what you would do differently. Be systematic in your thinking and planning. By going through this exercise for a current or recent incentive initiative within your organization, you will emerge more competent and confident to add incentive system design and development to your professional toolbox.

Motivational Interventions

In chapter 8 of *Training Ain't Performance* (pp. 128-130 and 133), we briefly introduced emotional interventions and discussed *motivation*. This is a somewhat slippery term with many connotations attached to it, so let's revisit it in greater depth. This will help you create some motivational interventions that, believe it or not, are relatively easy to develop and implement.

Motivation—What Is It?

Essentially, motivation is an internal state that triggers in us the desire to do something—"the push from within." Motivation drives us. It's a vital part of performance. It may be intrinsically driven—we want to do something because of our natural instincts and desires—or extrinsically stimulated—a reward that we would like to obtain is attached to successful performance. Because people are often very different in their interests and desires, what motivates one person may not be appealing at all to someone else.

Although the following examples are fairly superficial, we are asking you to decide whether the person would be intrinsically motivated to perform or would require some extrinsic motivational agent (check one).

Potential Performer	Required Task	Is Motivated Intrinsically	Requires External Motivating Agent
1. Teenager who loves sports, movies, and hanging out with friends	Wash dishes	☐	☐
2. Opera fan	Listen to a highly rated, recently released recording of "Aida"	☐	☐
3. Customer service agent who chose her career because she really wants to be of service to customers	Sell new products	☐	☐
4. Sales representative who likes nothing better than making a sale to a challenging customer	Sell new products	☐	☐
5. Manager who got her position because of superior technical capability and individual technical accomplishments	Coach weak performers	☐	☐

Here are the likely correct responses:

Potential Performer	Required Task	Is Motivated Intrinsically	Requires External Motivating Agent
1. Teenager who loves sports, movies, and hanging out with friends	Wash dishes	☐	☒
2. Opera fan	Listen to a highly rated, recently released recording of "Aida"	☒	☐
3. Customer service agent who chose her career because she really wants to be of service to customers	Sell new products	☐	☒
4. Sales representative who likes nothing better than making a sale to a challenging customer	Sell new products	☒	☐
5. Manager who got her position because of superior technical capability and individual technical accomplishments	Coach weak performers	☐	☒

Numbers 1 and 2 are fairly obvious. Few teenagers naturally want to wash dishes. An avid opera fan probably would wish to listen to a highly rated, new recording without some extrinsic agent. Number 3, the service-oriented agent probably wouldn't want to be a salesperson—so she'd need an extrinsic motivating agent that has meaning and value to her. Conversely, the sales rep in number 4 would most likely enjoy selling new products. In number 5, our guess is that the manager would not naturally wish to spend her time coaching weak performers, but this is a guess—it could go either way.

Our aim in the exercise above was to give you practice with the concepts of intrinsic and extrinsic motivators. Now let's apply and, to some extent, manipulate them.

Continuing with the term and concept of motivation, research indicates that there are three major components that affect it: value, confidence, and mood. Here is what we wrote in *Training Ain't Performance* (p. 128):

- *Value*—how highly a person values the desired performance. The more highly he or she values it, the greater the motivation.
- *Confidence*—how strongly a person feels she or he will be successful in performing. Under- or overconfidence lowers motivation. The optimal motivating state is one of challenge along with an expectation of success through applied effort.
- *Mood*—a person's emotional state when required to perform. The more positive the mood the more motivated. Workplace conditions and climate affect mood.

This leads directly to how the performance professional can intervene at the motivational level. Table 9-2 lists each of the three key factors and suggests a suitable form of intervention. It is predicated on two important prerequisites:

- You have conducted a front-end analysis and found evidence of a lack of motivation to perform as desired.
- You have investigated the lack of motivation (using interviews, observation, focus groups) and discovered that there is a lack of value attributed to the desired performance, a lack of confidence in being able to perform, an overconfidence that leads to neglect and errors, or a negative mood that depresses motivation—or perhaps a combination of these factors.

If these prerequisites have been accomplished, use Table 9-2 to determine your choice of interventions.

Motivation to perform begins with recruiting, selecting, and hiring the right people for the job. If there is endemic lack of motivation, examine the hiring and promotion criteria and practices. Although motivational interventions such as those listed in Table 9-2 can improve motivation, they can't overcome the innate characteristics of inappropriately selected performers.

Table 9-2. Motivational Interventions

Situation Requiring Intervention	Motivational Intervention
Lack of personal value	• Explain the value of the desired performance for performers, organization, and customers. Stress short- and long-term benefits. Use meaningful, concrete examples. • Demonstrate how others resembling the targeted performers have benefited from the performance. Give examples. • Explain the consequences of nonperformance. Avoid threats. • Demonstrate how desired performance can help performers achieve results they desire. • Use role models that the performers admire and trust to build value. • Reinforce all signs of highlighted interest or increased perceived value.
Lack of confidence	• Break the desired performance into smaller, simpler performances. Train, coach, and provide practice and feedback. Reward all progress, no matter how small. • Have people similar to the target performers describe and share their efforts and successes. Show that "others like you achieved success." • Focus feedback on the task, not the person. Patient practice and feedback about task performance, positively given, builds confidence.
Overconfidence	• Increase the challenge level. Provide more complex or difficult tasks. • Identify errors or lost opportunities resulting from overconfidence and have performers explain how these occurred. Have the performers generate quality checks. • Set artificial standards of quantity, quality, or time, and raise the bar to maintain the challenge.
Negative mood	• Analyze the environment to identify causes of negative mood. These might include job/security threats, harassment, inflexibility/regimentation, trivial and degrading practices, unnecessary restrictions or personal choices, sterile environment, unfair or discriminatory practices, cultural bias, bullying, favoritism, inconsistent practices, vague communications, and many others. • Eliminate mood depressors. • Build a positive atmosphere that enhances an individual's desire to perform. • Increase positive social activities and mutual support systems.

Putting Emotional Interventions Together

The overall environment and culture of the organization along with its myriad practices establish a large number of conditions affecting the emotional side of performance. The performance professional must attend to emotional factors that influence how people work and what they accomplish. When you are a performance professional, rebuilding the organization is beyond the scope of your job description. More realistically, when improved desired performance is the issue, you have the responsibility to identify all the major factors that affect the gap between desired and current performance. If in your front-end analysis or during later phases of your work you discover emotional factors at play, you must deal with them. Two main groupings of interventions are incentive systems and motivational changes. Both of these are less familiar to training and WLP groups. Now you have some guidelines and tools to help you grow in this emotional arena.

An Activity for You

Identify a person in the organization whose performance is not at the desired level. Conduct an informal front-end analysis. Determine if there is a motivational dimension to the lack of performance. If not, move on to another person until the motivational component appears. Using Table 9-2, determine which of the underlying motivational factors are present. Select the interventions you would apply. Share your findings with that person's manager. Implement the interventions. Monitor results and, without identifying the person in question, share the results with your WLP team.

Chapter Summary

This chapter dealt with a set of performance improvement interventions less well known than those of the previous two chapters. Emotional interventions stretch us as performance professionals. They also contribute immensely to the value we can offer our clients. In the course of this chapter,

- you were introduced to the emotional side of performance improvement with an explanation of why this is a road less traveled for most of us.
- you encountered the PIBI Model derived from research on incentive use and best practices in business and industry.
- you examined the eight "events" of the PIBI Model and acquired some new vocabulary—*task value, utility, efficacy,* and *agency.*
- you received a recipe for developing and implementing an incentive system.
- having examined an incentive system in action, you reviewed a past or current project in which an incentive system intervention might have been/might be relevant, and planned how you might intervene, using the PIBI Model and guidelines.
- you engaged your WLP team in an investigative exercise by examining a recent or current incentive program in your organization and determining, with the PIBI Model to assist you, how the team might have proceeded differently.
- you explored motivational interventions and, for practice, applied your learning to a person whose motivation was lacking.

With this chapter we conclude the examination of nonlearning interventions. In chapter 10 we turn to issues of consulting. A major transformation must take place to move from being a training group that responds to client requests by churning out training products to performing a more consultative service. This is what awaits you when you turn the page.

From Training Order-Taker to Performance Consultant

This chapter

- ◆ defines what it means to be a WLP consultant
- ◆ helps you determine what kind of performance consultant you are
- ◆ directs you in looking both backward and forward in your work to identify how you might have acted or will be able to act differently as a professional performance consultant
- ◆ provides you with a number of performance-consulting tools and guidelines.

Tools in this chapter include

- ◆ a consulting inquiry or request sheet
- ◆ a set of initial meeting guidelines
- ◆ a proposal outline
- ◆ guidelines for reporting to clients
- ◆ guidelines for making presentations to clients.

What Does It Mean to Be a "Consultant" in WLP?

In *Training Ain't Performance* (chapters 6 and 9), we helped you examine the current role you play and determine if it is more one of a training order-taker or one of a consultant focused on helping clients achieve performance results. Here's a quick way to assess yourself. Place a checkmark beside the description that more accurately fits you:

- ☐ **A.** I evaluate my success at work by the speed with which I develop training, the number of participants in my sessions, the scores they get on tests, the ratings my programs receive, and the number or percentage of trainees certified or the compliance requirements met.
- ☐ **B.** I evaluate my success at work by the measurable effect my interventions have in terms of results valued by my clients, their performers, my organization, and, when possible, our customers.

If you selected **A,** you are definitely in the training order-taker camp where success is judged by the speed and degree to which a training order is "filled." If you selected **B,** you are solidly in the performance-consulting camp where what matters is not what *you* did but what your performers and the organization accomplished. By assuming the role of "consultant" in the WLP world, you are no longer judged by activity alone, but by the valued accomplishments of your performers. It's a frightening position to occupy. In a sense you become the vehicle by which others arrive at success. But what you do is of immense value to *all* stakeholders, including you.

The Value Add of Performance Consulting

Examine the list below that presents some statements of the value that you add in assuming a performance-consulting role:

- ◆ You guide clients to separate the ends they wish to achieve from the intuitively selected (and often inappropriate or incomplete) solutions they ask for, and then you help them focus on those ends.
- ◆ You help your clients articulate success criteria and meaningful metrics to verify whether their valued ends have been achieved. This, in turn, enables them to display meaningful results to their managers, customers, and workers.
- ◆ You educate your clients, opening their eyes to an entire spectrum of means for attaining their goals.
- ◆ You offer a broad menu of interventions that equip your clients to attack their performance gaps more systematically than they could with simple "miracle cures." This increases their probability of performance success.
- ◆ You save time and money. Your aim is to achieve maximum impact at minimum cost in time, resources, and dollars.
- ◆ You help your clients, the targeted performers, and the organization optimally leverage their human capital potential by focusing on efficient attainment of results rather than on activities (such as training) that may be unnecessary or insufficient to do the job.

Your role as a consultant in WLP is so much richer than that of training order-taker. It's no wonder the training world is rapidly evolving in this direction.

Revisiting the Competency Areas and Critical Characteristics for Performance Consulting

In *Training Ain't Performance* (chapter 9, p. 139), we gave you a worksheet listing 16 performance-consulting competency areas. Achieving all of the value add we cited in the previous section requires that you build strong professional competencies to serve your clients most fully. In this *Fieldbook* we go beyond what we covered in *Training Ain't Performance* to clarify how each competency, in and of itself, adds value for your client, the performer, the organization, and, as appropriate, the customer. Review these competencies and their value here in Table 10-1. The information in the table serves two purposes: to reinforce your need to build strength in each competency; and

Table 10-1. Performance-Consulting Competencies and the Value Add

Competency	Value Add
1. Determine performance improvement projects that are appropriate to tackle	• Time and resources are almost always limited. By selecting only those projects that offer the highest potential for improved performance, the consultant helps clients achieve maximum success from the finite resources they possess. • By systematically analyzing requests for training and other interventions, the consultant gathers data and evidence on the worth of a project, thus helping avoid wasted effort on low-priority or inappropriate endeavors.
2. Conduct performance gap analysis	• When carefully conducted, the gap analysis should yield concrete evidence and specific data on the desired and current performance levels; factors affecting the gap; and appropriate, economical, feasible, and acceptable solutions and performance interventions. This diagnostic and prescriptive set of activities vastly increases the probability of success. • Performance gap analyses also lay the foundation for designing interventions, and they establish criteria for project success and suitable metrics to measure it.
3. Assess performer characteristics	• Performance solutions frequently are selected and developed without taking into account the characteristics, competencies, values, concerns, issues, and constraints of the performers. Accurate assessment of all of these dimensions increases the likelihood that interventions will be tailored to fit the performers. • The more closely the interventions match performers' characteristics, the more quickly and accurately the performers will achieve desired results.
4. Analyze the structures of jobs, task, and content	• Nice-to-know and even irrelevant tasks and content often are built unnecessarily into performance improvement interventions. This is called *overengineering* and is costly and wasteful. Ability to conduct job and task analyses and to analyze content for relevance helps maintain focus on necessary and sufficient development of performance interventions and support without gaps or waste.
5. Analyze the characteristics of a learning/working environment	• A context analysis (physical, ergonomic, social, management, cultural, administrative) identifying characteristics of the environment that may facilitate or inhibit performance helps ensure appropriate intervention design. • Analysis and identification of facilitating/inhibiting factors can result in avoidance of costly errors and wasted time or can leverage existing environmental elements for smoother implementation.
6. Write statements of performance intervention outcomes	• Clear outcome statements inform all stakeholders of what is to be achieved. The more clear the outcome statement, the higher the probability of attaining it.
7. Sequence performance intervention outcomes	• Creating timelines and time-and-action calendars with identified intervention outcomes helps team members coordinate their activities and provides a schedule of expectations for managers and performers. This can decrease costly delays or waiting times. • Each player in the project is always aware of what is happening and when outputs are due. This reduces teamwork inefficiencies and conflicts. The consultant makes planning easier.

(continued on page 152)

Table 10-1. Performance-Consulting Competencies and the Value Add (continued)

Competency	Value Add
8. Specify performance interventions and strategies	• This is the logical output of all prior analyses and preparation. Specifications, based on gathered data and information, guide all future activities. • A clear set of interventions and strategies facilitates budgetary and project management processes.
9. Sequence performance improvement activities	• The sequence of activities, when well laid out, helps in the planning and management of all development, implementation, and evaluation/monitoring activities. A well-developed sequence increases coordination and decreases time loss. • The sequence prompts smooth ordering and marshalling of resources for the project.
10. Determine resources appropriate for performance improvement activities and help obtain them	• Projects often fail because required resources are not accessible. The ability to specify requirements, obtain support for resource acquisition, and make it possible to acquire resources when they are required can contribute enormously to meeting project timelines and attaining project success.
11. Evaluate performance improvement interventions	• Evaluation is a weak area in most performance improvement projects. The consultant's design of both a formative and a summative evaluation system offers value in two important ways: — continuous monitoring to ensure performance interventions are being appropriately developed — data gathering to demonstrate performance intervention success (data that can be leveraged to garner support for future projects).
12. Create a performance improvement implementation plan	• The key to successful performance improvement projects is in their implementation. If begun early in a project, implementation planning increases field support, ensures adequate resources and facilities, and decreases last-minute barriers to implementation success. • A well-designed implementation plan foresees problems and prepares adequately for contingencies. Last-minute glitches vastly increase costs and produce time delays.
13. Plan, manage, and monitor performance improvement projects	• Generally, instructional designers and trainers are valued for their technical or presentation capabilities. Performance consultants also must be able to analyze, design, and present. But value add derives from a consultant's ability to make the project happen. By effectively planning, managing, and monitoring performance improvement projects, he or she helps maximize the investment in analysis and design/development. This is a benefit that enhances the consultant's credibility and trustworthiness, and helps clients achieve the greatest gains.
14. Communicate effectively in visual, oral, and written forms	• When a project is successful its success must be communicated in the most appropriate ways so that all stakeholders can understand what has been accomplished. This results in both sustained support for the current project and easier acceptance of future projects. • Clear communication throughout the project life cycle increases coordination, support, and commitment.

Competency	Value Add
15. Demonstrate appropriate inter-personal, group process, and consulting skills	• Many projects fail or are hampered by poor leadership and teamwork than by lack of talent and resources. Being able to deal with individuals and groups in an empathic manner is a high-value asset. Process consulting skills decrease barriers and open doors. The project flows more smoothly with fewer delays.
16. Promote performance-consulting and human performance improvement as a major approach to achieving desired results in organizations	• By demonstrating both performance improvement results and value-added characteristics of performance consulting, the consultant builds credibility as a professional and provides a high-ROI service to the organization. • Promotion of the field rebounds on the promoter. Both gain in the process.

to demonstrate to your clients, who are often impatient and want a "quick fix," that what you do benefits them beyond their current expectation levels.

In addition to the added value that the 16 performance-consulting competencies bring to a project and all its stakeholders, the competencies also define the 10 vital characteristics displayed by outstanding performance consultants. Table 10-2 summarizes these characteristics, drawn from *Training Ain't Performance* (p. 141). As in the previous table, we add here in brief form what value they provide to clients, performers, the organization, customers, and all other direct or indirect stakeholders.

As a performance professional—a performance consultant—you can effect large changes within your organization. These competencies and characteristics are your own personal targets. Keep in mind the added value that each one brings to you and your clients.

An Activity for You

You have examined the characteristics required of a performance consultant, as presented in *Training Ain't Performance* (p. 141) and in Table 10-2. Now let's bring things a little closer to home. Do you have the potential to be a good performance consultant? Assess yourself using Worksheet 10-1, but don't do it alone. None of us is the best judge of ourselves. We all require a credible outsider to maintain a balanced view of who we are. So, find a person you trust—a manager, mentor, colleague, client you know to be objective. *Together,* review the 18 items on the worksheet. For each quality listed there, check the box under the rating that you and your helper believe best describes you. Be sure to listen to the person helping you because your likely inclination will be to score yourself lower than you should. Most competent, skilled professionals underrate their own abilities. High achievers frequently feel that they're "frauds," pulling the wool over people's eyes. And a rare few of you will overrate yourself. Trust your rating partner.

It doesn't matter if you don't score "Got a Lot of It" on every quality. Few performance professionals do. For most projects you don't have to have all of these qualities at a high level—but of course it's worthwhile to strive for excellence.

Table 10-2. Performance Consultant Characteristics and the Value Add

Characteristic	Value Add
1. Is focused on client need: • never loses sight of the primary mission • is not swayed by enthusiasms or constraints • separates wants and whims from real needs • sticks to valued outcomes despite pressures	• This tenacity ensures that the client achieves results she or he desires. • By separating wants and whims from needs, the end result is of greater value to the client and the organization. • The performance consultant provides the steady hand on the tiller against the battering waves of enthusiasm and politics that can throw a project off course.
2. Is cause conscious, not solution focused: • is analytic • investigates systematically	• Decision making is based on data, hard evidence, and systematic sifting of facts. • Solutions are based on cause, not opinion.
3. Is able to maintain a system perspective: • accepts a holistic view • anticipates how change in one area affects other areas	• Balanced interventions are the result, with all major factors accounted for. • Simple solutions, although attractive, rarely result in long-term performance improvement. The system view weaves a tight web of interventions that are mutually supportive.
4. Is capable of involving others (authority figures, knowledgeable individuals) appropriately: • stresses complementary skills • draws strength from team diversity	• Through appropriate involvement of authority at the top, experts to lend credibility and accuracy, and team workers to develop interventions, the consultant maximizes individual and team efficiency.
5. Is organized, rigorous, and prudent: • lets credible data talk	• This characteristic builds trust among champions, clients, and other stakeholders, thereby increasing support for the project and smoothing the work. • This enhances the belief that the performance interventions will deliver as promised because decisions and actions are based on verifiable data.
6. Is sensitive to the need to verify perceptions: • performs reality checks with reliable people • checks interpretations two or three times	• By checking and rechecking understandings, the consultant builds support and ensures that the project is on the right track. • The investment in "verifying time" is more than compensated for by avoiding misinterpretations of information that lead down the wrong path.
7. Is able to sort out priorities.: • focuses on and sticks to business needs • avoids the seduction of technology	• All projects have the potential to slip off course when new, exciting "discoveries" or events are reported to the client. The consultant's ability to absorb the new information and sustain goal focus ensures that priorities are maintained. Dampening distractions, including technology hype, is a major asset the consultant with this characteristic brings to the project.
8. Is diplomatic and credible: • speaks and acts convincingly • overcomes resistance without creating animosity	• This characteristic takes the edge off of rejection or nonacceptance of nonessential recommendations. It helps maintain direction and support from all sources. It increases smoother implementation of interventions and attainment of performance goals without bitterness.
9. Is generous in giving credit to others: • highlights others' accomplishments • shares rewards and recognition of success	• This essential characteristic builds loyalty to the project and draws out the best from all players.
10. Is principled but flexible: • sticks to the bottom-line goal • bends to pressures and constraints without giving up the goal • accommodates client wants where and when feasible without losing sight of the desired result	• By maintaining a firm, fixed eye on the destination, the consultant can accommodate nondisruptive client desires, thus accomplishing two main goals: —producing valued performance success —satisfying and delighting the client.

Worksheet 10-1: Identifying Your Performance-Consulting Qualities

Instructions: Place a checkmark in the appropriate column to describe the amount of the quality you believe you possess or can develop.

Quality	Got a Lot of It	Got Some of It	Haven't Got It But Can Get It	Haven't Got It and Can't Get It
1. Performance-consulting expertise	☐	☐	☐	☐
2. Strong analytic skills	☐	☐	☐	☐
3. Ability to create workable solutions based on data	☐	☐	☐	☐
4. Ability to get along with a wide variety of people	☐	☐	☐	☐
5. Strong communication skills	☐	☐	☐	☐
6. Ability to work under pressure	☐	☐	☐	☐
7. Ability to meet deadlines	☐	☐	☐	☐
8. Good management skills	☐	☐	☐	☐
9. Integrity	☐	☐	☐	☐
10. A sense of responsibility	☐	☐	☐	☐
11. Ability to see things through the eyes of others	☐	☐	☐	☐
12. Professionally well groomed	☐	☐	☐	☐
13. Strength to maintain independence under pressure	☐	☐	☐	☐
14. Good listening skills	☐	☐	☐	☐
15. Ability to be a team player	☐	☐	☐	☐
16. Ability to inspire confidence	☐	☐	☐	☐
17. Ability to conduct an honest self-appraisal	☐	☐	☐	☐
18. Persistence	☐	☐	☐	☐

If you have many lower ratings, especially "Haven't Got It and Can't Get It" ones, these should be food for thought—and further self-appraisal. If you find a number of "Haven't Got It, But Can Get It" checkmarks, refer to the final two chapters of this *Fieldbook*. We have an array of resources for you that can help you "get it."

Ready? Turn to Worksheet 10-1 and check the appropriate boxes as you and your partner assess your consulting qualities. We'll wait here until you finish the self-assessment and then we'll score and debrief the experience.

Now comes the moment of truth: scoring yourself. If you have rated (or been rated) as "Haven't Got It and Can't Get It" on any of qualities 4, 5, 6, 7, 9, 10, 11, 14, or 18, consider these fatal flaws for performance consulting. Reflect on these responses. If they are truly accurate and you really "can't get it," it is likely that performance consulting is not for you. Work with or support other performance professionals, or look for other interesting career activities.

If you rated (or were rated) "Haven't Got It But Can Get It" on those same items, keep reading this *Fieldbook*. Pay special attention to the final two chapters and the Additional Resources section. Seek a mentor to help you develop.

A checkmark in either of those two columns for any other item indicates some restriction in taking on a performance-consulting assignment alone. Work with a colleague to shore up your areas of weakness until you gain strength and confidence. In the meantime, play to your strengths. Notice how many checkmarks you do have in the first two columns. Exploit and continue to build on those qualities.

Am I Doing It Right?

As you move more deeply into the performance-consulting role and build your performance capabilities, it is wise to monitor your efforts with your clients to ensure that you are "doing it right." Worksheet 10-2 can help you monitor your endeavors. Use it on a regular basis with each project. We have found it useful to sit down with the client and review each item either during a project or at the post-completion debriefing, or as a separate activity. This review invites dialogue, strengthens relationships, and yields useful feedback to help keep you on track.

The seven simple questions in the worksheet give a quick check on the quality and correctness of your work. They also offer the opportunity to make course corrections in your dealings with your client. Where you've answered "no" to a question, give some thought to appropriate corrective actions that you can take to improve your efforts. Remember that client feedback also gives you feed forward.

Handling Inquiries

As a training group, you probably receive inquiries and requests for services from a variety of people. You sort these requests into higher and lower priorities, decide

Worksheet 10-2: Am I Doing It Right?

Instructions: Check "yes" or "no" for each of the following questions. Briefly describe actions you can take to correct a "no" score or to heighten your performance on "yes" items.

In This Project, Have I...	Yes	No	Actions to Take
developed a performance improvement plan that reflects positively on the client and the organization?	☐	☐	
taken into account other client projects and work activities to ensure the plan's workability?	☐	☐	
ensured that all policies and procedures are being observed?	☐	☐	
verified that the work proposed and performed is consistent with client priorities?	☐	☐	
made sure that the performance improvement activities do not interfere with other performer responsibilities and activities?	☐	☐	
been meeting client-required deadlines?	☐	☐	
been serving the client in a professional, personable manner?	☐	☐	

what you can deliver, and follow up to respond in one way or another to the person who contacted you. As a WLP organization, however, you suddenly may find that you're inundated with a much broader array of inquiries or requests. It is essential that you and your team handle each of these inquiries systematically and professionally. Worksheet 10-3 can help you document each initial contact. Use it or a modified version every time you receive an inquiry or request for services.

This tracking sheet not only helps you document inquiries and requests, but also forms a database that you and your WLP team can review. Over time, the nature of the inquiries or requests will help shape your team's orientation and will serve as a base for resource planning and budgeting.

Conducting the Initial Interview

You are preparing for the initial interview with the potential client. What should you do? What should you keep in mind? And what do you do during the interview? Are there specific actions to take after the interview? These are the questions this section of the *Fieldbook* addresses.

Worksheet 10-3: WLP Support Inquiry/Request Tracking Sheet

Instructions: Each time you receive an inquiry about or a request for your WLP support services, complete this worksheet. Keep it in your files.

Name of inquirer/requester: _____

Department or administrative unit: _____

Contact information: _____

_____

Email address: _____

Telephone number: _____

Fax number: _____

Other: _____

_____

Date of inquiry/request: _____

Received inquiry/request by ☐ telephone   ☐ email   ☐ face-to-face contact

☐ other means—specify: _____

Contacted inquirer/requester by ☐ telephone   ☐ email

☐ face-to-face contact—specify circumstances: _____

Inquirer/requester found out about our services through _____

_____

_____

Potential of inquirer/requester as a client:

☐ Qualified prospect

General nature of the inquiry/request: _____

_____

_____

_____

_____

_____

☐ Unqualified because _____

_____

_____

☐ Referred to the following department: _____

Because _____

_____

_____

☐ Referred to the following outside service: _____

Because _____

_____

_____

Key words, terms, points to retain: _____
_____
_____
_____
_____
_____

Date, time, and place of follow-up meeting: _____
_____

Materials potential client will bring along: _____
_____
_____
_____

Materials performance consultant will bring along: _____
_____
_____
_____

Follow-up email or letter required: ☐ No   ☐ Yes
If "yes," specific points to mention: _____
_____
_____

Additional materials to include in mailing: _____
_____
_____

Inquiry/request sheet completed by: _____ Date: _____

The Purpose of the Initial Interview

As a performance consultant you have two main purposes for the interview:

1. To find out as much as you can about the problem, need, or nature of the client's interest and concerns so that you can propose your involvement in the project.
2. To sell yourself as the right person or team for the job (if that is the case).

You have to keep these two purposes uppermost in your mind. Everyone's time is valuable—including your own. The interview must be friendly, professional, and productive for both the client and you. Remember that most of your clients see you as the training person or group, so you have to reset their perceptions and expectations.

The Length of the Interview

The length of the interview should be commensurate with the potential of the project. Here are some recommendations:

- Before the interview, establish a reasonable length of time for meeting with the client. Stick to that allotment unless new developments occur during the interview itself.
- For new projects, plan to spend one to two hours in a first encounter, unless this is going to be a large-scale project and you have many people to meet.
- Don't lock yourself into a tight schedule of other activities on the day of the initial interview. Leave open time following the interview in case you and your client agree that more time is required. Ensure you have ample time after the meeting to review your notes privately and to clarify information gathered while it is still fresh in your mind.

Your Appearance and Image

This is a touchy subject. How you dress, style your hair, or speak is a personal matter that has little to do with competence. But as a performance consultant, you know that appearance and image count...sometimes a lot. Here are some simple, straightforward guidelines to follow:

1. First impressions count a great deal. Make the best impression you can.
2. Dress as neatly as possible. A polished appearance gives the impression of a person concerned with order and detail.
3. Dress in a manner similar to your potential client—usually one notch better—if you know how she or he dresses.
4. Act in a professional but not pompous manner. Express competence, confidence, and caring, but not conceit. You are there to help your client as a partner. Create a climate of comfort—relaxed alertness.
5. Be friendly, but not familiar. Try to understand your potential client—including aspirations and uncertainties with respect to the project. He or she is likely to tell you not only what the problem is, but also what the solution should be—probably training.
6. Build empathy and show that you understand and respect his or her concerns—perhaps even share many of them. But focus on desired performance outcomes and not on the means to secure them.
7. Above all, be yourself. If you have realistically assessed your qualities as a performance consultant and realized that you can handle the job, show who you and your team are and what you believe you can accomplish.

What You Should Learn from the Interview

At the interview you want to learn some very specific things:

1. Precisely what *problems* require solving? (Training itself is not a problem.) What will the end result look like? Focus on desired performance.

2. Exactly what are the client's expectations of you? What does she or he want you to do? You must work to shape those expectations.

3. What will the client consider to be indicators or confirmation that the project objectives have been met?

4. What particularly sensitive issues should you be aware of or watch for?

5. What potential problems may arise? Does the project have a high probability of success? Where are the traps?

6. Who is to be your main point of contact in the client's organization? Get her or his exact name, position title, and contact information. Often the person that you initially meet is not the person who'll coordinate and oversee the project.

7. Is there a back-up contact person? Secure the same information for this person.

8. In project terms, what authority does each contact person have?

9. Is there a specific budget allocated for the project? If not, discuss how this will be determined.

10. Is there a critical deadline by which the project must be completed?

In brief, you should come away from the interview with a clear understanding of what the client is looking for, who exactly represents the client, how much authority the client's representatives each have, what the size and scope of the project is (including the financial aspect), and what the client's expectations are concerning you.

What You Should Do at the Interview

The interview is more than a conversation. Here are some things to do—or avoid—during the initial interview:

1. Take notes. Record essential information so that you can refer to it later when you brief others or when you write the proposal (and there should always be some form of written proposal, even if it is brief and more resembles a letter of understanding that includes a proposed work itinerary). If you don't understand a point during the interview, ask the client to repeat what was said or to give an example of what he or she is referring to. Seek confirmation that you understood, or get clarification if you did not. Ask for copies of company documents that may be helpful later and include these with your notes. Be sure to refer to them in your notes so you will remember where they apply.

2. Don't give advice. Usually, you don't have enough information in the initial interview to make any recommendations. Stick to collecting information. This is critical. Be cause conscious, not solution focused. Remember front-end analysis.

3. Listen very attentively. Display interest by nodding, taking notes, or asking questions. Occasionally, at convenient spots, ask if you can review major points and understandings to verify that you have heard and understood correctly. As you listen, interject brief probing questions to clarify matters (such as, "Could you give me an example of that kind of error?" "Approximately how many?" or "How often does this happen?").

4. Respond honestly to any questions the client asks about your ability to handle the project. Your client may be concerned about your availability to give the project priority because of your other commitments. You will want to reassure the client that performance consulting is a planned activity for you or your organization, and that you can give the project the attention it requires. (This assumes that what you have now learned about the project leads you to believe that you can handle it without conflict.) Your client also may be interested in learning more about your prior experience doing similar work. Be prepared to discuss your and your team's competencies and experience. If possible, have work samples that you can show.

5. Share your needs and expectations. Feel comfortable sharing with the client the kinds of support you will require to complete the assignment successfully—such as an opportunity to meet senior managers; access to subject-matter experts, personnel records and company documents, and performers. The client must know what you need and what you expect. Let the client know the mode in which you operate—a collaborative approach involving the client organization throughout the project to ensure the greatest probability for successful implementation and maintenance. Remember: Collaboration and partnering are what performance consulting is all about.

At the end of the interview, ask the client to listen as you review what you have heard to verify that both of you are on the same wavelength. Check with your client to make sure that she or he has learned enough about you to make a decision about your appropriateness for the project. Review these key elements:

- what triggered the inquiry or request
- what the desired performance should look like
- the client's perception of current performance
- success criteria and credible metrics to demonstrate success. (Nowhere do you state what the solutions will be.)

Closing the Interview

The interview is coming to an end. If you sense that the potential client wishes to engage your services, give some general information on how you feel you both should proceed next. Ask if he or she would like to go ahead with the project. Offer to send a statement of understanding or a proposal (which we deal with next) outlining tasks, timelines, and the budget if appropriate.

If the client is anxious to get started and makes a verbal commitment, state that you, too, want to go ahead with the project. Be careful about agreeing to timelines and costs. Be extremely tentative. Again, state that you will send correspondence confirming exactly what you can and will do, in what timeframe, and at what costs.

If you and your client decide that a proposal is required before any decision can be made, indicate that you will submit a brief but very specific proposal. Obtain the following clarifications:

- that you can call your contact person if you have any additional questions
- exactly when the proposal should be submitted, and in what format
- if there are specific pieces of information or documents that must be included with the proposal.

Shake hands (if appropriate) at the end of the interview. Thank the client for her or his time and interest in meeting with you, and be sure to leave a business card.

Get the letter of understanding or proposal in by the deadline. If no deadline was set, create one very close to the initial interview, and submit the document before your memory of key issues fades.

Speaking of proposals, we can now move on to the next section that deals with them.

Mastering the Proposal Process

From inquiry/request to interview to proposal—that's the normal sequence, although in performance consulting, you soon discover that very little occurs "normally." Nevertheless, most projects, at some point, do call for a proposal in one form or another. How do you prepare one with maximum impact and minimum pain? That's what this section will help you accomplish.

What Is a Proposal and Why Is It Necessary?

A proposal is simply a written document that describes the performance-consulting assignment you are *proposing* to undertake. It applies equally to internal and external performance professionals. It spells out exactly what you will do if you and your team get the green light. The proposal includes the timeframe of your performance and the costs associated with your services.

After the initial interview in which the client and you discussed needs and generally defined the project, your next step takes the form of a proposal. This is almost always standard operating procedure. It finalizes the agreement by tying all the loose ends together and forms the basis for a contract. Whether you are an internal or an external consultant, a clear proposal is one of the hallmarks of a performance professional. If well written, it tends to increase the client's confidence in your ability to successfully produce.

What Do Proposals Look Like and What Should They Contain?

For the type of consulting you will most likely be doing, letter proposals are usually sufficient. A letter proposal is just like any other letter, except that it contains all the elements that lead to a clear understanding of the consulting assignment. In writing proposals, bear these tips in mind:

- Keep the structure of the proposal clear and logical. Headings that identify each major section help accomplish this objective.
- Use a professional but friendly style of writing.
- Write your proposal to reflect your client-meeting conversation and the outcomes you arrived at together. (That is why we suggested copious note-taking at the initial meeting.) If new ideas (no matter how brilliant) come to you between the interview and the proposal submission, do not include them in your proposal without first testing them with your potential client. For example, if you decide that running a couple of focus groups with the client's employees would help facilitate the analysis you are proposing, don't just write these into the proposal. Check first. There may be very valid reasons, such as cost, time constraints, or confidentiality, that make this type of activity inappropriate.
- Check the proposal with the potential client before sending it. It is in everyone's best interest that the proposal be right on target even before you turn it in. It may be difficult or impossible to make changes later.

Your proposals will vary in length, depending on the project and what the client's expectations are. In general, proposals should contain the sections described below, but it is quite okay to delete one or more of the sections or add a heading or two, as your performance-consulting assignments dictate. Keep in mind that the following headers are elements that are found in most proposals. At least initially, follow this model quite closely.

An Opening

An opening is just a simple statement that you are writing to submit your ideas for the project under discussion. Refer to your client meeting and to the client's request for this proposal. A paragraph should suffice, although you may want to handle this in a very short cover letter and make the proposal a separate document.

Background and Understanding of Need

In this section you describe the background of the consulting situation, the nature of the problem or opportunity, your client's assumptions, and other general facts about the case. A single page is usually enough for this section.

The purpose of this part of the proposal is to reassure the client that you have a good understanding of the background of the situation and the need. If in the initial meeting you suspected there might be causes of the problem (other than those expressed by the client) that should be investigated or needs that have not been identified, it's important to address these. For example, if the client's analysis of the situation has led her or him to conclude that a training program is needed to overcome the problem, and you have reason to believe there may be other critical factors affecting the situation (perhaps unclear expectations, lack of feedback, lack of performance standards), your concerns should be expressed, with due caution. If the cause of the problem turns out to be different or greater than what your client suspected, the solution and implementation will have to vary as well. You have a responsibility to convince the client that these causes have to be explored before you write an official proposal. This means some form of front-end analysis is desirable. Remember: It is important to build and maintain a positive and open communication bond with your client from the outset.

Objectives

This half-page section, presented in bullet-point format, should be a precise statement of the objectives of the consulting engagement—what exactly your client will learn or receive as a result of your work.

Deliverables

You may be wondering what the deliverables are in this context. In brief, they are the finished products your client will receive. Here you describe—very succinctly—what the finished products will be (for example, documents, reports, training programs, job aids, policy and procedure manuals). These may be tentative at this point if you have not yet done front-end work.

Methodology

State what methods you will be using to accomplish the objectives. If several methods are possible, list them and explain why you selected the method you did. This is particularly important if your client is unfamiliar with performance consulting and expects design and development to start immediately.

There is a tendency in this section to use highly technical language. Avoid it unless your client also possesses technical expertise and vocabulary. Done in a concise manner—and that is the way it should be—a half-page to a full page should be sufficient.

Potential Problems

This section is optional but vital if you foresee potential problems—anything that could limit or detract from achieving the objectives. Documenting these here should prompt the client to reduce the possibility of their occurrence. It also serves as a safeguard if unavoidable problems cause delays, increased costs, or inability to do the assignment as originally described.

Schedule

This section may be as simple as stating a deadline date for the deliverables or as complex as a full-blown timeline detailing the project from commencement through follow-up. Use your own judgment based on the complexity of the assignment. When in doubt, include more details. Be careful with project management software. The outputs can sometimes confuse more than clarify.

Cost and Payment Information

Cost information should contain both fees (if your group bills clients) and expenses (if they apply). Payment information should include how much you expect to receive and when you would like to receive it. Bear in mind that most performance-consulting projects have a startup fee followed by payments at established intervals. Your payment schedule should be laid out so that the client can budget accordingly. Organizational guidelines prevail here.

Capabilities and Resources

In this section include a concise statement of your capabilities, previous clients, and similar problems you have handled. Be sure to include bios of yourself and others who likely will have key roles on the project. Make them short; a paragraph or two for each is fine. Also devote a paragraph in this section to your WLP organization. Share its key features and accomplishments with your potential client.

Authorization to Proceed

This is an optional section that enables you to convert a proposal into an agreement. It should include a statement indicating that signing below authorizes you and your team to proceed with the consulting assignment. Add space for the client's signature, title, and the date.

Exhibit 10-1 summarizes the key elements generally included in a performance-consulting proposal. Use its outline as a template for your initial proposal writing.

The first proposal you write will be tough. After that, it's a breeze. Why? Because some sections are standard, such as Capabilities and Resources. Other sections, such as schedules and cost and payment information, are "boilerplate"—you plug in relevant information that pertains to the project in question. Here are a few more points worth noting about the value and use of proposals:

- The proposal makes an excellent decision-making instrument. Because it states exactly what you will do, by when, and at what cost, it gives all the critical information required to make a decision about proceeding with a project. Proposals provide a written document that can be altered, if changing conditions warrant (such as new budgetary constraints or changes in priorities affecting timelines). A decision to accept a proposal in its original (or altered) state is a commitment to the project. It ties the client into the decision. When this is accomplished, everyone can move ahead.
- The proposal is an excellent management tool when the decision has been reached and the commitment to proceed made clear. Both client and consultant benefit from the proposal documentation because it spells out milestones and metrics by which to monitor the project and manage the conditions it entails: Are work timelines being met? Are payments forthcoming on schedule? Is the agreed-to methodology being followed?

Exhibit 10-1: Proposal Template

Opening
- Purpose of proposal
- Reference to client meeting(s) and request for proposal
- Outline of proposal contents

Background and Understanding of Need
- Background of the situation and nature of problem or opportunity
- Initial assumptions and general facts (from client)
- Findings from initial investigations (for example, front-end analysis)
- Issues, concerns and assumptions
- Initial conclusions

Objectives
- What will be accomplished, in specific terms:
  —what will be done
  —what results will be achieved

Deliverables
- Completed tangible artifacts:
  —reports
  —designs
  —prototype materials
  —final materials
  —implementation plans
  —evaluation plans
  —other items as appropriate

Methodology
- List and description of all methods used to accomplish objectives:
  —analysis methods
  —facilitation methods
  —management methods
  —design and development methods
  —implementation planning methods
  —evaluation methods
  —other methods as appropriate

Potential Problems
- Resource requirements
- Access to key people and data
- Security restrictions
- Budgets
- Conflicts in the organization
- Competing priorities
- Resistances
- Other issues as appropriate

Schedule
- Tasks
- Timelines
- Deliverables due dates
- Sign-offs

Cost and Payment Information
- Fees
- Expenses
- Payment schedule
- Special considerations and/or understandings

(continued on page 168)

Exhibit 10-1: Proposal Template (continued)

Capabilities and Resources
- Statement of WLP capabilities
- Client lists and testimonials
- Descriptions of similar projects and outcomes
- Names of project team members, their bios, and their assigned project roles

Authorization to proceed
- Brief statement converting proposal to commitment
- Spaces for authorization signatures, titles, and dates

Summary
- Review of key proposal elements
- Thanks for invitation to propose

Preparing Project Reports

One of the seemingly not-so-fun parts of performance consulting is the preparation and delivery of reports. But clients usually require them. If they are spending the money, time, and resources, at some point they will demand that reports be submitted. So let's tackle the topic of report writing. By the end of this discussion, you'll have useful tools and guidelines for producing those project reports on your own.

Some Advantages of Report Writing

Before being turned off by this aspect of performance consulting, examine some of the ways you benefit by preparing these reports:

- You get a chance to document what you've done. The end product of your consulting may appear insignificant (maybe just a new procedure for ordering vegetables), but your report can demonstrate how complex the task was, how ingenious the solution, and how valuable the organizational impact of your accomplishment.
- You get your "day in court." The report enables you to speak your mind and say, recommend, or forecast what you professionally believe to be true.
- You produce a concrete document that you can reuse in a number of ways later—on other projects, in articles submitted to professional journals, or in conference presentations (with client approval, of course); in performance appraisals; and for coaching purposes.
- Preparing the report prompts you to review and reflect on your work, and draw personal conclusions about how the project went and what you will do in the future.

Why Write a Report?

You write the project report for lots of reasons:

- to document what has been done to date in terms of what was proposed
- to inform the client of progress and/or problems

- to summarize information
- to lay out alternatives for decision making by the client organization
- to justify steps that were taken
- to describe, synthesize, and clarify accomplishments.

What Types of Reports Are Required?

These are the two types of reports that most usually are requested:

1. *Intermittent progress reports.* The delivery dates for these reports and their volume and content should be specified in the proposal or in a contract.

2. *Final reports.* These summarize what occurred from the start of the project to its completion. They usually end with conclusions and recommendations for future projects, project maintenance, or organizational action.

Other reports you may find yourself working on are

- *technical reports*—usually stating the problem, giving the background, and briefly laying out the planned methodology. They go on to create a blueprint of technical details (with justification) where necessary, and give information and a plan that relevant client organization personnel or contractors can understand and use.

- *survey or research reports,* which open with a problem or question statement, lay out background information, describe the methodology (usually with sample forms, questionnaires, and interview protocols in the appendixes), provide the data analysis, detail the results and possible interpretations of the results, and end with conclusions and recommendations.

- *focus group or interview reports,* which generally include a statement of the problem, an understanding (or background) of the problem, methodology and objectives, a list of meetings, the names of people present or interviewed (unless anonymity is called for), a description of what came out of the meetings or interviews, and your conclusions and recommendations. (Meeting or interview protocols usually go in an appendix.)

- *literature-review reports*, which are fairly rare, include an introduction to major questions requiring answers from the relevant literature, a rationale for asking these questions, a list of relevant sources, the literature review methodology, the review itself (with partial conclusions along the way), and overall conclusions to be drawn from the literature. If required, the report may make recommendations. It should contain an annotated bibliography of all reference materials. Including copies of critical articles or sections of reports in an appendix is useful.

- *financial reports,* which generally are very brief, detail expenses with respect to budgetary allocations. A financial or accounting person must work with you in preparing these reports, both the periodic and the final ones. The client often has a specific format or accounting forms that you must use. Get these from the client and conform to them 100 percent.

Who Writes the Reports?

If you are the primary performance consultant and "doer" on the project, you generally are responsible for writing the reports. You can, however, ask for assistance or even assign other people to write specific sections, such as

- the client or members of the client organization to provide internal data, examples, and documents
- WLP colleagues to write a brief piece on an aspect of the project they know best
- certain administrative units in your organization to provide statistics, policies, equipment numbers and prices, and the like
- other specialists or assistants working with you on the project and knowledgeable about certain aspects of it.

Don't be shy about asking various people to contribute. But also know that you will have to edit what they write and pull it all together into a consistent style and format.

How Should the Report Be Written?

Here are a few tips about the style and appearance of your reports:

- Keep as your motto "less is more." Be as brief as possible without leaving out important information.
- Go for clarity more than for literary style. Use clear, clean, short active sentences that say what has to be said.
- Omit needless words. Get someone to read your report and cross out superfluous words.
- Be specific. No vague stuff. "This section presents 14 sample menus for people with diabetes," not, "In this section we attempt to offer a variety of menus for the diabetic patient."
- Put the guts of your report into the verbs—make it action oriented. Use fewer adjectives and adverbs (such as "In the training seminar, participants role-played management and administrative personnel," instead of "In the training seminar, participants took the interesting roles of management...").
- Avoid "fancy" words or technical jargon that only look like they are trying to impress.
- Write in the active voice. "This project produced 12 output specification sheets," rather than "Twelve output specification sheets were produced by this project."
- Keep paragraphs short.
- Use graphs, charts, tables, and pictures wherever possible, and comment on them briefly.
- Get an editor to revise your report for
  - consistency and style
  - grammar, spelling, and punctuation

- clarity
- unnecessary verbiage
- overall professionalism and comprehensibility for the intended reader(s).

What Should the Report Include?

Each report has its own set of requirements. For most interim reports, the format in Exhibit 10-2 works well.

Interim reports have one purpose: to keep the client informed and up-to-date. Keep them short. Unless you have a long and complex project, your interim reports should run from three to 10 pages plus appendixes.

Final or major reports are a different matter. According to the size and scope of the project, a major report could run from a few pages to several hundred. Most performance-consulting reports, when required, are brief. An analysis of our last 20 projects shows that we had

- one requiring four interim reports and one final report
- five requiring final reports of no more than 25 pages
- three requiring a large final report that included all accomplishments—approximately 250 pages
- 11 requiring no final reports, but for which we produced assorted memos, summary documents of varying lengths, and products.

Exhibit 10-2: Interim Report Template

Title page
- Name of project
- Name of client organization
- Author(s) and affiliation/s
- Period covered by report
- Report number (#1, #2,...)
- Date of report submission

Table of Contents (for reports of 15 pages or more)

Introduction
- Outline and/or specification of objectives worked on during reported time period
- Actions taken (in bullet-point form)

Accomplishments (in bullet-point form)

Concerns
- Project
- Personnel

Financial Report (use client formats and guidelines)

Recommendations

Appendixes
- Drafts of materials or reports
- Sample plans
- Meeting minutes
- Useful documents

Exhibit 10-3 is a sample template outline for a performance-consulting final report. It can be applied or easily adapted for most projects.

As to appendixes, the general rule is, if an item breaks the flow of the report and cannot be placed in a succinct table or figure, place it in an appendix. Often, appendixes are more voluminous than the body of the report.

In closing our discussion of final reports, we want to remind you that their dual purpose is to document what you and your team accomplished and to inform the client and stakeholders as succinctly but specifically as possible what they received for the money, resources, time, and effort invested.

Making Presentations

A major part of performance consulting is making presentations. Why? For almost the same reasons as writing reports: to document; to inform; to summarize; to lay out alternatives; to build support; to justify, report, synthesize, and clarify; and to inspire, convince, and sell the human performance improvement approach.

Two critical differences between reports and presentations are these:

1. A report stands alone and depends entirely on its content. A presentation not only depends on its content, but also on you and the way you present that content.
2. A report may or may not be entirely read or alternatively studied. You have no control over that. In a presentation you have greater control over your clients' and others' attention.

As a performance consultant your three main purposes for making live or virtual oral presentations are

1. *to persuade:* convince your listeners to examine the data, draw conclusions similar to yours, avoid focusing on means and fix attention on ends, and invite them to act as required to achieve desired performance outcomes
2. *to inform:* give decision makers or project stakeholders the information required to teach them something that they ought to know
3. *to report progress or lack of it:* bring key players up-to-date so they don't encounter surprises.

Sometimes more than one purpose guides a presentation. Regardless of purpose, use the checklist in Worksheet 10-4 for all of your presentations. It helps you build a portrait of your audience, decide on your timing, and verify the environment before creating your presentation.

Generally, presentations in the human performance improvement domain contain four main sections. Variations abound, of course, but if you and your WLP team are relatively new to the field, the presentation plan contained in Exhibit 10-4 may prove helpful.

Exhibit 10-3: Final Report Template

Title page
- Name of project
- Name of client organization
- Author(s) and affiliation(s)
- Date of submission
- Note at bottom of page as follows: "Final report submitted in accordance with the requirements of contract #ABC1234-1, issued July X, 2XXX."

Acknowledgments Page
- Recognition of those who contributed to the project
- Thanks to individuals, groups who supported the project

Table of contents (for reports of 15 pages or more)

Executive Summary (2-3 pages for reports of 20 pages or more)
- Key points from each report section
- Clear, concise list of conclusions and recommendations

Introduction (1-3 pages)
- Project need
- Project purpose
- History and context of performance improvement situation
- Critical events that triggered the project
- Important decisions that stimulated the project

Statement of the Problem or Overall Project Objective
- Problem to be solved or nature of the project
- Rationale for performance-consulting approach
- Useful background information

Project Methodology
- Front-end analysis and rationale
- Intervention selection and rationale
- Intervention development and rationale
- Evaluation, monitoring, and maintenance with rationale

Project Objectives (cover the following for each objective)
- The objective itself
- Activities
- Deliverables/products
- Results
- Conclusions

For this section, draw heavily from interim reports.

Project Conclusions
- Accomplishments
- What was not accomplished
- Overall project conclusions with explanations

Recommendations
- Further actions
- Further decisions
- Time and action calendar (if appropriate)

Appendixes
- Protocols, policies, plans, transcripts of interviews, detailed analyses, lengthy evaluation tables
- Sample materials produced
- Financial reports

Worksheet 10-4: Presentation Checklist

Instructions: Use this checklist to prepare for your presentation. Check off each task as you complete it.

Presentation title: _____

Purpose of presentation: ☐ persuade ☐ inform ☐ report progress

Date and time of presentation: _____

Location of presentation: _____

1. Audience characteristics:
   - number of participants identified ☐
   - position and status of participants identified ☐
   - key participants identified ☐
   - attitudes toward project and presenter(s) identified ☐
   - conflicts among participants identified ☐
   - general character of group (active/passive) identified ☐

2. Resources, constraints, timing:
   - amount of allocated time confirmed ☐
   - time of day selected and confirmed ☐
   - size and type of room selected ☐
   - presentation equipment ordered and tested ☐

3. Expectations of presentation and presenters:
   - presentation topic accepted and communicated to all ☐
   - qualifications of presenter(s) communicated ☐
   - presentation outcomes defined ☐
   - subjects to avoid identified ☐
   - style of presentation selected ☐
   - expectations of audience participation and actions identified ☐

4. Level of participant knowledge of presentation topic, issues, and human performance improvement:
   - range of participant knowledge about project verified ☐
   - level of sophistication/naiveté about human performance improvement verified ☐
   - specific points of opposition among participants identified ☐

Presentations are both challenges and opportunities for you as a performance consultant. They give you the opportunity to display what you have done, can do, and believe in as a performance professional. Well-organized and -delivered presentations can do a great deal to make your performance-consulting projects flow more smoothly as your reputation and that of your WLP team grows.

An Activity for Your WLP Team

Take the content of this entire chapter to your team. Review all key points and study the worksheets and exhibits. Select and, if needed, adapt all those that appear valuable to exploit. Make decisions on what to do and how to act moving forward.

Exhibit 10-4: Presentation Plan

Opening (brief, clear, and attention getting)
- Provocative question or strong affirmation
- Empathy builder to draw the participants toward you
- Statement of purpose with rationale
- Statement of specific objectives—expectations of what the participants will accomplish as a result of the presentation

Body (moves participants along to the attainment of objectives)
- Presentation of each objective, including
  —clear statement
  —clear, direct structure
  —clear statistics, examples, and anecdotes to highlight and support key points
  —visuals, as appropriate, to clarify, support, and lead participants along
  —clear, logical arguments, conveyed with conviction

Summary/Conclusion (the "finale" that helps participants draw appropriate conclusions and make desired decisions)
- Review of key points
- Presentation of conclusions (with crispness and conviction)
- Emphasis on urgency and importance of conclusions
- Recommended actions
- Summary of action requirements and a firm, credible, even dramatic (if appropriate), close

Questions and Answers (to explain and defend—but don't be defensive)
- Crisp, brief responses, in order, to questions posed (anticipated and prepared for in advance as possible)
- Response to questions within presentation timeframe
- Avoidance of debate
- Respectful responses to questions, regardless of quantity or tone of question
- Firm, specific responses
- Explanation of follow-up for questions that cannot be answered immediately

Chapter Summary

What a large chapter, and what a vast subject! Becoming a performance consultant is far more challenging than taking training orders. It's significantly more strategic. It makes greater demands on you. It also offers immense rewards for both you and your organization. In this chapter

- you defined what it means to be a consultant in WLP.
- you reviewed the value add that you bring to your clients and organization in your performance consulting role.
- you revisited the performance-consulting competencies and critical characteristics from *Training Ain't Performance*, and pinpointed how each of these adds value for all stakeholders.
- you assessed your performance-consulting potential and drew conclusions about yourself.
- you reviewed a worksheet to help you determine whether you are carrying out your performance-consulting role correctly.

- ◆ you gained a job aid to help you handle inquiries and requests for your WLP services.
- ◆ you examined a series of guidelines and tools to assist you in handling initial client interviews, writing proposals, preparing reports, and making presentations.

Although this appears so demanding, it really is a natural extension of what you currently do. Yes, it requires stretching and growing, but it's enormously worthwhile for you and your organization. Both of you benefit. The payoff will endure long into the future.

While all of this is still fresh in your mind, turn to the next chapter. It focuses on the performance consultant–client relationship. It's the companion chapter to this one.

Managing the Client–Performance Consultant Relationship

This chapter

- ◆ introduces the crucial issue of managing the client–performance consultant relationship
- ◆ reviews three alternative performance-consulting roles and recommends which one is most advantageous to all
- ◆ provides guidance on maintaining a collaborative relationship
- ◆ helps you avoid potential conflicts
- ◆ suggests activities for you and your WLP team in which you decide how to manage your client relationships
- ◆ recommends a road map to relationship success.

Tools in this chapter include

- ◆ guidelines for creating a WLP philosophy statement
- ◆ guidelines for establishing and maintaining a collaborative relationship
- ◆ a road map for mutual success.

Managing Your Client Relationships

This is a hot chapter. Handle with care. All human relationships are fraught with potential opportunities for great joy...and grief. The client–performance consultant relationship is no different from work, friendship, neighbor, or even live-together relationships in terms of the potential for sharing and conflict. Hence the need for a chapter that offers some guidelines to help you manage the relationship successfully. Although we draw on the ideas and writings of other consultants to guide us, most of the content of this chapter comes from our experience and our hearts.

Managing Your Client and Getting Your Client to Manage You

Managing the client–consultant relationship requires you to take a philosophical and practical stand on how you believe such a relationship should be handled. We have our own firm position: "All our clients either are our friends or become our friends." This doesn't mean we want to go dancing with them every Saturday night. But what it does signify is that there is more than a financial and technical relationship between us. We want to look forward to seeing our clients as much as we look forward to doing business with them. We want them to be pleased that we are their performance consultants. We may work with some of our clients only once or a very few times, but we want our and their memories of having labored together to be ones of mutual satisfaction.

Before we get too emotional, please consider the practical reasons for this philosophy:

- Satisfied clients collaborate rather than confront. Less time and energy are lost through controversy or suspicion.
- We can cut through formalities and red tape, and get things moving more quickly.
- We can share concerns and take concerted action to overcome obstacles.
- We can all let our guard down, and get frank answers and real data.
- We can negotiate flexibility on timelines when we desperately need it.
- We get testimonials, support, and repeat business, even during organizational budget-tightening times.

There is a price to pay for this "friendship philosophy." Just as with any friends, you can never let your clients down.

An Activity for Your WLP Team

As a team, you must adopt a philosophical stand. You have to "create an image and an approach" in your relationships with your clients, and then you must discipline yourselves to communicate it and live up to it. We provide space below to write your philosophy and approach to performance consulting. As a group, decide on your WLP philosophy (for example, "We are totally committed to the client's best interest and to achieving for the client and the organization results that are measurable and demonstrable. We do not jump to solutions before determining valued client performance requirements and systematically analyzing all the factors that affect desired outcomes. We are professionals whose success is determined by our clients' successes. We see ourselves as our clients' valued performance partner."). Then decide as a group how your relationships will be governed every time you consult with clients and client groups (for example, "We listen to our clients, but challenge assumptions. We verify and make decisions based on data and verifiable evidence. We operate as a consultative, professional partner with our clients. We place our clients' interests above our own. Our dealings with our clients are friendly, and we want clients to be as happy working with us as we are with them."). Be consistent with your organization's image and policies.

Philosophy:

[ ]

What this means in terms of relationships with clients:

[ ]

What you wrote forms the foundation on which you'll build your consulting practice. Please revisit it from time to time to determine if it truly reflects your professional stance and is serving both your clients and you as it should. You may decide to revise it as your experiences deepen.

From Philosophy to Practicality

How do you manage your clients? And what can you do to help them manage you? When Harold was president of a professional society, he wrote an article that summed up many of the issues rather well. Instead of paraphrasing it, we adapted it slightly and include it for you here (Exhibit 11-1). Although penned a number of years ago, what he wrote then remains true today.

A clear consulting philosophy certainly helps you manage the client-consultant relationship. But you have to do some practical things as well, many of which are alluded to in Exhibit 11-1. This is a hot and critical item in performance consulting. The nature of the relationship will have a highly significant impact on the quality of your results.

Consulting Models

What kind of a performance consultant are you anyway? Are there different relationship roles that consultants play in dealing with clients? Answer: yes. Most of the literature on the topic tends to break consultant roles into three types. We like the terms Peter Block used in his book, *Flawless Consulting*: expert, pair of hands, and collaborative.

Our point of view is that the performance-consulting roles you play are situational—that is, they depend on the circumstances and the type of client you deal

Exhibit 11-1: Good Clients and Bad

I'm thinking of giving up performance consulting. Premature retirement due to breakdown. No, no, I am only joshing, but I must admit that a couple of my clients are getting beneath my professional cool, calm, and collectedness and are hastening me toward a place in a rest home. One has imposed on me impossible deadlines; a second keeps changing tasks; a third never pays his bills on time. I would love to berate all these bad clients and tell them how they are responsible for making me a mental wreck. But the truth of the matter is (alas!) it really is my own darn fault!

Training in the Technology of Performance Consulting

Why am I sharing my woes with you? Because in my travels and during professional conferences I frequently spend many an hour having my ear bent by one colleague or another bemoaning her or his dismal treatment at the hands of an ungrateful client. Martyrdom seems to come with the trade.

To some extent, this is understandable because our training is in the learning and performance technologies we employ. We study and practice task analysis, media selection, performance audit, job aid design, and other useful professional skills. I have yet to attend a class on "Client Training" or on "How to Avoid Getting Mangled by the People You Work For." No one ever taught me how to negotiate a contract, or build in sign-off points, or even how to bill a client. And because of this, many of us—myself certainly included—may be fine at applying the tools of our trade, but we end up as less than rank amateurs in our business relationships with our clients.

Is This Message Aimed Only at External Consultants?

No way. Even internal consultants (and I have just witnessed this inside a large corporation) within an organization experience many of the same problems as external consultants: lack of clarity about the missions and/or tasks, unrealistic budgeting, vague or impossible deadlines, unclear assignment of responsibilities, lack of sign-off points, uncertainty as to who holds copyright exclusiveness or nonexclusiveness of right to content or materials use, field trial and revision responsibilities, confidentiality...I could go on and on.

Who's Responsible for the "Goodness" or "Horridness" of Our Clients?

I don't want to assume the mantle of responsibility for all the world's ills, but I do believe that a large measure of responsibility for ensuring that our clients are "good" resides with us. Let us remain coherent with our performance-consulting philosophy: if the system we create does not work and the targeted performers cannot do the job, it is our fault. We are professionally committed to this principle and, barring major unforeseen factors, we accept the responsibility to analyze the system in which learning and/or performance is to be improved, design suitable interventions based on our analyses, and then verify and revise those interventions until they work. Ditto for clients.

If we are performance professionals, we had better clean up our acts with respect to the ways we both manage and are managed by clients. We need to build in systems and safeguards that protect our clients and ourselves from communications (and nervous) breakdowns. This means

- drawing up formal (but not necessarily legal) documents that clearly and unequivocally specify the milestone and scope of the project.
- putting in writing the responsibilities, duties, and perhaps even major tasks for both consultant and client.
- drawing up timelines that are realistic—not just wished-for. My experience has been that we generally do not allow enough time for our clients to study our draft documents thoroughly and generate useful feedback.
- creating very complete budgets that carry no hidden surprises for client or consultant. Many outside consultants get into financial difficulties because they underestimate the cost of a project to land a contract. That does no one any good.
- specifying a number of intermediate, formal sign-off points. These indicate that the client has approved the intermediate product (such as the task analysis, the objectives, or the interventions).
- specifying invoicing and payment due dates, and penalties for late payments.
- specifying the legalities surrounding the content and rights to the final products. These include content or even project confidentiality; right to reuse the content or format of the final product; exclusive-use rights; copyright ownership; royalties; even whose names go on the finished products, where, and in what font size.
- clarifying later rights and responsibilities for reproduction, revision, periodic monitoring, and other legal/technical points.

There is probably a lot more that could be added. However, I am not an expert myself. Experience is my teacher—and let me assure you, I am finding it to be a very tough instructor.

To Any Clients Who Are Reading This

What I suggest for the performance consultant is very useful for the client as well. Support the people who are dealing with your problems; collaborate with them on specifications, budgets, timelines, and payment schedules. These actions benefit you in the long run. If the client-consultant relationship runs smoothly, everyone's energies can be focused where they ought to be: on the success of the project.

To Conclude

We pride ourselves on our professionalism in the learning and performance domains. To practice our professionalism we must create conditions with our clients that will help us achieve their goals as effectively and efficiently as possible. That means becoming better client managers. Theoretically, just like our learners, all our clients should reach criterion. There should be no bad clients if we correctly prepare the people with whom and for whom we work.

Now all I have to do is follow my own advice.

with. We borrow from Hersey and Blanchard's situational leadership approach (see Blanchard, Zigarmi, and Zigarmi, 1999) to describe our perception of consulting roles and relationships.

Picture three rectangles arranged thus:

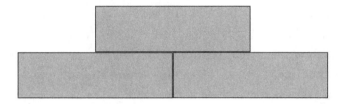

Let's label them as follows:

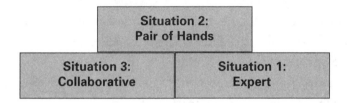

Each of these blocks stands for a different consulting situation and, hence, a different role that you play. In situation 1, the Expert role, your client brings you in because "you know how to do it." Her or his approach is one of "I need this; do whatever it takes to get it done. It's your responsibility. Keep me informed. I'll make the final decisions if you figure it out to my (and my organization's) satisfaction." Here are some examples of Expert tasks:

- develop a training program on basic sales skills
- set up a coaching program for our managers
- give us a set of reference materials and job aids for this new software
- create a feedback system for improving quality care
- set up a Leadership Institute with university help.

Essentially your client wants you to take responsibility and get it done with a minimum of fuss or involvement on his or her part. In the pure form of this role, the client generally is "unwilling and unable" to collaborate. He or she only makes yes/no decisions. You do all the work. If some analysis has to be done, then you do it. "Show me the bottom-line results" is this client's mantra.

Situation 2, the Pair of Hands role, brings you in as a helper. In this case, the client feels he or she could really do the job with internal resources, but has none available (nor the time). This is a particularly sensitive role because the client actually may have the expertise (although perhaps not as much as he or she believes) and a different viewpoint from your own. The client retains control and has you doing parts of the project under close supervision. These are some typical client remarks:

- "Here are some of my customer service vignettes, roughed out. Clean them up and make me 10 more of these. I'd do it myself, but I'm swamped."
- "Here are problems I've identified in our billing information flow. Untangle each of these and show me how you would fix it. I can use the help. I'll see which ones I like and then I'll get you started on the next steps."
- "I've presented this incentive proposal to improve performance to the board. They've approved it. I need you to follow my lead to help make it work."
- "These are the objectives I want the personnel to attain in our new Sexual Harassment program. I don't have time or personnel to get everyone onboard. I'd like ideas from you on role-plays."

A client like this wants control—perhaps even wants to do it all—but is limited by time and internal resources. As the performance consultant, you operate as his or her extra pair of hands. In this situation, your client is willing to do the job but unable because of constraints.

Finally, in situation 3, the Collaborative role, your client seeks an equal partnership in which there is a clear delineation of roles and responsibilities. You have skills and knowledge needed by the client's organization. She or he has access to internal resources and decision makers, and knows the goals and politics of the system. Her or his expertise, capabilities, and roles differ from yours, and you complement one another. The collaborative relationship may go like one of these examples:

- "We have to get our administrative personnel up to speed on the new budgeting system." The client's role is to provide data, arrange accessibility to internal personnel, review analyses, and design documents that you, the consultant, create and deliver. You work together to build the learning and performance support system and the materials required.
- The client wants to establish new hospice services. She provides patient data, personnel resource data, and demographic and financial information. You help prepare plans for bringing onboard existing and new personnel for the hospice service. Together you fit needs and resources with the requirements of the plan to make sure that it will work when launched.

Your collaborative client wants success and wants you to help achieve it. The relationship is one of mutual sharing, with each person contributing what he or she knows best. By the time you leave, much of the relevant knowledge you possess has been transferred to the client. What you produced is a product of both your efforts. Situation 3 has you dealing with a client who is both able and willing to collaborate.

The figure here depicts the three types of clients and the consultant role each expects you to assume:

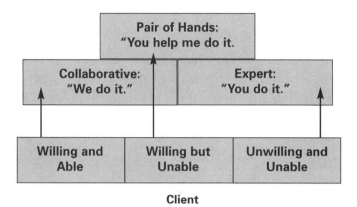

It's obvious that the most rewarding client-consultant relationship is collaborative (situation 3), especially for performance consultants. Not all clients (and, unfortunately, not all consultants) are able and willing to do it together in a spirit of collaboration. Why? Because...

The Client...	The Consultant...
• Wants to maintain control and discipline	• Wants to do things his way without interference
• Feels threatened	• May feel threatened
• Doesn't like outsiders	• Is a snob
• Resents paying another department	• Feels if she gets paid, she should do all the work
• Has hang-ups about consultants	• Has hang-ups about clients
• Is insecure	• Is insecure
• Is afraid of criticism for being too friendly	• Is afraid of losing that "outsider's objectivity"
• Feels that you pay people to do work	• Feels that familiarity may breed contempt
• Believes he doesn't have time	• Believes it's faster to do it alone
• . . . and many more	• . . . and many more

That's foolish thinking for both parties, and it's very unproductive.

As a performance consultant, you should do your utmost to move the client to a collaborative mode. If she or he brings you in as the "Ms. or Mr. Fix-It" with an "I'm hands off and you do the job" attitude, move the client to take on increased responsibility and ownership along the way. If you are viewed as "another pair of hands," manage the client to obtain a more equitable balance between the two of you and to enable the client to profit from your performance expertise.

In long-term consulting relationships with our clients, we eventually succeed (sometimes with great effort) in moving to collaboration. In all cases when this happens, our clients and we have come out winners.

How to Acquire and Maintain That Collaborative Relationship

This part of the chapter is tough. It's difficult to communicate the thousand-and-one little things you do to create and maintain a balanced relationship. It takes strategizing and diplomatic maneuvering, good will, sensitivity, and occasional assertiveness to get there. No formula replaces experience and trial-and-error-learning, but here are some things you can do to get started. Coupling these actions with *who* you are and *what* you already know about human relationships should take you the rest of the way.

1. Before meeting the client, set the stage for the relationship. Create expectations that
   - make all of your WLP team's publicity and correspondence reflect your collaborative style.
   - demonstrate your ability to collaborate in every activity or event. Establish your reputation.
   - prompt you to do your homework on the client. Learn enough that you can call on her or his strengths and accomplishments when you meet.
   - let everyone know you believe that a client's success is *your* success.
   - emphasize in your proposal the type of relationship you feel will produce the best results for your client. Always emphasize accomplishments the client and her or his group value.

2. In the initial meeting(s) with the client, model appropriate collaborative behaviors, such as these:
   - Listen carefully.
   - Ask questions about the organization and reinforce answers with comments such as, "I'm pleased you have this information. It will really help the project."
   - Ask what resources, time, and personal investment your client wishes to put into the project. Reinforce collaboration.
   - Provide brief examples of how past clients have "won," working closely with you (without bragging, of course).
   - Set up expectations and ground rules you believe in, and negotiate them with your client.
   - Say, "Here is what you can expect from an outsider."
   - Emphasize that although you, as a learning and performance support professional, may have expertise and credibility, you can't achieve the trust that an insider has automatically. You need internal support.
   - Leave your client with the understandings that he or she can count on your collaboration, and that you earnestly want a reciprocal arrangement.

3. When the project is under way, cultivate collaboration in the following ways:
   - Reward/reinforce your client for collaborative moves.

- Ask for assistance if you have a "hands-off" client, or for greater professional autonomy if you are being used as a "pair of hands." Reinforce all client behaviors that move both of you in the right direction.
- Speak up. Be frank when you feel the relationship is in trouble. Ask, if you sense the client is uneasy; address the discomfort. Speak up tactfully if you are feeling abused.
- Share credit for accomplishments and blame for mishaps.
- Take time to get to know your client, while focusing interactions on the project. Share his or her aspirations and frustrations without becoming either a confessor or a co-plotter.
- Be flexible. Don't hide behind the contract. Make changes that will accommodate client needs without hurting you. If necessary, renegotiate times, costs, and deliverables.
- Be a model for your client. Let your conduct guide her or his behaviors toward you.

4. Maintain a spirit of collaboration in the following ways:
   - To the end of the project and beyond, be a collaborator and a partner to the client. Share in the spirit of project ownership.
   - Call or meet after the conclusion of the project to demonstrate your interest and concern in the client's satisfaction.
   - Be available after the project to give advice or help solve problems.
   - Call or send a note of congratulations if the project gets good press or your client achieves special success.

5. Finally, from the beginning to the end of your collaboration,
   - test your ideas with your client
   - never surprise your client—prepare him or her for new ideas and changes
   - show your integrity and stick to what you believe in
   - keep out of client organization politics
   - maintain confidentiality
   - don't gossip about your clients or their personnel
   - don't show off, and keep your language level appropriate
   - don't overburden your client with unnecessary details, and don't omit necessary ones
   - respect commitments.

Some Final Thoughts on Client-Consultant Relationships

As with any relationship, you and your client will share both good times and bad. What can you do to maintain this relationship successfully?

- Work things out together.
- Become true friends. Go for a long-term relationship.
- Be respectful of personal confidences that you share. Don't say anything to anyone that might injure your client, your organization, or you.

Avoiding Conflict

Despite all the sound advice we have shared with you, conflicts will arise. Try to anticipate them. Handle them proactively. Below are some conflicts we've faced and how we try to avoid them today:

- *Potential conflict:* Client feels inadequate, threatened by knowledge or skills the performance consultant possesses. Client acts belligerently.
  Ways to avoid: Don't brag or show off. Be respectful of the client's capabilities and show interest in them. Reinforce their worth without patronizing. Show the client how her or his input helps the project progress.
- *Potential conflict:* Client wants all the credit.
  Ways to avoid: Let the client have any organizational credit, but fight for a byline and recognition of your contributions, for repeat business, and for referrals. Trade off credit for testimonials and references.
- *Potential conflict:* Client feels you don't understand that "it's different here."
  Ways to avoid: Listen. Probe for what the client feels is unique about his or her environment. Note differences. Collaboratively seek acceptable solutions while you maintain integrity.
- *Potential conflict:* Client wants something you consider unethical.
  Ways to avoid: Explain your position and the reasons for it. Seek a middle ground. Ask for the request in writing, and say you'll check with your organization. Be ethical and above-board right from the start.
- *Potential conflict:* You and the client disagree on the quantity or quality of the deliverables.
  Ways to avoid: Create a clean, clear, comprehensible contract. Review all deliverables and time commitments before signing the contract. Negotiate as much as possible before you sign, rather than after.

Do your homework on the client. Find out about "red flags," "minefields," and other potential dangers. There are many ways of doing this. The most common is to inquire of trusted sources about the client. This may include colleagues or other departments that have had dealings with the client and her or his group. Internal documents describing the client organization and its responsibilities/accomplishments are also useful. Informal meetings with members of the client's team to learn about the group often can lead to disclosures that might not be commonly known. You must treat this information cautiously, however. Listen and learn, but be prudent about what you learn until you obtain hard facts. Walk softly but forthrightly as the professional performance consultant you are. You can set and maintain the tone of a successful client-consultant relationship.

Building a Successful Client-Consultant Relationship

Exhibit 11-2 describes the steps you and your client can take together to ensure project success. Share this information with your client early in the relationship and discuss how to make each step work.

Exhibit 11-2: Steps along the Road to Successful Client-Consultant Relationships

1. Establish early a clear, shared understanding of the factors that triggered the need to work together.

2. Create together a shared vision of what success means—what it should look like concretely. Document this vision.

3. Set ground rules for developing open communication. Reassure each other that you will keep one another informed of what is happening; unanticipated events; and changes affecting the work, concerns, and successes.

4. Draw up mutually acceptable success criteria and suitable, feasible metrics for demonstrating success. Revisit these regularly.

5. Find ways to demonstrate mutual support and respect.

6. Meet periodically to revisit the final goal so that it is never lost from sight in the midst of activities.

An Activity for Your WLP Team

This chapter has focused on the working relationship with clients. Many of the points raised are just as applicable to training professionals as they are to performance consultants, but the stakes are higher in performance consulting.

When we take training orders, we still have a great deal of discovery to undertake. We have to work closely with our client's personnel. Collaboration is needed. Understanding who commands and who obeys is clear in order taking. In performance consulting, however, the relationship is not as obviously defined. Yes, you serve the client's needs, but your role is more that of trusted advisor. You don't just take orders and you don't just produce. Rather, you test client assumptions. In fact, there is a high likelihood that what you ultimately recommend and help produce may be very different from what the client initially requested. This creates its own special set of dynamics.

Review the content of this chapter with your team. Identify changes you all believe will have to be made in future client dealings as you evolve toward the performance consulting model. Decide what you must do to prepare your clients if you foresee significant relationship changes, and document this. If appropriate, role-play possible scenarios. Assume the roles of various known clients and test your relationship-building skills as a performance consultant. Debrief these activities and draw conclusions.

Chapter Summary

We have been focusing on process consulting skills. In the chapter

- ◆ you investigated the somewhat delicate area of client–performance consulting relationships.
- ◆ you examined three alternative performance-consulting models and saw why the collaborative model is the most advantageous to all (although you'll have to operate in the other two modes occasionally).

- you studied guidelines for maintaining collaborative relationships with clients, and encountered a few conflict cases that we coupled with suggestions for handling them.
- you received a set of steps you and your client can follow to build a successful relationship that produces a winning outcome.
- you closed with a team activity to help you develop a workable approach for managing client relationships.

Onward now to a more technical chapter on evaluating results. Chapter 12 contains a few more return-on-investment strategies beyond those described in *Training Ain't Performance.* They offer additional means for you to demonstrate your contribution to your clients' and organizations' successes.

Evaluating Results

This chapter

- briefly reviews the rationale for evaluating the impact of your performance improvement projects on organizational results
- describes two methods for demonstrating results to clients and senior management.

Tools in this chapter include

- a procedure for demonstrating performance improvement ROI in "soft," or not readily quantifiable, performance areas
- a method for demonstrating impact credibly through journaling and surveys.

Rationale for Evaluating Project Impact

Two recent reports from ASTD presented results that troubled us deeply. Yes, we already knew what the reports revealed, but it still hurt to see the information in print. The first publication was the State of the Industry Report 2005 (Sugrue and Rivera, 2005) that again confirmed how few organizations (approximately 2 percent) systematically verify the impact and/or ROI of their learning and performance support efforts. The second report (O'Driscoll, Sugrue, and Vona, 2005) was an in-depth study of CEOs', CFOs', and other "C"-level managers' perceptions about learning and performance support activities in their organizations. The good news is that high-level managers generally are pleased with what is being done and they value WLP activities. The bad news is that they are not looking for ROI reports from their training or WLP departments. Why not? They're not convinced that such evaluations can be done well and they don't believe the effort is worth the cost.

That second report almost hurts more than the first. These same senior respondents would never accept other departments, such as engineering, operations, or information technology, not providing a business case for proposed expenditures and projected ROI as well as follow-up reports on bottom-line results. Not expecting this from training/WLP has two serious negative consequences:

1. It generates a lack of respect for what we do. Without demonstrable, meaningful results that link to the bottom line, we take a back seat to the big players—those who can show value for dollar. We take on the role of support personnel—helpful but not to be counted on to make "real" differences.

2. It leaves us vulnerable when the crunch comes. Organizations hold on as long as possible to those groups or individuals who make a critical contribution to survival. Without data on impact, we're not on the essential-players list. In recent years we've seen two giant corporations shed thousands of employees. The axe fell with disproportionate weight on the workforce learning and performance support teams.

Our position in the face of this is simple. We must demonstrate bottom-line results and significant, meaningful ROI for our activities. Whether it is asked for by senior decision makers or not, we cannot escape this duty. We are only seen to be as valuable as the results we produce.

ROI—To Be or Not to Be

In *Training Ain't Performance* (chapter 10), we made the following two assertions:

1. You're in competition. Money in organizations is scarce and growing more so as global competition forces everyone to become leaner and, unfortunately, meaner. With this has come a widening demand to demonstrate the worth of performance interventions and the return-on-investment in learning and performance.

2. The purpose of calculating worth and ROI is to help clients, decision makers, and stakeholders decide on whether to fund your performance improvement recommendations. Worth and ROI are financial concepts, so calculate these only when you can boil down performance outcomes (valued accomplishments) to economic terms.

In the first statement, the widening demand derives from the competitive forces we face. Asked for or not, the demand is there and growing. In the second statement, the troublesome part is in making calculations only when you can boil down performance outcomes to economic terms. How do we deal with the need to write better proposals, improve presentation skills, or develop leadership in senior managers? How do we "boil down" these sorts of demands to "economic terms" and demonstrate ROI? These are important questions, so let's attack them.

Boiling Down Performance Improvements to Economic Terms

We can divide desired performance improvements or changes into three basic categories: (1) those with clearly identifiable economic outcomes, (2) those that require conversion and manipulation to identify economic outcomes, and (3) those for which economic outcomes are almost impossible to discern directly. Examine the following list. Check the *1* beside easy-to-identify economic outcomes items, check the *2* beside those that require more effort, and check the *3* beside those improvements for which it would be difficult to measure direct economic outcomes.

Desired Performance Improvement	Category		
	1	2	3
A. Sell 20 percent more of Product X	☐	☐	☐
B. Reduce wastage by 6 percent	☐	☐	☐
C. Improve the quality of sales proposals	☐	☐	☐
D. Transform 10 percent of customer service calls into sales	☐	☐	☐
E. Improve telephone etiquette	☐	☐	☐
F. Improve project management skills	☐	☐	☐
G. Reduce team conflicts	☐	☐	☐
H. Develop coaching skills	☐	☐	☐
I. Improve leadership skills	☐	☐	☐
J. Eliminate order errors	☐	☐	☐

Here are our answers (although we admit that arguments can be made for different answers, depending on context):

Category 1:	A, B, D, J	All four have easily defined values attached to them and can be connected to dollars relatively quickly.
Category 2:	C, F	By comparing the success rate of "quality proposals" with those considered poorly written, you can establish an average value for high-quality proposals. This can be converted to dollars. Similarly, by comparing time and cost losses for poorly managed projects (for example, cost of time, over-budget costs, lost sales due to project delays) with well-run ones, you can calculate value.
Category 3:	E, G, H, I	These are all more nebulous. We suspect that a thorough front-end analysis would eliminate some of these. If they are indicated, however, we recommend a different evaluation/measurement approach to calculating ROI—an approach that we'll describe later in the *Fieldbook*.

For Category 1 items, chapter 10 in *Training Ain't Performance* provides plenty of guidance and tools. So here we'll turn directly to Category 2 items.

Calculating ROI in the Soft Skills Domain

There are books recommending various methods for calculating ROI, and we've listed several in the Additional Resources at the back of this volume. Here we present a method that has been demonstrated to work. It was developed by Schneider and Wright (1990). We've modified their approach somewhat. These are the steps you will follow in applying it:

Step 1. Determine what percentage of the performer's time is spent on performing the targeted task. Have several performers maintain a journal for one to two weeks at random time periods. Analyze the listed tasks to calculate time spent and percentage of total work done. An alternative method is to conduct a job analysis, list all job tasks, and have random samples of performers identify tasks performed each day and the amount of time spent on each. The simplest (but least accurate) way is to bring together a focus group of performers to estimate approximate time spent, and then convert their estimates to percentages of work time. As we move through the steps here, we'll illustrate with an example based on the journaling method.

Example: Making Effective Presentations

Six managers of the 1,150 in the company kept journals of their activities for two weeks. Analysis of the journals showed that an average of 8 percent of their time was spent making presentations (range 5 to 12 percent).

Step 2. Develop criteria for assessing desired performance. These criteria are generally quality, quantity, time, and cost, but other specific criteria may be included. In a typical situation, five to seven criteria are sufficient.

Example: Making Effective Presentations

Together, a team of four senior managers, three acknowledged company top presenters, and a consultant met to establish six criteria for what constitutes a "winning presentation"—one that achieves its goals and advances the company.

Step 3. Establish a baseline of current performance. This is done through either surveys, observation, examination of random samples, or 360-degree assessment techniques.

Example: Making Effective Presentations

To assess current presentation quality levels, an evaluation instrument based on the criteria established by the team of senior managers, top presenters, and the consultant (with a 10-point scale for each criterion) was created. Participants at all presentations in the company were handed evaluation sheets for each presentation and asked to rate the presentations. The sheets were collected, scored, analyzed, and converted to percentages. The baseline mean was 58 percent, with a range of 12 to 98 percent.

Step 4. Based on the recommended interventions derived from the front-end analysis, implement these interventions to improve or attain desired performance from targeted performers.

Example: Making Effective Presentations

The front-end analysis produced the following recommended interventions: individual assessment; training; job aid templates to design effective presentations; standards, self-evaluation, and peer evaluation; instruments; and video practice sessions with feedback. All managers went through the assessment, received opportunities for training and coaching, produced presentations, practiced with peers and coaches, were videotaped, and received both oral and written structured feedback using feedback forms.

Step 5. After a suitable time period has elapsed following intervention implementation, again collect performance data using the same methods you used in Step 3 when you established your baseline.

Example: Making Effective Presentations

With the same six-criteria evaluation instrument used for collecting baseline data, participants in all company presentations were given evaluation sheets and asked to rate each presentation as before. The sheets were collected, scored, analyzed, and converted to percentages. This time the post-intervention mean score was 82 percent, with a range of 52 to 100 percent.

Step 6. Calculate the difference between the baseline and the post-intervention means. Multiply the difference by the percentage of total performer work represented by the activity. Multiply the result by the average performer's annual salary. This represents the average monetary or value improvement obtained for each performer. Multiply the individual improvement figure by the number of performers to obtain the total estimated performance improvement (value) in dollars (*estimated* because you are dealing with averages).

Example: Making Effective Presentations

The difference between the pre- and post-intervention means was 0.58 to 0.82—or 0.24. Because making presentations constitutes, on average, 8 percent of managers' jobs, 0.24 x 0.08 = 0.0192. The average manager salary is $85,000 annually. By multiplying 0.0192 x $85,000, we discover that the value of the improved manager presentation performance = $1,632 per manager. For 1,150 managers, this represents an overall value to the company of $1,876,800 per year. Most impressive!

Now for some comments. First, we don't know what the true impact of better presentations is in our example. If the result is improved sales, better worker performance, or reduced turnover, the value could and most probably would be much greater. This approach is absolutely the most conservative form of value estimation. Nonetheless, $1,876,800 per year is not bad.

A second point is that in the "soft skills" areas, such as making presentations or conducting performance approvals, the impact tends to have a relatively long life. Think about this. If you gave poor presentations and then improved as a result of assessment, training, coaching, practice, and structured feedback, you would probably continue at the improved level for a long time. In this example let's assume that, with turnover and changes, the impact lasts for a conservatively estimated three years. The value over three years now becomes $5,630,400 (3 × $1,876,800) just based on managers' salaries.

Point number three is that with the value calculated, you can easily calculate worth and ROI just as described in chapter 10 of *Training Ain't Performance*. For illustrative purposes, we'll assume that each manager received an average of two days worth of training, coaching, and practice with feedback. Because we're dealing with base salaries, we only calculate the cost of two base salary days per manager as a start. We divide $85,000 by the number of true annual working days (for example, 230): $85,000 ÷ 230 = $370 per manager workday. Let's also say that the total program cost was $195,000. This includes training and coaching, design, instructors, facilities, equipment, materials, and administrative costs. In the following box are all the ROI calculations:

1.	Total manager training time costs ($370 per day x 2 days x 1,150 managers)	$851,000
2.	Total program costs	$195,000
3.	Total costs	$1,046,000

4. Our formula is $ROI = \dfrac{V\ (Value) - C\ (Cost)}{C\ (Cost)} \times 100$

Therefore, $ROI = \dfrac{\$5,630,400 - \$1,046,000}{\$1,046,000} \times 100$

438.28%

This is a great return on investment!

If you would like to demonstrate how quickly you pay back the entire investment, here is the calculation:

$$PB\ (Payback) = \frac{C\ (Cost)}{V\ (Value) \div M\ (Months)}$$

$$= \frac{\$1,046,000}{\$5,630,400 \div 36}$$

$$= 6.69\ months$$

Based on the performance improvement, you can recoup the entire expense in less than seven months.

A fourth point deals with another interesting and highly useful number—the *standard deviation* (SD)[1]. We won't go into a discussion of statistics, but here is what

---

1. Standard deviation is a statistical way of describing the spread around the mean or arithmetic average of a set of numbers. Because it is "standard," one-third of the set of numbers always falls to one side of the mean and one-third always falls to the other side. The larger the size of the SD (in our example, it was 19.3 before intervention), the bigger the spread in performance. The smaller the size of the SD (in our example, it was 10.2 after intervention), the greater the consistency of performance. In our example, not only is the post-intervention mean higher (82 percent compared to 58 percent), but the size of the SD is smaller—less spread away from the mean—which suggests there is more consistency of performance.

the SD can do for you. When you establish your baseline of performance, you can ask that the mean *and* the SD be calculated. A great many software packages do this for you automatically. Calculate the mean and SD following the performance intervention too. The SD shows how spread out from the mean all the individual scores are. Let's return to our example of making effective presentations. Suppose what you found was this:

Scores on Making Effective Presentations		
	Mean	**SD**
Before the performance improvement intervention	58	19.3
After the performance improvement intervention	82	10.2

What this tells you is that two-thirds of your managers scored between roughly 39 percent and 77 percent before your performance interventions, and two-thirds scored between approximately 72 percent and 92 percent following intervention. (The percentage of managers who fall ±1 SD from the mean is always two-thirds. This statistical constant never varies because you essentially are dealing with one group divided into three equal portions—those who are below, at, and above the mean.) Not only is the mean after your performance improvement venture dramatically higher, but there also is much greater consistency now in the way your managers perform. They're making better presentations more consistently! You and your client should break out the champagne.

A Note of Caution

All of the preceding discussion concerning Category 2 performance improvement projects is simply an attempt to demonstrate ROI. It is founded on several assumptions:

- The estimate of percentage of work time is accurate.
- The assessment of performers is accurate.
- The dollar amount attributed to the activity derived from performer salaries and percentage of total work is meaningful.

The more solid the basis for these assumptions, the more credible the results. It is essential that you do your homework to ensure the highest level of credibility in each case.

It's important to remember that there are secondary benefits derived from improved soft skills—and these benefits aren't included in the calculations discussed above. We should expect better presentations to generate a number of benefits that affect the bottom line (benefits such as greater sales, more informed workers, a clearer sense of project goals and progress that reduces time to completion). Defining the bottom-line value of these secondary benefits requires going after the performers and tracking examples of these benefits. They all are grist for your ROI mill.

The Highly Intangibles—What to Do?

We are now going to address those performance improvement goals for which calculating ROI seems at first glance to be almost impossible. Examples: improve leadership skills, improve telephone etiquette. What do we do with these?

We begin with a disclaimer. In our experience these performance improvement projects generally emerge from the "wise" heads of decision makers. They're based on the latest miracle cure (like empowerment, management-by-walking-around, you-can-negotiate-anything, or reengineering). We have a list of approximately 100 of these great big ideas. All of them have kernels of usefulness but, like the cabbage diet, they are rarely sensitive to the whole array of factors affecting performance (or weight and fitness). Often, reports of something that worked elsewhere triggers enthusiasm to apply it here. Benchmark studies, books, and keynote speeches all generate sudden activity. The dollars mysteriously appear, and the race is on.

A "bad experience" suffered by a senior decision maker is another catalyst for a performance improvement project. If a bank's executive VP makes a call that's poorly handled by a branch clerk, it can launch a corporate-wide venture on improving telephone etiquette. If the CEO makes a purchase that goes awry at one of the company retail stores, the 450 stores in the chain can be plunged into a "stellar customer service" program.

Please forgive our cynicism here, but sadly we've seen many important performance issues set aside in pursuit of what we considered to be wasteful adventures. Our comments aside, here is what we can do to demonstrate ROI when our front-end analyses (or pressures) lead us into less directly measurable types of projects.

The Journal Method

This method works well for most Category 3-type projects. It's simple in strategy but difficult in execution. If done correctly and well, however, the results are highly credible for two reasons. First, journaling provides first-hand quantitative data. Second, journaling often provides anecdotes that bring to life the results of your interventions. Here's how this works.

Step 1. As part of the implementation plan for your basket of interventions, you develop clear instructions on tracking results. You also designate a person (and here is where university interns from local learning and performance programs are extremely helpful) to monitor journaled results on a weekly basis.

Example: Leadership Program for All Middle- and Senior-Level Managers

Your company has conducted a form of "needs analysis" and determined that there is a leadership gap. The result of this gap is that decisions either are not made or take too long, opportunities are wasted, timidity causes inefficiencies, talent is lost, and many other negative things occur. Charged with developing a six-month-long leadership program, your client turns to you for assistance. You analyze the situation, and then design and develop the program. In the process you build in a journaling and monitoring system. You assign an intern to gather data each week from the 70 participants in the program. Participants meet once every three weeks for four hours. They leave each session with tasks to perform, a mini action plan, and a journal.

(continued on next page)

They are told that they will be contacted each week by email and asked to report on actions they took or decisions they made as a result of the program. They also will be asked to calculate the value of each action or decision to the company.

Step 2. When this project is set in motion, participants track their activities and decisions that are directly linked to the program. The monitor sends a weekly email and follows up to ensure all participants respond. The monitor collects the journaled information in a summary report, some of which (the nonconfidential portions) are released to participants as the program continues.

Example: Leadership Program for All Middle- and Senior-Level Managers

Each week the intern sends this email and form:

Please fill in the form below as a follow-up to your last Leadership session. Include all actions you took and decisions you made that directly relate to the program since it began. Please estimate as accurately as possible the financial impact of each action or decision.

Action/Decision	Linked to Which Part of the Leadership Program?	Estimated Financial Impact	How You Calculated or Estimated This	Nonfinancial Impact

The monitor collates all the information into a summary report that is distributed at each session (minus confidential portions) to share ideas, demonstrate impact, and stimulate actions.

Step 3. At the conclusion of the program, journaling with ongoing data collection may continue for a specified period. At a predetermined time, a final report containing the recorded financial and nonfinancial impact of the performance improvement program is released, along with an estimated ROI calculation.

Example: Leadership Program for All Middle- and Senior-Level Managers

The program continues for six months. It includes clear definitions of what "leadership" is and what is expected of managers as leaders. It provides training, job aids, processes, benchmark practices, work assignments, data collection and reporting, visits to other organizations, expert guidance, reading, and other elements. At the conclusion, journaling and monitoring continue on a monthly basis for three months. The performance improvement team produces a report on what resulted from the program. The report provides data derived from participants as well as other sources (such as sales figures, wastage reports, costs, market penetration progress reports, turnover figures). Most important, it gives financial and nonfinancial results, complete with ROI. The estimated ROI shows that for the $950,000 spent on the program (including participant time off the job minus the fully loaded cost of $280,000), the estimated value of financial impact is close to $130,000,000 to date. The estimated financial ROI [ROI = (V − C / C) x 100] is 1,268 percent. Whether or not this is completely accurate, the ROI is very obviously high and supported by participant explanations of calculations. And then there are the nonfinancial benefits reported....

As we mentioned, the strategy is relatively simple but the execution is tedious and demanding. Nevertheless, this is an extremely worthwhile venture that you and your WLP team should consider applying to a strategic performance improvement program.

On a methodological note, it is not necessary to gather data from all performers, especially when they are numerous. You can select a random sample of 20 performers (but the sample must be *truly* random), and focus on data collection from those 20. Then, with suitable modesty, generalize to the entire population. This is much more workable, but does diminish somewhat the drama and, unfortunately, the credibility, despite its likely relative accuracy.

An Activity for You

As we noted earlier, demonstrating a positive effect on the bottom line is the most useful means for furthering the WLP cause and building both credibility and support for your organization. According to the ASTD State of the Industry Report (Sugrue & Rivera, 2005), only 3.2 percent of organizations offer their management and clients projected ROI (business cases) and even fewer—2.1 percent—calculate actual ROI. This is both a sad statement about WLP practice and a clarion call to you to be among the best through your performance improvement professionalism.

Examine your upcoming projects. Select one that offers potential for calculating both projected and actual ROI. It can be in any of the three categories described in this chapter, but if this is your first attempt, remember that Category 1 projects offer the most solid numbers. Look for a supportive client, and explain why you are doing this. Demonstrate benefits. Then go for it. Consult *Training Ain't Performance* for job aids you can use to calculate costs, value, worth, ROI, and payback period.

An Activity for Your WLP Team

When you have identified a project for which you will track costs and calculate value and ROI, share this with your WLP team. Gather suggestions and insights from them. If possible, sign up recruits to assist you in your efforts. Keep the team informed as you progress. Encourage similar ventures from your colleagues.

Chapter Summary

This chapter led you more deeply into ROI country than did *Training Ain't Performance*. The approach was to share alternative means for calculating ROI. In the soft or less tangible areas, estimates and self-reports are, unfortunately, the realities with which we must deal. Although that makes our results less than perfect, those results still indicate important contributions to the organizational bottom line. Please bear in mind that many other seemingly hardline groups face the same barriers: marketing, advertising, operations, sales, and information technology all build business cases on assumptions and best estimates. Even after a project is completed, their reports include the data they are able to assemble. For example, there are few highly positive ROI reports on Enterprise Resource Planning (ERP) software implementations into which many large corporations have poured many millions of dollars. We often read in the press about seemingly wondrous ROIs projected for corporate acquisitions and mergers (apparently concluded on the basis of expert financial advice and calculations) that turn out not to be so brilliant—or accurate. We contend that our performance improvement efforts and contributions can be far more accurately demonstrated than many other groups with longer records of doing it. We encourage you to try it. You simply will be amazed!

This chapter

- began with a rationale for evaluating the impact of your performance improvement efforts—to demonstrate results and contributions to organizational success.
- described two methods for demonstrating ROI beyond those presented in chapter 10 of *Training Ain't Performance*.
- gave you procedures and examples of those two methods.
- encouraged you to integrate ROI calculations into one of your projects and share progress and results with your WLP team.

To close the core content of this *Fieldbook*, we return to the beliefs and myths we hold and often perpetuate in our professional work. In *Training Ain't Performance*, chapter 11 (pp. 173-188) offered a dozen "hit or myth" statements, and you decided if each was a "hit" (true) or a "myth" (false). All turned out to be pretty much mythical. The next chapter returns to these statements, and adds a "beyond" aspect to them.

Hit or Myth:
Facing the Facts

This chapter

- ◆ reviews the 12 myths about performance improvement presented—and demythologized—in *Training Ain't Performance*
- ◆ adds recommendations for counteracting the perpetuation of myths
- ◆ helps you and your WLP team to commit to productive actions that fit with your organizational environment.

Tools in this chapter include

- ◆ a hit-or-myth worksheet that includes the 12 myths from *Training Ain't Performance*, presents key findings to counter them, offers recommendations for practice, and leaves space for you and your team to enter productive actions that fit your organizational culture and setting.

The Amazing Power of Myth

You drop a mirror that smashes into hundreds of fragments. Quick, what's your first thought? Is it "Oh no! What a mess" or "Oh no! Seven years of bad luck"? When we pose this question to our conference and workshop participants, about 70 percent admit that they first think of seven years of bad luck.

Superstition is powerful. It's perpetuated by peoples' belief in superstitions or, because they've heard the superstition expressed so often, by a feeling that it can't hurt to be cautious. We knock on wood to keep away "bad luck" or carry an amulet to invite good fortune. Almost all of us say "Bless you" when someone sneezes. (Just try a quiet sneeze in an elevator and listen to how many strangers utter this very thoughtful expression.) Its purpose includes everything from preventing the devil from entering your throat to keeping your heart beating.

We still find a large number of myths and superstitions circulating in our organizations today. In chapter 11 of *Training Ain't Performance*, we delivered a dozen of them to you. We also presented arguments against each of the myth statements. In this chapter of the *Beyond Training Ain't Performance Fieldbook*, we take you one step farther to the *application* level. We'll revisit each myth and the key findings about it, and then we'll present recommendations for practice. Your job, and that of your team, will be to bring these recommendations to life.

An Activity for You

Study the statements in Worksheet 13-1. Examine the findings and recommendations associated with each myth. Think about your work, your clients' performers, past successes and failures, the culture of your organization, and your own capabilities. For each myth statement, enter *at least* one action you can take to better align your performance improvement practices with what is recommended. You're not limited to one action. Feel free to enter as many as you believe feasible. If you're already doing some things that align with the recommendations, enter these and pat yourself on the back. We salute you in advance.

Separating yourself and your organization from beliefs and practices that are part of the culture isn't easy, but it's surely worthwhile to put aside what isn't going to help achieve results that everyone values. When you complete the worksheet, pause, reflect on how far you've come, and congratulate yourself for assuming this professional leadership role.

An Activity for Your WLP Team

When you have completed your own set of actions (either actual or projected) in Worksheet 13-1 and reflected on how you can counteract the myths while advancing your professional cause, meet with your team. Have them do the Hit or Myth exercise on page 176 of *Training Ain't Performance*. Debrief their choices using the text in chapter 11 (pp. 175-184). Then share Worksheet 13-1 from this *Fieldbook*. Show your action entries, and ask the team to build on these. Record their suggested (or actual) actions. When completed, circulate a list of these actions to your entire team to stimulate professional practice based on research.

As a further activity, you and your team can become myth-buster sleuths. Identify practices in your organization that you feel are not productive. Performance appraisal is a great place to start. Go to the Internet to find research and best practices data to debunk the myths underlying unproductive, even counterproductive, practices.

Worksheet 13-1: Myths Versus Facts, and the Actions You Will Take to Counter Myths

Myth Statement	Findings	Recommendations	Actions
1. To achieve higher overall worker performance, hire for job-specific competencies rather than characteristics.	• The notion that the most competent people will perform best is not accurate. • Outstanding companies, such as Southwest Airlines, Singapore Airlines, People Soft, and Enterprise, do not always seek out the most competent employees. They focus on cultural fit, ability to work in teams, service orientation, and other essential characteristics. • The most competent may move on more rapidly to new opportunities. • Research indicates that cultural fit and compatibility with an organization's values are strong predictors of work performance and retention—stronger than job-specific competencies.	• Study your top (exemplary) performers to isolate common success characteristics. • Establish characteristics criteria for hiring and promotion. • Employ performance-based hiring/promotion procedures that include emphasis on characteristics, work values, and organizational cultural fit. • Monitor reasons why employees are let go. Track failure as well as success characteristics.	
2. Increases in job satisfaction tend to result in improved worker performance.	• There is a strong body of research evidence indicating that the correlation between job satisfaction and worker performance is "illusory." • Information on job satisfaction can bias performance appraisals. • Managers tend to rate more highly the performance of employees they have hired than the performance of employees others have hired. • Effective management of work patterns, encouragement, support of more intensive work, and job challenge appear to produce higher performance than does investment in supporting "job satisfaction."	• Do not use job satisfaction ratings as indicators of high workplace performance. • Employ, as feasible, objective supervisors and managers to assess worker performance. • Set objective criteria and standards for measuring performance, but ensure that expectations are clearly communicated, meaningful to performers, and accompanied by timely and specific feedback. • Focus on management of work patterns, meaningful challenges, encouragement, and support more than on happy, satisfied workers.	
3. On average, high performers are about 30 percent more productive than average performers.	• Research studies suggest that high performers are 40 percent to 70 percent more productive. • Two recent studies in automotive sales by the authors suggest that top performers are over 200 percent more productive in sales than average performers. • Effective management of the work environment (expectations, feedback, resources, incentives, selection, consequences) tends to raise the performance level of all employees while it reduces disparities among them.	• Talent management is essential. Identify top performers and ensure support and encouragement accompanied by meaningful challenges. • Study high performers to determine success criteria. Apply these to the selection and management of workers. • Focus on environmental factors that affect overall performance to reduce wide performance variability.	

(continued on page 204)

Worksheet 13-1: Myths Versus Facts, and the Actions You Will Take to Counter Myths (continued)

	Myth Statement	Findings	Recommendations	Actions
3.	On average, high performers are about 30 percent more productive than average performers. (continued)	• Top performers tend to exhibit a higher degree of "desirable characteristics" and competencies than do average performers.		
4.	Personality-type inventories used for selection purposes are strong predictors of performance success.	• Research suggests that "typing" through personality tests is unstable, despite its wide use. Over time, different results are obtained. • There is little consistency of definition/meaning for personality types across published instruments. • A National Research Council controlled study found that 60 percent to 80 percent of subjects changed their personality-type classification over a five-week period. • Performance-based hiring procedures tend to be better predictors of performance success than do personality tests.	• Conduct job analyses using top performers to identify exemplary performance. • Identify characteristics of exemplary performers. Use these for selecting new performers for a job. • Avoid making decisions based on personality inventories alone. • Define success criteria and metrics, develop performance interventions to achieve success, and monitor performance with feedback and support to performers.	
5.	When people select work goals on their own, their motivation to achieve them is greater.	• Research indicates that people willingly accept and buy into assigned work goals if those who set the goals are perceived as trustworthy and credible, if the goal is personally meaningful, if the goal inspires belief and confidence, if it applies to everyone evenly and fairly, and if it calls for outstanding results. • Research indicates that assigned, credible goals are at least as motivating as those selected by individuals and teams if, in addition to all the items cited above, performers are encouraged to select appropriate means for achieving them.	• Ensure that credible performance goals are set by respected people. • Ensure that goal achievement expectations are communicated clearly, meaningfully, and fairly to all. • Ask performers for input to determine means for achieving performance goals—especially top performers. • When you assign a goal, be sure to provide the needed support for achieving it.	
6.	In the early stages of learning to solve problems, extensive practice in problem solving is more effective than studying worked-out solutions to problems.	• A great deal of recent research supports the study of already-worked-out problems as more efficient and effective ways of increasing problem-solving performance, especially in early stages of learning.	• Identify common, relatively straightforward problems that performers will encounter, and present these problems with workable solutions. • Provide models of solutions, and analyze them with performers. • Provide practice applying model solutions to new problems.	

Myth Statement	Findings	Recommendations	Actions
6. In the early stages of learning to solve problems, extensive practice in problem solving is more effective than studying worked-out solutions to problems. (continued)	• New, complex learning overloads the short-term memory's capacity to handle information. Learning efficiency declines. • Worked-out sample problems decrease learning effort and promote more efficient transfer to new problems. • Caution: This is more often the case for novices than for advanced performers who require considerable problem-solving practice for proficiency.	• Increase difficulty levels as you fade out solutions. • Share new solutions generated by performers.	
7. Pay-for-performance is a fair way of rewarding superior performance.	• Although the concept appears good and fair, research shows that numerous problems arise in application. Key problems are these: — Pay for performance (PFP) is often administered within certain salary ranges, based on a fixed pool of money. Eventually, top performers reach a ceiling and rewards for higher performance vanish. — On interdependent work teams it becomes difficult to match performance to individuals. Perceived fairness becomes an issue. — Perceptions of performance in PFP systems rather than objective measures enter into decisions. Research shows bias and subjectivity influencing payment decisions. — Rewarding individuals is sometimes viewed as being done at the team's expense. This can breed resentment and occasional sabotage. — PFP often encourages a focus on short-term results rather than long-term strategies.	• Apply PFP principles prudently, with careful design and administration. • Re-examine the PIBI Model in chapter 9, and follow guidelines and principles derived from incentive research and best practices. • Above all, ensure fairness and equitable practices in paying for performance. • Bear in mind the results of one study: Most PFP plans share two common attributes—they absorb vast amounts of management time and resources, and they make everybody unhappy (Mercer 1997, p. 61).	
8. Organized, supervised work teams tend to outperform self-managed teams.	• More than 20 years of research overwhelmingly supports self-management. • Workers who manage themselves decrease the time and costs required for management to do it. • There is closer work coordination, less slacking off and absenteeism, and higher productivity on self-managed teams.	• Identify best practices in self-managed teams and examine the feasibility of applying them in your work context. • Develop incentives for self-managed teams. • Identify ways of loosening controls in highly managed work teams. Shift internal team management to workers.	

(continued on page 206)

Worksheet 13-1: Myths Versus Facts, and the Actions You Will Take to Counter Myths (continued)

Myth Statement	Findings	Recommendations	Actions
8. Organized, supervised work teams tend to out-perform self-managed teams. (continued)	• Workers share ideas, implement needed changes immediately, and share in benefits; they take greater ownership. • Self-management reduces levels of supervision and administrative tracking and speeds up execution of tasks. • Other benefits of self-managed teams include increased loyalty, innovative practices, and new hires brought up to speed more quickly without formal training.	• Track productivity indexes for both types of teams if they exist within your organization, and disseminate findings to senior decision makers.	
9. Immediate feedback for improving performance on complex tasks is more effective than delayed feedback.	• Numerous studies comparing immediate and delayed feedback suggest that immediate feedback works well with simple or familiar tasks. With complex tasks, delayed feedback (from hours to days) appears to be more effective. • Constraints of short-term memory suggest that the working memory component is soon overloaded by details of a complex task. Feedback separation appears to be beneficial.	• Provide means for giving immediate feedback on simple or familiar tasks. • Delay feedback in complex task execution. Test for optimal delays. • Regardless of timing, provide feedback on performance. This is essential for achieving desired performance. • Provide corrective feedback to improve performance, and confirming feedback to maintain performance, but never provide them simultaneously. • Focus feedback on the task, not the performer. • Follow the principles in chapter 8 of this *Fieldbook* to create feedback systems.	
10. We are pretty accurate judges of our own specific knowledge and performance capabilities.	• We know what we can and cannot do in highly overt tasks: fly an airplane, speak French, swim five miles. But we are poor judges of our very specific skills and knowledge (convert a service to a sales call, soothe an angry customer) or capabilities (judge a person's honesty, make a smart investment). • Research experimentally demonstrates the poor "calibration" (the correlation of confidence rating about specific skills and knowledge with actual performance) in judging ourselves.	• Do not be overly influenced by what performers say they can do. Observe, test, and obtain results. • Identify key required behaviors and accomplishments, and provide opportunities for practice and feedback, regardless of performer preferences. • Measure performance; do not rely on the word of the performers or their managers to make performance improvement decisions.	

Myth Statement	Findings	Recommendations	Actions
10. We are pretty accurate judges of our own specific knowledge and performance capabilities. (continued)	• Similar findings occur in judgments about "how much I learned" compared with test scores that reveal how much was learned. • Research also shows that we do not acquire skills and knowledge better from preferred instructional approaches than nonpreferred methods. Practice and feedback are key.		
11. Executives who clearly recognize the importance of investment in their employees tend to spend more on developing employee performance capabilities and measuring results.	• An in-depth survey of 250 executives (including CEOs) across a wide variety of industries showed that this was not the case. • CEOs in the survey ranked employee retention as one of the top two measures of value creation for their companies, but did not present this in the formal reporting of expenditures, did not measure factors affecting retention, and cited costs and poor management systems for not doing so. • Although 85 percent of executives cited the critical importance of investment in their employees, less than 35 percent admitted that they put their money where their convictions lay.	• Although it is important to reinforce executives and CEOS for making supportive statements, do not count on such affirmations to translate into financial commitments. • Demonstrate credible ROI backed by solid data to obtain senior management investment. • Calculate the ROI of your performance improvement projects. Be strategic. In chapter 10 of *Training Ain't Performance* and chapter 12 of this *Fieldbook*, review methods for doing this.	
12. As more companies have become concerned about the return on their learning and performance improvement investments, activities to measure ROI have increased.	• Despite increased pressure to produce ROI data, companies have not shown more effort to demonstrate results. ASTD's State of the Industry reports indicate a downward trend. In 2005 only 3.2 percent of reporting companies stated that they calculated projected ROI, and only 2.1 percent actual ROI (Sugrue & Rivera, 2005).	• What is not measured is frequently neglected. Evaluate the results of your performance improvement interventions to demonstrate on-the-job application and improved results. Include ROI figures. • Identify clients interested in demonstrating gains and ROI. Collaboratively calculate results and publish these in company newsletters, industry journals, and other media.	

Chapter Summary

This chapter

- reviewed a dozen myths from *Training Ain't Performance*.
- provided recommendations for countering all of those myths.
- encouraged you to list actions that are feasible within your organization and that take you away from myth-based performance improvement practices.
- had you play the Hit or Myth game from *Training Ain't Performance* with your WLP team, debrief it, expand feasible actions for going beyond the myths, and encouraged you and your team members to become myth detectives.

We are asking a lot of you because we believe that the effort you invest will provide huge returns to you personally and to your organization. This requires not only investment in making the effort, but also in increasing your own professional performance capabilities. That's the subject of the next chapter that focuses on strengthening you professionally.

Beyond Training Ain't Performance: Ongoing Growth and Development

This chapter

- ◆ returns to the start of *Beyond Training Ain't Performance* and has you and your WLP team assess, for a second time, where you currently are and where you want to be on seven *Training Ain't Performance* dimensions
- ◆ recommends, with guidelines, setting up a support system for your environment
- ◆ helps you diagnose facilitating and inhibiting factors in moving from training to performance
- ◆ helps you exploit facilitating factors and eliminate inhibiting ones
- ◆ recommends, with suggestions, forming a *Training Ain't Performance* study group
- ◆ provides a performance instrument and guidelines for use in planning your professional development and growth.

Tools in this chapter include

- ◆ a *Training Ain't Performance* individual evaluation, identical to the one you used in chapter 2
- ◆ a *Training Ain't Performance* evaluation of your organization, also identical to the one in chapter 2
- ◆ an Actions to Take in Building a Support System worksheet to help you create ways to support your progress toward becoming the performance support organization you would like to be
- ◆ a Support System Action Plan to make sure you develop an effective support system
- ◆ a Personal Facilitating and Inhibiting Factors template to help you sort through what will help you grow and develop and what potentially can hold you back
- ◆ a Personal Actions to Exploit Facilitating Factors and Decrease Inhibiting Factors worksheet

- an Organizational Facilitating and Inhibiting Factors worksheet to help your team isolate system elements that can either help or hinder team advancement
- an Organizational Actions to Exploit Facilitating Factors and Decrease Inhibiting Factors worksheet
- a performance instrument and guidelines to help plan your professional development and growth.

In chapter 2 of this *Fieldbook*, you and your WLP group had an opportunity to conduct a *Training Ain't Performance* self-assessment. The instrument you used had seven dimensions to it. You indicated where you currently are on each of these dimensions and where you want to be. Without looking back at your earlier answers, assess yourself again now that you have begun applying the principles, guidelines, and tools of both *Training Ain't Performance* and the *Beyond Training Ain't Performance Fieldbook*. We've reproduced the instructions and instruments for you in this chapter. Remember, do it on your own first (Assessment 14-1). Then, preferably, you and your team do the second one (Assessment 14-2). When you've completed these, go back and look at your completed assessments from chapter 2. Take note of any differences.

To complete Assessment 14-1, take the following steps:

1. For each dimension, read the descriptions at both ends of the continuum.
2. For each dimension, using pens or pencils of different colors, place an "X" on the continuum at those points you consider to be your own *current* state (one color) and your own *desired* state (second color). Be consistent. Always use the same color for *current* and the same second color for *desired*.
3. When you have placed all of your Xs in both colors, use a ruler to join all Xs in the *current* color and then join all Xs in the *desired* color. You'll have two (probably zig-zag) vertical lines. Here is an example (current = solid line; desired = dashed line).

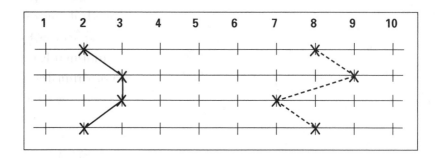

Assessment 14-1: *Training Ain't Performance* Individual Evaluation

Dimension	State A	1	2	3	4	5	6	7	8	9	10	State Z
My mission	To train learners based on client requests, stated needs, and/or organizational decisions											To build and support performance in ways all stakeholders value
How I am viewed by management and clients	Primarily as a deliverer of knowledge and skills content											Primarily as an expert and a partner in helping achieve desired, valued performance from people
Work style	Reactive; gatherer of training requests/requirements, and deliverer of instruction according to client demands											Proactive; partner-consultant helping clients define needs, and select and apply a range of interventions that build and support performance success
Products and services	Training programs and curricula; manuals and reference guides for learning											Performance gap analyses; consulting services to improve and support performance; broad range of performance support interventions; performance evaluation
Needs assessment process	Gather leader and client perceptions of training and development needs											Front-end analyses; performance discrepancy analyses; business case/return-on-investment studies
Evaluation process	Measure learner reactions to training; provide statistics on numbers trained/certified											Demonstrate bottom-line performance, business value, and return-on-investment
Accountabilities	I am measured on how well and how many I train											I am measured on my bottom-line impact—my measurable contributions to organizational goals and objectives

Assessment 14-2: *Training Ain't Performance Organizational Evaluation*

Dimension	State A	1	2	3	4	5	6	7	8	9	10	State Z
Our mission	To train learners based on client requests, stated needs, and/or organizational decisions											To build and support performance in ways all stakeholders value
How we are viewed by management and clients	Primarily as deliverers of knowledge and skills content											Primarily as experts and partners in helping achieve desired, valued performance from people
Work style	Reactive; gatherers of training requests/requirements, and deliverers of instruction according to client demands											Proactive; partner-consultants helping clients select and apply a range of interventions that build and support performance success
Products and services	Training programs and curricula; manuals and reference guides for learning											Performance gap analyses; consulting services to improve and support performance; broad range of performance support interventions; performance evaluation
Needs assessment process	Gather leader and client perceptions of training and development needs											Front-end analyses; performance discrepancy analyses; business case/return-on-investment studies
Evaluation process	Measure learner reactions to training; provide statistics on numbers trained/certified											Demonstrate bottom-line performance, business value, and return-on-investment
Accountabilities	We are measured on how well and how many we train											We are measured on our bottom-line impact—our measurable contributions to organizational goals and objectives

4. Note the discrepancies between the two zig-zag lines. A distance of three or more points between *desired* and *current* states on any dimension suggests that you have a lot to do to move from where you are to where you want to be.

The instructions for completing Assessment 14-2 are very similar to those for the Individual assessment. However, it is best done by a group of interested parties. Pull together fellow team members, your manager, and, if possible, a client or two whom you regularly serve. Allow for ample discussion while making up your minds on where to place the Xs.

1. For each dimension, read the descriptions at both ends of the continuum.
2. For each dimension, use pens or pencils of different colors to place an "X" on the continuum at the point the members of your group believe should be your training, learning, or WLP organization's *desired* state (one color) and at the point they consider to be your training, learning, or WLP organization's *current* state (second color). Ensure consistency in the use of the two colors.
3. When all Xs have been placed in both colors, use a ruler to join the Xs in the *current* color and then join all the Xs in the *desired* color. Once more, you should end up with two irregular vertical lines. Here's an example (current = solid line; desired = dashed line).

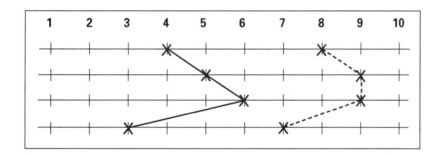

4. Note the gaps between the two zig-zag lines. A distance of three or more points between *desired* and *current* states suggests that your organization has a lot to do to move from where it is to where it would like to be.

Were there any significant *current* or *desired* changes for you or your organization compared with your selections in chapter 2? We don't anticipate large changes for you, personally, with respect to *desired* performance, but we do hope that *current* is beginning to edge closer to *desired* for you, and that your organization has progressed in its *desired* thinking. With time, you should experience greater convergence between *current* and *desired* states on all seven dimensions. Please self-assess again in four to six months and then two to three times annually. Doing so will keep you thinking about what more there is that all of you can do to become a WLP organization as you would wish it to be.

Building a Support System for Your Environment

Trying by yourself to become an effective performance improvement professional simply may lead to frustration. You need support to be successful within your organization. So do your colleagues. Here are some suggestions for building your and your group's support system. It's a starter list that should trigger ideas of your own.

An Activity for You

Read through the list in Worksheet 14-1. Check off those items that have appeal and are feasible in your environment. Cross through those that do not apply. Add your own actions to this list. Place your checkmark in the appropriate columns.

An Activity for Your WLP Team

Share with your group the list of retained actions (including your additions) in Worksheet 14-1. Ask if they would keep all the actions you retained and if they would place the checkmarks as you did. For each action your group retains, figure out what is needed to make it happen. Prioritize the actions on the list. Then develop a time and action plan for each. Assign responsibilities. Worksheet 14-2 can help with this.

Facilitating and Inhibiting Factors in Moving from Training to Performance

Progressing toward the *desired* state from where you currently are as indicated in your *Training Ain't Performance* assessment is an evolutionary process. It always takes longer than you think it should.

To reduce the time—and the obstacles—you must carefully analyze your current environment and practices. You also have to assess objectively your current competency levels, resources, expectations, and myriad other factors that can influence your practice. One way to start is to make a list of existing factors that you feel can facilitate the transformation from training to performance. Then do the same list-making for inhibiting factors.

An Activity for You

Start with yourself. Be totally honest. List physical, emotional, spiritual, intellectual, social, professional, personal, and other factors or issues that either facilitate or inhibit your personal transformation. Forewarned is forearmed. Use Worksheet 14-3. Make each list as exhaustive as possible.

If you've been rigorously honest with yourself, both lists should be fairly long. Unfortunately, the inhibiting factors column often ends up somewhat longer. Nevertheless, this is your reality. Your next step is to decide how you can go about exploiting the facilitating factors and eliminating or at least decreasing the inhibiting ones. Worksheet 14-4 can help you do this.

Worksheet 14-1: Actions to Take in Building a Support System

Instructions: Read the list of actions in column 1 and cross out any that have no appeal or are not feasible in your work setting. For all remaining actions, place a checkmark in the appropriate column beside each action listed below. Add descriptions of other actions that are interesting or feasible in your work setting and place checkmarks for them.

Action	We Already Do It	We Can Easily Do It	This Will Take Effort	This Will Be Almost Impossible to Do But We Can Try
Create a performance improvement resource library and encourage use of it.				
Hold in-house workshops/seminars on performance improvement issues and have the entire group attend.				
Read articles, highlight key passages, copy the articles, and circulate them to team members and clients.				
Target individual, "open" clients with whom you can collaborate, build success, and then leverage results with other clients.				
Hold "show-and-tell" meetings at which you and your colleagues share performance improvement successes and difficulties with clients and managers.				
As a team, attend professional performance improvement conferences and share with one another what you learned there.				
Develop in-house projects that enhance professional growth (for example, calculate ROI of performance improvement projects; create a "best practices" task force).				
Take a senior manager to lunch and educate him or her about the performance improvement group's aspirations and potential impact on the bottom line. Offer concrete suggestions. Seek support.				
Enroll in external courses and programs related to performance improvement. Share learning and resources with others. Encourage others to enroll.				
Join local, national, and international learning and performance organizations (such as ASTD and ISPI). Attend meetings. Become active in local chapter events. Share what you learn.				
Create links to other, similar external groups in organizations, both related to your industry and outside of it.				

(continued on page 216)

Worksheet 14-1: Actions to Take in Building a Support System (continued)

Action	We Already Do It	We Can Easily Do It	This Will Take Effort	This Will Be Almost Impossible to Do But We Can Try
Establish relationships with internal and external mentors who can help you and your team develop professionally.				
Celebrate performance improvement successes you and your team members achieve.				
Informally assist one another on performance issues and projects. Create an informal support network.				
Document what works. Share the knowledge practices, models, examples, templates, and designs with others. Develop a Website that everyone in your training group can access.				
Submit for professional awards if you or your group has had a successful performance improvement initiative. If you win, publicize it to build credibility and support for your endeavors.				

Worksheet 14-2: Support System Action Plan

Action	Start Date	End Date	Person Responsible	Other Contributors	Resources Required

Worksheet 14-3: Personal Facilitating and Inhibiting Factors

Instructions: List your physical, emotional, spiritual, intellectual, social, professional, and personal factors that can facilitate or hinder your transformation as a performance improvement professional.

Facilitating Factors	Inhibiting Factors

Worksheet 14-4: Personal Actions to Exploit Facilitating Factors and Decrease Inhibiting Factors

Instructions: Describe the actions you can take to make the most of those personal factors that facilitate your transformation and those actions you can take to decrease or eliminate the factors that hinder your transformation.

Facilitating Factors	Actions to Exploit
Inhibiting Factors	**Actions to Eliminate/Decrease**

The following exhibit presents several examples to trigger your own ideas:

Facilitating Factors	Actions to Exploit
• New manager who seems to want us to improve our results • Recent best-practice study of performance support in our industry shows great results • Tuition reimbursement program	• Meet with manager. Show tools from this *Fieldbook* and obtain support. • Make copies, highlight key leverage points, and circulate them. • Enroll in local university performance improvement certificate program.
Inhibiting Factors	**Actions to Eliminate/Decrease**
• Budget reduced by 5 percent • Already have a heavy workload • I've got a great reputation as a trainer	• Show how addressing some of our problems and opportunities with less expensive performance improvement interventions can decrease time and save money. • Meet with manager to discuss current workload; show where certain tasks can be transformed into more productive ones. • So why am I troubled? I can still do training, but can add to my reputation by showing fabulous performance improvement results.

An Activity for Your WLP Team

As you did for yourself, now extend your thinking to your organization. Using Worksheets 14-5 and 14-6 as a group, list facilitating and inhibiting factors first. Then list actions to exploit facilitating factors and eliminate or decrease inhibiting ones. If you feel it is appropriate, share your personal lists from the work you did above.

The lists and actions you and your group have generated are extremely valuable as you move forward from *current* to *desired* states. Keep these close at hand and refer to them frequently to maintain the progress. As you exploit the facilitating factors and work to reduce or eliminate the inhibiting elements, changes will occur more rapidly.

Form a *Training Ain't Performance* Study Group

Training Ain't Performance and the *Beyond Training Ain't Performance Fieldbook* are resources to be *used*. One way of using them is to create a study group. Ask each person to accept responsibility for leading the discussion about one chapter or topic. Set a calendar of meetings (live or virtual) when the group can gather to discuss what they read, tried, and discovered as they went through the assigned material. The discussions should include

- ◆ what are the key concepts, principles, or practices?
- ◆ how do these add value to learning? to performance? to our organization?
- ◆ what conclusions should we draw based on our readings or experiences?
- ◆ what action plans can we create?
- ◆ how do we verify results of our actions?
- ◆ how do we obtain required approvals and support?

Worksheet 14-5: Organizational Facilitating and Inhibiting Factors

---

Instructions: List the group's physical, emotional, spiritual, intellectual, social, professional, and personal factors that can facilitate or hinder its transformation as a performance improvement team.

Facilitating Factors	Inhibiting Factors

Worksheet 14-6: Organizational Actions to Exploit Facilitating Factors and Decrease Inhibiting Factors

Instructions: Describe the actions the group can take to make the most of those factors that facilitate its transformation and those actions it can take to decrease or eliminate the factors that hinder its transformation.

Facilitating Factors	Actions to Exploit
Inhibiting Factors	**Actions to Eliminate/Decrease**

These are suggested questions only . . . starting points for your ongoing growth and development.

Plan Your Professional Development and Growth

Before we conclude this important chapter, we want to provide you with a means and tool for creating and monitoring your own professional development plan (PDP). Any time is the right time to put this development plan in place. It begins where you are now and lays out steps to take you where you want to go. In Worksheet 14-7 you'll find a format for creating your PDP.

Here are the steps to follow:

1. Identify and list performance areas requiring development:
   • technical
   • work practices
   • interpersonal.
2. Identify and list areas of strength to enhance.
3. List career aspirations—future positions or opportunities.

Worksheet 14-7: Creating Your Professional Development Plan

Instructions: Fill in column 1 and then complete the other columns for each entry you have made in column 1.

	Internal Activities, Experiences, Assignments	External Activities, Courses, Events	Self-Regulated Activities	Start Date	Checkpoint Dates	Success Criteria
Performance areas requiring development:						
Strengths to enhance:						
Career aspirations:						
Subjects of special interest:						

4. List subjects of special interest to be pursued.
5. Beside each listed item, prescribe internal activities, experiences, and assignments; external activities, courses, events; self-regulated activities that are appropriate to achieve a successful outcome.
6. List start dates and checkpoint dates.
7. Describe your success criteria.

When you've created your PDP, it's up to you to *work* that plan. Set realistic but challenging goals for yourself. Monitor your performance against the plan, gently bring yourself back on track if you stray. Modify the plan as you see fit. Reward yourself for your progress and accomplishments.

Chapter Summary

What a heavy-duty chapter! Let's review what happened.

- ◆ You assessed yourself and your organization again, just as you did in chapter 2 of this *Fieldbook*. You then were able to compare perceptions of *current* and *desired* states for you and your WLP group then and now.
- ◆ You reflected on how to build a support system for yourself and for your group. You generated actions to take in both cases and created action plans for making these happen.
- ◆ You identified facilitating and inhibiting factors in your environment with respect to moving to your desired states. Once more you created action plans to exploit facilitating factors and eliminate or decrease inhibitors.
- ◆ You concluded the chapter by considering suggestions for setting up a *Training Ain't Performance* study group.

In this chapter we gave you a number of ideas and support materials. These should help you as you leave us. But before we say "goodbye and good luck," we give you one last action item. Review this chapter a second time very soon. Select from it what you can feasibly do for ongoing growth and development for yourself and your colleagues. Get started now. Don't let inertia work against you. Organize with your teammates. Get your management onboard. Use the tools and suggestions in this chapter, and move yourself and your WLP support team to a new level by making significantly more contributions to your organization.

In the next chapter we turn to external support systems that can help you and your organization make the transition.

External Support Systems

This chapter

- ◆ examines ways the external world beyond your organization can assist you in reaching new performance improvement heights
- ◆ explains the value of joining local or industry-based performance improvement associations
- ◆ suggests benefits to you for joining national and international performance improvement societies
- ◆ describes value to be gained from attending workshops and conferences and from forming relationships with colleges and universities
- ◆ encourages you to read professionally in the field, and gives you some excellent starting places to explore
- ◆ lays out the benefits of networking
- ◆ welcomes you to continue the dialogue with the authors.

This final chapter adds an external dimension for supporting your ongoing progress toward becoming a *Training Ain't Performance* organization—one that achieves the performance improvement that leads to valued results for all stakeholders. The first recommendation we offer is our strongest one: *become active professionally outside your company.*

Join a Local or Industry-Based Performance Improvement Association

We suggested in the previous chapter that joining a performance improvement society offers self-development benefits. We return to this and add that being part of such a group provides an external support system for you and your organization. Such groups

- ◆ share best practices
- ◆ obtain speakers at a much lower cost than your own organization would have to pay

- keep members current on what's happening in the field
- provide collegiality when support is needed
- act as a sounding board for your issues, concerns, and ideas
- usually give out awards for member (individual and organizational) accomplishments, and these reinforce your and your team's efforts while they validate and enhance them
- offer an opportunity for networking, which leads to recruitment of talent and hiring of consultants and freelancers, and which opens possibilities for your own future career moves.

These associations can be local, with members representing a wide range of industries. This type of diversity encourages cross-pollination of ideas. Industry-based associations focus on concerns similar to those of your own organization. Learning and performance improvement associations exist in the pharmaceutical, financial, railway, high-technology, and telecom industries as well as many others.

An Activity for You

Contact your local Chamber of Commerce to identify associations in your area. Also contact ASTD at www.astd.org, the Canadian Society for Training and Development (CSTD) at www.cstd.ca., or the International Society for Performance Improvement (ISPI) at www.ispi.org for information on local chapters in your geographic region. (ASTD and ISPI also have chapters in many other countries.) To locate industry groups, the best way to start is with an Internet search. You will discover a broad array of professional support groups.

An Activity for Your WLP Team

Create a list of potential local associations to explore. Gather information and set up a file on each one. Circulate these files among your colleagues. Hold a meeting to discuss impressions and reactions. Assign individuals to explore further and report to the group. Finally, select a local and/or industry association in which to become active. If the association has the potential to support your WLP organization, not only become active but also accept increasing leadership positions. You will grow individually and your organization will reap the rewards of your expanding vision and capabilities.

Join a National or International Performance Improvement Society

We have already mentioned ASTD and ISPI. Both of these produce publications and reports that are of immense benefit to performance professionals. Their fees are reasonable. Their conferences are extremely professional and provide continuing learning opportunities for you and your team. They also offer workshops and certificate programs to enhance performance capabilities in a variety of relevant areas.

Attend Workshops and Conference Events

There are dangers in becoming too internally fixated on your work. Attending local and national workshops and conferences opens one's eyes to new avenues. Often the materials from these events can constitute the basis for significant change in your work setting. We recommend getting on email lists from ASTD, ISPI, and industry/local associations. Their periodicals also announce learning and conference events. Webinars are a growing vehicle for professional development. Their advantage is that you need not travel to learn from external courses. Fees are generally low, and the quality is becoming better as Webinar software increases in simplicity of use and sophistication of interaction and delivery.

Get Certified

ASTD offers a Human Performance Improvement (HPI) Certificate Program. It provides professional development for aspiring performance consultants. This program helps you

- develop marketable skills that enable you to move beyond training
- gain experience using tools designed to cultivate performance improvement competencies
- learn from experienced performance consultants and practitioners
- demonstrate your commitment to performance improvement
- enhance your reputation for providing results-oriented solutions.

For more information on ASTD's HPI Certificate Program, visit www.astd.org /astd/education/hpi_certificate_program.

ISPI offers a Certified Performance Technologist (CPT) designation, which helps employers and clients identify practitioners who have proven they can produce results through systematic performance improvement processes. For practitioners the CPT credential helps assess their ability, focus their professional development efforts, and recognize their capabilities.

A CPT designation provides a professional label that is respected worldwide. A certification says you are a member of a profession. Your name is placed in a registry of CPTs. The designation program is based on globally accepted standards of human performance technology.

The 10 Standards of Human Performance Technology are drawn from the key principles that form the foundation of the field. They require application of systematic processes to improve performance. These standards ensure that the certified performance technologist conducts her or his work in a manner that includes

1. an unwavering focus on results
2. systematic examination of performance improvement situations while maintaining a system view of the global context with its competing pressures, resource constraints, and anticipated organizational changes

3. the addition of value from how you do your work and the work itself
4. development of partnerships or collaborations with clients and other experts, as required
5. systematic assessment of the performance opportunity or problem
6. systematic analysis of the work and workplace to identify the causes or factors that limit performance
7. systematic design of appropriate interventions or specification of the requirements to eliminate or decrease performance gaps
8. systematic development of all or some of the performance interventions
9. systematic implementation of the basket of performance improvement interventions
10. systematic evaluation of the processes employed and the results achieved.

CPTs also adhere to a universally accepted code of ethics intended to promote appropriate professional practice. To be certified or recertified, an applicant must sign a statement of agreement with the principles on which the code is based, principles that guide the performance improvement process:

* adding value
* using validated practices
* collaborating with others
* continuously improving ones proficiency
* demonstrating integrity
* upholding confidentiality.

CPTs are committed to continued growth and development in their profession. There is a requirement for periodic recertification. ISPI offers conferences, institutes, and workshops that support the standards of human performance technology and the code of ethics and that provide the means for recertification.

To learn how you can become a CPT, visit ISPI's Website at www.certifiedpt.org/.

Create Relationships with Colleges and Universities

Educational institutions have large amounts of expertise and resources on hand. Costs for using these resources are often less than your internal ones. Your local college or university may have software specialists and studios with which you can contract to develop and deliver Web-based learning and performance support tools and systems. Subject-matter experts can help enhance content. Students, acting as interns, can increase your ability to undertake projects for which you have insufficient resources. You also contribute to the students' learning. Often, an intern becomes a potential recruit for your team.

Read

Build your knowledge of the training field and acquire tools for improving your organization's performance by reading books and periodicals on relevant topics.

Training Ain't Performance contains a large reading resource section. Beyond that list there is a vast body of reading materials, far too many to cite here. As learning and human performance support continue to grow in importance, books and magazines are increasing rapidly. Below is a list of publishers who specialize in these topical areas. We recommend that you research the following sources:

- ASTD Press—www.astd.org/astd/Publications/books /astd_press_books.htm
- ISPI—http://performance.ispi.org/source/library /ordershome.cfm?section=orders
- HRD Press—www.business-marketing.com/store/hrd.html
- Pfeiffer—www.pfeiffer.com/WileyCDA/Section/id-101552.html
- Berrett-Koehler—www.bkconnection.com/
- CEP Press—www.cepworldwide.com/storefront.asp

With respect to magazines, we recommend

- *T+D* (ASTD's monthly magazine)— www.astd.org/astd/publications/td_magazine
- *Infoline* (ASTD's series of tips and tools)— www.astd.org.astd/publications/infoline/infoline_home
- *Performance Improvement Journal* (ISPI's monthly journal)—www.ispi.org/
- *Performance Improvement Quarterly* (ISPI's quarterly academic publication)— www.ispi.org/
- *Workforce Performance Solutions*—www.wpsmag.com

Build a Network

Local and industry associations are certainly excellent means for creating professional networks. Beyond these we recommend searching through your own organization for kindred spirits, people who are committed to human performance improvement and the impact this can have on results. Where do you find them? Almost anywhere. Here, however, is a high-probability starter list:

- human resources personnel (for example, compensation, benefits, incentives)
- other groups in your organization with a performance improvement mandate (such as information technology, sales, manufacturing, safety)

- individual contributors who are committed to and actively engaged in performance improvement initiatives
- organizational development and organizational effectiveness specialists
- human factors/ergonomics specialists
- work process specialists.

An Activity for Your WLP Team

Brainstorm with your group to identify internal network contacts of value to or in support of the directions you wish to take your WLP team. Include key influencers, informal leaders, union leaders, and managers who may champion your cause.

Outside your organization are like-minded thinkers in your industry, local professionals, and national/international thought leaders. Most are open to exchanges of information. Exploit all of these potential links.

Stay in Touch

This brings us to the end of our *Beyond Training Ain't Performance Fieldbook*, but not to the end of the dialogue we've established with you. We're always open to chatting with you and helping support you. Our Website is www.hsa-lps.com. There you can find free articles to download and a newsletter you can receive online at no cost.

This *Fieldbook* is a tool-based resource for you. Use it. Let us know how you're doing. We wish you the best of success in improving your, your clients', and your organization's performance!

A Lexicon of
Human Performance Improvement Terms

Action procedure: A sequence of steps that leads to the completion of a task.

Actuals: What a target population currently knows and does. Used when performing a needs assessment or front-end analysis. *Actuals,* as a term, is often replaced by *current state.*

Analysis procedure: A systematically organized sequence of steps that leads to the breaking down of an issue, case, situation, task, or object into its constituent parts.

Aptitudes: General or specific capabilities of the learners/performers. In an instructional design context, subject-matter competence (for example, basic math skills, Level II systems administration, or certification plus a minimum of three years' experience) is often included as part of aptitudes. The term *aptitudes* is also used for *ability to perform.*

Assessment certification: The process of providing clear evidence of an individual's competence in specific job skill areas through the use of validated verification procedures.

Attitudes: Sustained feelings toward the required learning or performance, specific instructional methods/media, and/or the learning/performance context, or toward training in general.

Audit trail: A documented record of all steps and activities undertaken to create and implement a learning or performance intervention. It fulfils two purposes: creates a running example for others to consult, and documents the development of the intervention in case of legal challenge after implementation.

Automaticity (or automated procedure): Procedure that consumes none or very few cognitive mental resources. Automated procedures operate so fast that a person is literally unaware that the procedure has been used. In effective learning, new behaviors are reproduced to the point of automaticity (unthinking accurate action). The individual (for example, a hockey player, an actor, or an auctioneer) generally lacks conscious control over the procedure and cannot verbalize or explain exactly what or why something is being done.

Behavior: Something a person does that involves an action, usually in response to some external or internal stimulation.

Behavior modeling: Learners acquire new behaviors first by observing live or televised models displaying ideal behaviors and then by rehearsing the behaviors they've seen. Learners receive information on their behavior, generally through structured feedback (via observation checklists, video recording and playback). This cycle is repeated as the model is faded out until learners have mastered the behavior.

Blended solutions: Intelligent intervention combinations, seamlessly integrated to produce desired learning and performance outcomes. Blended solutions combine elements from various intervention strategies into a single, integrated package. Often a blended solution will incorporate elements from traditional instructor-centric strategies with one or more technology-based strategies such as e-learning or performance support tools plus a feedback system, incentives, and other environmental or motivational interventions.

Case study: Learners receive information about a situation or case either orally, through written or mediated materials, or a combination of these. Individually or in teams, learners examine the facts and incidents of a case, critically analyze those facts, and develop solutions. Case studies work best when several are used within a program. Cases may be close-ended (have only one best solution) or open-ended (have any number of best solutions as long as they are well supported or require group consensus for resolution).

Causes: Reasons for lack of optimal (desired) performance.

Checklist: An instrument for physically checking off the presence/absence of items. In a learning and performance context, checklists frequently are used to observe behavior and accomplishments. Checklists also can be used for tracking the frequency of behaviors.

Classroom instruction: Instructor-led, group-based learning. It may take the form of a school-type classroom or teaching laboratory. The term is usually associated with "live," face-to-face instruction, but also can be applied to interactive distance learning.

Client: Someone who requests an intervention; someone we serve professionally; someone who receives training or performance support from the workforce learning and performance group to achieve valued results from workers.

Competency: An ability that is usually required for a job. This is in contrast to a *skill*, which is simply an ability to do something and which may take many forms (psychomotor, verbal, artistic, analytical). To define competency requirements, you analyze a job; to decide if a person's skills match the competency requirements, you analyze the person. Competencies should not be confused with *characteristics*—those traits that people exhibit as part of "who they are." In the work setting, it is almost impossible to alter a person's characteristics. We often hire for characteristics and train for competencies.

Context analysis: Analysis of the setting and conditions in which training or a performance improvement intervention is to occur. This is key to ensuring successful implementation of the intervention.

Decision procedure: A sequence of steps that leads to a judgment or conclusion.

Declarative knowledge: Knowledge that tells us who, what, why, when, where, and how. It is "talk-about" knowledge. Declarative knowledge breaks down into facts (such as, Montreal is a city), concepts (such as a triangle), and principles (such as, what goes up must come down).

Delivery system: The integrated grouping of media and other support mechanisms for carrying instruction to the learner. Delivery systems include self-paced, multimedia learning kits; satellite delivery video classrooms; multitask simulator trainers; and the Internet. In its simplest form, a delivery system can be a live instructor with a blackboard or even a book.

Documentation: Published products, such as print records, books, manuals, training programs, and performance support tools that store information. These can be produced as hardcopy publications or in such physical formats as videotapes, audiotapes, CD-ROMs, DVDs, online help, and other electronic forms.

Education: Activities, either deliberately designed or naturally experienced, that foster the development of general mental models and values. These form the foundation for how one views the world. They also create the basis for consistent behavior and decision-making patterns.

e-Learning: A generic label used to describe any learning materials delivered via the Web. Also, frequently referred to as *Web-based training* or *online learning*. The Web can deliver any existing type of instruction: live (synchronous) instruction via video; self-paced (asynchronous) computer-based-technology/multimedia-like or print-like materials with or without interactivity, tracking, and feedback; and collaborative learning activities such as online discussions (synchronous or asynchronous) among learners and instructors. In some cases, use of CD-ROMs and DVDs is included with e-learning.

Electronic performance support system (EPSS): A highly dynamic and complex performance support tool and system. EPSS guides the performer to attain a desired result.

Feelings: Sensations and opinions about a task, problem, person, or situation. It is important to identify feelings when conducting a front-end analysis because these will strongly influence selection and implementation of learning and performance interventions.

Fluency: The speed/agility that one strives for when a basic behavior or level of performance has been achieved. Distinguishes masters from novices.

Focus group: An informal, small-group discussion designed to obtain participants' perceptions, experiences, ideas, response to, and beliefs about a defined topic.

Formative evaluation: An evaluation conducted while a program or intervention is under development to improve its effectiveness.

Front-end analysis: A rigorous set of activities that, when fully applied, gathers data permitting the identification of desired and actual performance states. It includes clear indications of what the nature of the gap is and it identifies potential solutions—both instructional and noninstructional—for closing the gap. It is a term and methodology originally created by Joe Harless.

Human capital: The sum total of all knowledge, experience, and human performance capability an organization (or an individual) possesses that can be applied to create wealth.

Human performance technology (HPT): A recognized body of professional knowledge and skills whose aim is the engineering of systems that result in accomplishments valued by the organization and all stakeholders. The goal is human performance improvement. HPT is a disciplined professional field that is systemic in its vision and approach, systematic in its conduct, scientific in its foundation, open to all forms of intervention, and focused on achieving valued and verifiable results.

Implementation planning: Development of a plan for installing, applying, and maintaining an instructional program or set of performance interventions to ensure that there are no delays or missing support systems. This involves identifying all groups that will contribute to some aspect of the implementation and those that will be affected by it or its consequences. It also includes contingency planning.

Incentive: Something valued by an individual or group that is offered in exchange for changed or increased performance.

Incentive system: An organized program of rewards offered to motivate people to perform in specific ways.

Instruction: A set of organized activities intended to create changes in learners that permit them to generalize (that is, apply and adapt) what has been learned to new instances.

Instructional event: A learning activity designed to help learners plan, select relevant information, connect new information to prior knowledge, hone their skills through practice, and/or monitor their performance.

Instructional format: The overall design or approach for organizing a complete course or program.

Instructional method: Means for externally supporting the mental processing required for learning. An instructional method also may compensate for mental-processing or motivational deficits. It is the active ingredient for triggering learning.

Instructional strategy: A structure or design that permits a number of instructional methods to be organized and delivered to learners (for example, role-play, interactive lecture, case study, structured on-the-job training).

Instructional systems design (ISD): The main, disciplined, and systemic approach to engineering effective learning systems. It offers a mental model as well as documented procedures for how to approach the engineering of learning interventions that achieve desired, verifiable results.

Intervention: A deliberately conceived act or system specifically designed to bridge the gap between current and desired performance states. It can be complete unto itself or part of a basket of interventions. It is strategically applied to produce intended performance results. An intervention may add a performance support element or may remove an obstacle that prevents performance from occurring.

Knowledge management: The collection of processes that govern the creation, dissemination, and use of knowledge. In the current business world, knowledge has become a critical competitive asset that must be fostered, captured, stored, and shared. This requires systems that search, record, protect, and disseminate knowledge throughout an organization and across communities of practice.

Learner analysis: Identification of learner characteristics that must be taken into account for instruction to be effective. This includes background and aptitudes with respect to what is required, attitudes, learning and language preferences, and (if appropriate) tool skill abilities and deficits.

Learner-controlled instruction (LCI): A strategy that shifts power from instructor to learner. Learners receive a learning map that specifies required performance and measures along with a repertoire of resources. These may include materials specifically designed for learning or simply informational documents. Resources usually include people with whom the learner may interact or consult. Learners decide when they are ready to demonstrate performance capability, often through some form of test or work effort. LCI programs usually take place at designated model work sites where personnel have been trained to provide support, coaching, and feedback. In most cases the training or performance support department is involved in certifying performance capability.

Learner verification: The process of verifying with actual or simulated learners the effectiveness of an instructional program.

Learning: A change in cognitive (mental) structures that results in the potential for behavior change. Learning is a genetically coded ability that enables organisms to adapt to local, changing conditions in the environment.

Learning management system (LMS): Management system for online (and sometimes other forms of) learning. One type is essentially a check-in/check-out database system that keeps track of student registration and progress. Some LMSs have their own built-in assessment functions. One can run course materials of any kind within these check-in/check-out systems. A second type of LMS is one that provides a more complete set of functions not only for registration and tracking, but also for organizing materials within courses and integrating content with communication tools, multimedia resources, and integrated assessments, self-tests, and quizzes.

Live instruction: Instruction provided mainly by an individual or team face-to-face with learners (trainer, guest speaker, facilitator, master performer, and so forth). Activities may include lecture, question-and-answer session, demonstration, guided practice (including a laboratory situation), or any other learner-teacher interaction. Live instruction may include use of instructional media aids.

Mediated instruction: Generally used to describe all forms of instruction delivered by means other than a live instructor in a face-to-face context. Mostly denotes instruction provided via video and/or computer.

Motivation: An internal state that impels or drives a person to action. Motivation is strongly influenced by the value a person attributes to the action (the higher the value, the greater the motivation), the confidence of the person (under- or overconfidence decreases motivation), and the mood of the person (positive mood increases motivation). In learning and performance, motivation plays a key role along with ability and prior knowledge.

Multimedia: Combinations of media (visual, auditory, tactile) integrated to deliver an instructional message.

Needs analysis: A generic term for identifying gaps between ideal and current states.

Needs assessment: The initial analytic activity to identify and characterize gaps between desired and actual states. This term is often associated with Roger Kaufman of Florida State University. In his gap model, you begin by verifying if there is a gap between desired and actual outcomes of your system. If yes, you backward chain to identify gaps at the outputs, products, processes, and input stages. This enables you clearly to display all the gaps in the system and trace backward to initial causes. Needs assessment helps identify where gaps exist, at a mega (societal), macro (organizational), or micro (local) level.

Objective: A statement that presents in specific terms what learners or performers will be able to do as a result of a designed or specified learning experience or performance intervention. Also referred to as *instructional objective* or *performance objective,* depending on context.

On-the-job training: Training conducted within the work environment by a job expert, usually involving one or a small group of trainees.

Optimals: Visions of desired knowledge or performance.

Peer learning system: A strategy that provides structured materials to learners who then teach their peers using the materials. Peer learning requires clearly defined objectives, materials for peer teachers/tutors, evaluation instruments, and an instructor or facilitator to provide guidance and feedback.

Performance: A function of behavior and accomplishment. Performance includes what one does and the result of what one does. The behavior portion is the "cost" part of performance—the effort expended to attain the accomplishment. The accomplishment is the "benefit"—the desired or valued outcome.

Performance analysis: The initial analytic effort to identify and characterize gaps between desired and actual performance states. Also referred to as *gap analysis.*

Performance consulting: The set of professional activities one engages in to identify gaps in performance—either opportunities or problems—that affect an organization's results and to prescribe appropriate interventions. The key focus of performance consulting is the attainment of desired organizational results through people. The main body of professional knowledge that supports the performance consultant is HPT.

Performance engineering principles: Principles that govern the practice of human performance technology. They codify what science has discovered about human performance in the workplace. Authors who have enunciated these principles include George Geis, Thomas F. Gilbert, Geary Rummler, and Joe Harless.

Performance gap: The gap between actual performance and desired or optimal performance.

Performance management: The array of activities for identifying required performance for individuals or groups, setting and communicating expectations, monitoring activities and outcomes, providing appropriate feedback, and documenting results. It may include a provision of incentives and consequences.

Performance support: Means of providing resources, information, and assistance within the job environment to help individuals and teams achieve desired results.

Web-based tools encompass a wide range of performance support possibilities: interactive job aids to assist in completing forms or performing work steps; online help for computer-based systems; interactive forms that support a predefined work flow and allow data to be carried forward to related forms or work steps; interactive content retrieval systems to provide rapid access to business-critical knowledge assets; and refresher content on previously acquired skills and knowledge. Managers, supervisors, and colleagues also are key agents of performance support.

Performance system: A system made up of a number of elements that interact with one another to ensure that people perform as desired in the workplace.

PIP (potential for improving performance): The ratio of the worth of exemplary (W_{ex}) performance to the worth of typical performance (W_t), usually expressed as PIP = W_{ex}/W_t.

Procedural knowledge: Knowledge that allows us to perform—generally to do something automatically so that we do not seem to be "thinking about it" (for example, riding a bicycle, touch typing, troubleshooting a system). Procedural knowledge includes analysis, decision, and action procedures.

Prototype: A model set of materials in a form that can be transformed through testing and refinement into a final, produced program package.

Return-on-investment (ROI): Result of a calculation that compares the value of what an investment achieves with its cost. In the human performance context, it provides a concrete means for demonstrating the value of human performance interventions and the increased value of human capital. The general formula for calculating ROI is ROI = (value − cost/cost) × 100. The result is expressed as a percentage.

Reusability: The term is now part of a new vocabulary that includes reusable information objects, reusable learning objects, reusable nuggets, and so forth. The assumption is that if we can create content and place it in an information repository in discrete chunks each time we develop information packages and/or learning programs, then we can go into this repository, withdraw relevant chunks for a particular group or individual, combine these into coherent packets, and deliver them to anyone, anywhere, at any time.

Self-study: Learners receive materials designed specifically for instruction according to the logic of learning. Learners interact solely with the material and engage in active responding. The materials may be print, computer-mediated, interactive video instruction, multimedia, and so forth. Feedback on accuracy generally is immediate and continuous.

Solutions: Means for attaining optimal performance.

Stakeholder: A person or group who has a vested interest in a project's outcome.

Structured on-the-job training (SOJT): An instructional strategy that requires the participation of training personnel, job supervisors, skilled practitioners, and learners. Learners receive objectives and guidelines from the workplace learning and performance group and are released to the job. Job supervisors monitor progress and ensure the availability of skilled workers to act as on-the-job trainers. The skilled practitioners who have been trained as structured on-the-job trainers guide learning activities and provide feedback.

Summative evaluation: An evaluation conducted to determine the effectiveness of a program or intervention. Summative evaluation provides a statement of how well the program or intervention worked.

Systematic: Elements are considered in a step-by-step, organized fashion.

Systemic: All elements are regarded as they interrelate, not piecemeal or in isolation. This viewpoint encompasses all the parts of the system working together to produce a unified, customer-desired result.

Task analysis: The breaking down of an overall task into its constituent components. The task analysis lays out the framework on which the instruction will be built. It provides a complete detailed portrait of all subtasks that must be mastered to attain desired overall performance.

Task interference: Activities that inhibit attainment of priority tasks. As an example, filling out reports and attending meetings can become task interference for achieving sales goals.

Technology: The application of scientific and organized knowledge to achieve practical ends.

Time-and-action planning: A form of planning procedure and tool that lays out a set of tasks required to achieve a goal, with start and end times for each task. It may include designated people responsible for completing each task.

Training: A set of activities designed to change behaviors in very specific and predetermined ways. If training is properly done, learners are able to reproduce the targeted behaviors. The more effective the training, the more efficiently the new behaviors are reproduced—more rapidly, with fewer deviations, and under increasingly varied and more difficult conditions—to the point of automaticity (unthinking but accurate action). The term *training* often encompasses all deliberately designed learning activities, and may cover instruction and education as well.

Training evaluation: The objective assessment of training results. It asks the question, "Did training create differences in the way things are?" This is a process of systematically gathering and examining data to answer a variety of questions about a training initiative (for example, are trainees learning new knowledge and skills? What is the impact on bottom-line business outcomes? What is the ROI?).

Training system: A number of elements that interact with one another to generate learning that results in desired performance on the job.

Transfer: The application by the learner of the skills or knowledge acquired in learning to the work context.

Use level: This refers to acquired knowledge that is not just stored at the "memory level" for recognition or recall purposes, but at the application level. In the former case, the learner is able to identify or talk about what she or he has learned. In the latter case, the learner is able to apply knowledge—actually do something with it (that is, discriminate between examples of good and poor customer service; calculate a discount on a customer's bill; transfer a call to another extension).

Validity: The degree to which a measuring tool actually measures what it is intended to measure.

Value: The amount buyers consider appropriate to pay for an item of goods, a commodity, or a service; the right price.

Valued accomplishment: A result obtained that the organization, the person performing, and all other significant stakeholders consider desirable.

Virtual classroom: A learning "environment" that involves the use of technology to enable instructors to reach a geographically dispersed audience without incurring travel and collateral expenses. Almost anything an instructor can present in a live, face-to-face environment can be duplicated in a virtual classroom.

Virtual team: A geographically dispersed work team that relies on interaction conducted mainly via computer and telephone with minimal, if any, face-to-face contact.

Worth: The ratio of value to cost.

Worth analysis: An analytic procedure that calculates the extent to which there is a financial benefit for closing the gap between actuals and optimals. The general formula for calculating worth is worth = value/cost. A ratio greater than 1 suggests that "it's worth it."

Worthy performance: Performance (the combination of behaviors and accomplishments) that is "worth it" from a cost or expenditure perspective. Worthy performance (P_w) is performance in which the value generated is substantially greater than the cost of generating it.

Structured On-the-Job Training in Developing Nations

Structured on-the-job training (SOJT), adapted to a developing-nation environment, can improve significantly the performance capability of workers, and do so at low cost.

Globalization and competition in products and services have created enormous pressures to increase productivity. Developed nations have risen to the challenge. The same is not true for the developing world where the context of poverty does not permit similar investment in productivity to enable workers to compete internationally. Within developing nations a rich source of capital exists—human capability. The problem is how to organize and exploit this potential source of wealth.

The project reported here examined the opportunity for and appropriateness of SOJT in developing nations and describes a pilot effort in one African nation, Cameroon.

SOJT is a systematically planned process for designing and carrying out training. Learning takes place at the work site. Experienced workers serve as trainers and provide specific feedback on task execution. There are detailed training plans. The entire effort is integrated and orderly. It is a complete, unified system.

Implementing SOJT in Cameroon

The annual per capita income in Cameroon is US$764, which makes it one of the poorest nations. Cameroon is typical of many developing nations: high rates of poverty and unemployment; large foreign ownership; low productivity.

Adapting SOJT to the culture of Cameroon demands analyzing the technical capabilities of potential SOJT trainers, adopting teaching strategies that fit their backgrounds, exploiting cultural values and practices that enhance the SOJT experience, and verifying linguistic/ethnic compatibility.

The adapted SOJT model was tested to answer three questions: Is it effective in building performance capabilities of workers, compared with the usual training approach? Is it cost and time efficient, compared with the usual practices? Do management and employees have favorable attitudes toward SOJT, compared with the usual practices?

A controlled study compared SOJT to traditional training center (TC) preparation. The TC group did not gain in speed from pretest to posttest, despite six weeks of training (see Table A-1).

Table A-1: Pretest and Posttest Trial Times of All Tasks

Group	Pretest	Posttest
SOJT group	Mean: 27 min. 30 sec. Range: 25–30 min.	Mean: 15 min. 40 sec. Range 14–17 min.
Control group	Mean: 27 min. 30 sec. Range: 25–30 min.	Mean: 27 min. 15 sec. Range: 25–30 min.

Table A-2 compares costs of the two training approaches. The SOJT cost 25 percent less than did the TC training.

Table A-2: Training Costs in Cameroon Francs

Item	SOJT Cost	Posttest
Trainer salary	0*	680,000
Bonus for training	400,000*	0
Trainee salaries	600,000**	720,000
Development of training	100,000	60,000
Total Cost	1,100,000	1,460,000

*SOJT trainers continued their regular jobs but received training bonuses. Training Center trainers were fully dedicated to training.

**SOJT trainees trained 15 days; control group trained 30 days. SOJT trainees worked, and so had higher salaries. $600,000 and $720,000 are based on 12 trainees each.

Table A-3 displays the results of a Likert scale type instrument used to determine trainee and trainer attitudes toward the SOJT. All recommended that the company adopt this training approach.

General Conclusions from the Project Trial

SOJT demonstrated its effectiveness, efficiency, lower cost, and high satisfaction ratings. The projected organizational benefits (ROI) are a shortened learning curve, improved worker efficiency, and lowered incident rates (for example, damages, time/cost of clean up, lost productivity). Based on the 43 percent better performance of SOJT subjects, the immediate daily benefit was calculated at 46,440cfa in savings. Add in decreased incidents (no SOJT incidents; one control group incident

Table A-3: SOJT Satisfaction Scores*

Group	Instructor Scores	Trainee Scores
SOJT procedure	100	100
SOJT structure	100	95
SOJT use of time	95	98
SOJT relevance of content, method	81	81
Overall Satisfaction	94**	89

* Maximum score = 100.

** Interviewed instructors expressed great satisfaction with bonuses and increased status as SOJT instructors.

valued at 27,000cfa). Extrapolating over a year, a 3,000,000cfa investment to train 36 workers could yield a 33,000,000cfa savings (1000 percent ROI).

A final note on lack of improved TC group performance. The control group spent considerable time attending classroom lectures. There was little practice. Equipment was inadequate and obsolete. Practice space was different from the work site.

Summary and Conclusions

SOJT appears to be a "natural" solution for developing countries. It is relatively inexpensive, does not require specialized expertise to create and implement, and has demonstrated very high return in terms of learning transfer and productivity pay-off. Solutions such as SOJT—low cost and high yield—offer developing nations an effective means for meeting global marketplace competition.

Additional Resources

This *Beyond Training Ain't Performance Fieldbook* has drawn from both the authors' professional experiences and numerous published sources. Many of the source materials we have used make wonderful additional reading for you and your WLP team. Our list of recommended readings could extend over many pages. However, we have been selective in our entries to create a starter list for you. In almost all cases, the titles of the books, reports, and articles we have included are descriptive of their contents. We sincerely thank the authors of these publications for enlightening us and providing us with the foundation for this *Fieldbook*. They have helped us understand so much more about WLP than we ever could have achieved alone. Their contributions to our professional lives have been great, and we strongly recommend that you now turn to them for guidance and growth.

Axelrod, E. L., H. Handfield-Jones, and T. A. Welsh. "War for Talent, Part Two." *McKinsey Quarterly* 2001.

Banker, R. D., J. M. Field, R. G. Schroeder, and K. K. Sinha. "Impact of Work Teams on Manufacturing Performance: A Longitudinal Field Study." *Academy of Management Journal* 39(1996): 867-90.

Batt, R. "Outcomes of Self-Directed Workgroups in Telecommunications Services." In P. B. Voss, ed., *Proceedings of the Forty-Eighth Annual Meeting of the Industrial Relations Research Association.* Madison, WI: Industrial Relations Research Association, 1996.

Becker, F., and F. Steele. *Workplace by Design: Mapping the High-Performance Workscape.* San Francisco: Jossey-Bass, 1994.

Becker, G. S. *Human Capital: A Theoretical and Empirical Analysis with Special Reference to Education,* 3d edition. Chicago: University of Chicago Press, 1993.

Blanchard, K., D. Robinson, and J. Robinson. *Zap the Gaps! Target Higher Performance and Achieve It!* New York: William Morrow, 2002.

Blanchard, K., P. Zigarmi, and D. Zigarmi. *Leadership and the One-Minute Manager.* New York: William Morrow, 1999.

Block, P. *Flawless Consulting: A Guide to Getting Your Expertise Used,* 2d edition. San Francisco: Jossey-Bass/Pfeiffer, 2000.

Boulton, R.E.S., B. D. Libert, and S. M. Samek. *Cracking the Value Code: How Successful Businesses Are Creating Wealth in the New Economy.* New York: HarperCollins, 2000.

Broad, M. L. *Beyond Transfer of Training: Engaging Systems to Improve Performance.* San Francisco: Pfeiffer, 2005.

Broad, M. L., and J. W. Newstrom. *Transfer of Training: Action-Packed Strategies to Ensure High Payoff from Training Investments.* Reading, MA: Addison-Wesley, 1992.

Brown, L. *Designing and Developing Electronic Performance Support Systems.* Boston: Digital Press, 1996.

Chee, L. S. "Singapore Airlines: Strategic Human Resources Initiatives." In D. Tarrington, ed., *International Human Resource Management: Think Globally, Act Locally.* New York: Prentice Hall, 1994.

Clariana, R. B. "Differential Memory Effects for Immediate and Delayed Feedback: A Delta Rule Explanation of Feedback Timing Efforts." Paper presented at the Annual Convention of the Association for Educational Communications and Technology, Houston, TX, 1999. (ERIC Document Reproduction Center ED 430 550.)

Clark, R. E. "Motivating Performance." *Performance Improvement* 37, no. 8 (1998): 39-47.

Clark, R. E., and F. Estes. *Turning Research into Results: A Guide to Selecting the Right Performance Solutions.* Atlanta: CEP Press, 2002.

Combs, W. L., and V. F. Salvatore. *The Targeted Evaluation Process: A Performance Consultant's Guide to Asking the Right Questions and Getting the Results You Trust.* Alexandria, VA: ASTD Press, 2000.

Crawford, R. *In the Era of Human Capital: The Emergence of Talent, Intelligence, and Knowledge As the Worldwide Economic Force and What It Means to Managers and Investors.* New York: HarperCollins, 1991.

Davenport, J. O. *Human Capital: What It Is and Why People Invest It.* San Francisco: Jossey-Bass, 1999.

Dean, P. J. "Thomas F. Gilbert, PhD: Engineering Performance Improvement With or Without Training." In P. J. Dean and D. E. Ripley, eds., *Performance Improvement Pathfinders: Models for Organizational Learning Systems,* vol. 1. Washington, DC: ISPI, 1997.

Dickelman, G. J. *EPSS Revisited: A Lifecycle for Developing Performance-Centered Systems.* Silver Spring, MD: ISPI, 2003.

Drucker, P. F., R. Eccles, J. A. Ness, T. G. Cucuzza, R. Simons, A. Dávlla, R. Kaplan, and D. Norton. *Harvard Business Review on Measuring Corporate Performance.* Boston: Harvard Business School Press, 1998.

Edvinsson, L., and M. S. Malone. *Intellectual Capital: Realizing Your Company's True Value by Finding Its Hidden Brainpower.* New York: HarperCollins, 1997.

Elliott, P. H. "Job Aids." In H. D. Stolovitch and E. J. Keeps, eds. *Handbook of Human Performance Technology: Improving Individual and Organizational Performance Worldwide.* San Francisco: Jossey-Bass/Pfeiffer, 1999.

Esque, T. J., and P. A. Patterson. *Getting Results: Case Studies in Performance Improvement.* Amherst, MA: HRD Press, 1998.

Farquar, J. D., and J. W. Regian. "The Type and Timing of Feedback Within an Intelligent Console-Operations Tutor." Paper presented at the Conference of the Human Factors and Ergonomics Society, 1994.

Fishman, C. "Whole Foods Teams." *Fast Company* April-May 1996: 104.

Fitz-enz, J. *The ROI of Human Capital: Measuring the Economic Value of Employee Performance.* New York: AMACOM, 2000.

Ford, J. K., and D. A. Weissbein. "Transfer of Training: An Updated Review and Analysis." *Performance Improvement Quarterly* 10, no. 2 (1997): 22-41.

Fried, Y. "Meta-Analytic Comparison of the Job Diagnostic Survey and Job Characteristics Inventory As Correlates of Work Satisfaction and Performance." *Journal of Applied Psychology* 76, no. 5 (1991): 690-98.

Friedlob, G. T., and F. J. Plewa *Understanding Return on Investment.* New York: John Wiley & Sons, 1996.

Fuller, J., and J. Farrington. *From Training to Performance Improvement: Navigating the Transition.* Washington, DC: ISPI, 1998.

Gilbert, T. F. *Human Competence: Engineering Worthy Performance.* Washington, DC: ISPI, 1996.

Glenberg, A. M., A. C. Wilkinson, and W. Epstein. "The Illusion of Knowing: Failure in the Self-Assessment of Comprehension." In T. O. Nelson, ed., *Metacognition: Core Readings.* Boston: Allyn & Bacon, 1992.

Graham, L. *On the Line at Suburu-Isuzu.* Ithaca, NY: ILR Press, 1995.

Halal, W. E., ed. *The Infinite Resource: Creating and Leading the Knowledge Enterprise.* San Francisco: Jossey-Bass, 1998.

Hale, J. *Performance-Based Management: What Every Manager Should Do to Get Results.* San Francisco, CA: Pfeiffer, 2003.

———. *The Performance Consultant's Fieldbook: Tools and Techniques for Improving Organizations and People.* San Francisco: Jossey-Bass/Pfeiffer, 1998.

Harless, J. *An Ounce of Analysis Is Worth a Pound of Objectives.* Newnan, GA: Harless Performance Guild, 1970.

———. *Analyzing Human Performance: Tools for Achieving Business Results.* Alexandria, VA: ASTD Press, 2000.

Harmon, P. *Business Process Change.* San Francisco: Morgan Kaufmann Publishers, 2002.

Hatcher, L., and J. L. Ross. "From Individual Incentives to an Organization-wide Gainsharing Plan: Effects on Teamwork and Product Quality." *Journal of Organizational Behavior* 12 (1991): 174.

Iaffaldano, M., and P. A. Muchinsky. "Job Satisfaction and Job Performance: A Meta-Analysis." *Psychological Bulletin* 97, no. 2 (1995): 251-73.

Jacobs, R. L., and M. J. Jones. *Structured On-the-Job Training: Unleashing Employee Expertise in the Workplace.* San Francisco: Berrett-Koehler, 1995.

Kaufman, R. E., H. Oakley-Brown, R. Watkins, and H. Leigh. *Strategic Planning for Success: Aligning People, Performance and Payoffs.* San Francisco, CA: Jossey-Bass/Pfeiffer, 2003.

Kearny, L., and P. Smith. "Workplace Design for Creative Thinking." In H. D. Stolovitch and E. J. Keeps, eds., *Handbook of Human Performance Technology: Improving Individual and Organizational Performance Worldwide.* San Francisco: Jossey-Bass/Pfeiffer, 1999.

Keller, J. M. "Motivational Systems." In H. D. Stolovitch and E. J. Keeps, eds., *Handbook of Human Performance Technology: Improving Individual and Organizational Performance Worldwide.* San Francisco: Jossey-Bass/Pfeiffer, 1999.

Kern-Dunlap, L. "Effects of a Videotape Feedback Package on the Peer Interactions of Children with Serious Behavioral and Emotional Challenges." *Journal of Applied Behavior Analysis* 25, no. 2 (1992): 355-64.

Kravetz, D. J. *Measuring Human Capital: Converting Workplace Behavior into Dollars.* Mesa, AZ: Kravetz Associates Publishing, 2004.

Lee, D.M.S. Job Challenge, "Work Effort and Job Performance of Young Engineers: A Causal Analysis." *IEEE Transactions on Engineering Management* 39, no. 3 (1992): 214-36.

Locke, E. A., and G. P. Latham. *A Theory of Goal Setting and Task Performance.* Englewood Cliffs, NJ: Prentice Hall, 1990.

Mager, R. *What Every Manager Should Know about Training: Or I've Got a Training Problem and Other Odd Ideas.* Atlanta: CEP Press, 1996.

Mannheim, B., Y. Baruch, and J. Tal. Alternative Models for Antecedents and Outcomes of Work Centrality and Job Satisfaction of High-Tech Personnel." *Human Relations* 50, no. 12 (1997): 1537-62.

Mercer, W. *Leader to Leader.* 1(Winter 1997): 61.

O'Driscoll, T., B. Sugrue, and M. K. Vona. "The C-Level and the Value of Learning." *T+D* October 2005: 70-75.

Olson, N. "Realism of Confidence in Witness Identification of Faces and Voices." Unpublished PhD diss., Uppsala University, Sweden, 2000.

O'Reilly, B. "The Rent-a-Car Jocks Who Made Enterprise #1." *Fortune,* October 1996: 128.

O'Reilly, C. A., J. A. Chatman, and D. F. Caldwell. "People and Organizational Culture: A Profile Comparison Approach to Assessing Person-Organization Fit." *Academy of Management Journal* 34 (1991): 487-516.

Paas, F.G.W.C. "Training Strategies for Attaining Transfer of Problem-Solving Skill in Statistics: A Cognitive Load Approach." *Journal of Educational Psychology* 84 (1992): 429-34.

Pfeffer, J. *The Human Equation: Building Profits by Putting People First.* Boston: Harvard Business School Press, 1998.

Phillips, J. J. *Return on Investment in Training and Performance Improvement Programs,* 2d ed. Burlington, MA: Butterworth-Heinemann, 2002.

Phillips, P. P. *The Bottomline on ROI: Basics, Benefits, and Barriers to Measuring Training and Performance Improvement.* Atlanta: CEP Press, 2002.

Pittenger, D. J. "The Utility of the Myers-Briggs Type Indicator." *Review of Educational Research* 63 (1993): 467-88.

Robinson, D. G., and J. C. Robinson. *Strategic Business Partner: Aligning People Strategies with Business Goals.* San Francisco: Berrett-Koehler, 2004.

———. *Performance Consulting: Moving Beyond Training.* San Francisco: Berrett-Koehler, 1995.

Rossett, A., and J. Gautier-Downes. *A Handbook of Job Aids.* San Diego, CA: Pfeiffer, 1991.

Rothwell, W. J. *The Intervention Selector, Designer and Developer Implementor.* Alexandria, VA: ASTD Press, 2000.

———. *ASTD Models for Human Performance Improvement: Roles, Competencies and Outputs.* Alexandria, VA: ASTD Press, 1999.

Rummler, G., and A. Brache. *Improving Performance: How to Manage the White Space in the Organization Chart,* 2d ed. San Francisco: Jossey-Bass, 1995.

Sasaki, Y. "Individual Variation in a Japanese Sentence Comprehension Task—Form, Function, and Strategies." *Applied Linguistics* 19, no. 4 (1997): 508-37.

Schnackenberg, H. L., H. J. Sullivan, L. R. Leader, and E.E.K. Jones. "Learner Preferences and Achievement Under Differing Amounts of Learner Practice." *Educational Technology Research and Development* 46 (1998): 5-15.

Schneider, H., and C. Wright. "Return on Training Investment: Hard Measures for Soft Subjects." *Performance & Instruction* 29, no. 2 (1990): 28-35.

Schoarman, F. D. "Escalation Bias in Performance Appraisals: An Unintended Consequence of Supervisor Participation in Hiring Decisions." *Journal of Applied Psychology* 73 (1998): 58-62.

Schultz, T. W. *Investing in People: The Economics of Population Quality.* Berkeley: University of California Press, 1981.

Seagraves, J. *Quick! Show Me Your Value: A Trainer's Guide to Communicating Value, Connecting Training and Performance to the Bottom Line.* Alexandria, VA: ASTD Press, 2004.

Shaiken, H., S. Lopez, and I. Mankita. "Two Routes to Team Production: Saturn and Chrysler Compared." *Industrial Relations* 36 (January 1996): 31.

Smith, P., and L. Kearny. *Creating Workplaces Where People Can Think.* San Francisco: Jossey-Bass, 1994.

Smitter, J. W., H. Collins, and R. Buda. "When Ratee Satisfaction Influences Performance Evaluations: A Case of Illusory Correlation." *Journal of Applied Psychology* 74, no. 4 (1989): 599-605.

Stewart, T. A. *Intellectual Capital: The New Wealth of Organizations.* New York: Doubleday, 1997.

Stolovitch, H. D. *Best Practices in Learning and Performance Support.* Los Angeles: HSA Learning & Performance Solutions, 2000.

Stolovitch, H. D., R. E. Clark, and S. J. Condly. *Incentives, Motivation and Workplace Performance: Research and Best Practices.* New York: SITE Foundation, 2002. (Available at www.ispi.org)

Stolovitch, H. D., and E. J. Keeps. *Front-End Analysis and Return on Investment Toolkit.* San Francisco: Jossey-Bass/Pfeiffer, 2004.

————. *Training Ain't Performance.* Alexandria, VA: ASTD Press, 2004.

————. *Engineering Effective Learning Toolkit.* San Francisco: Pfeiffer/Wiley, 2003.

————. *Telling Ain't Training.* Alexandria, VA: ASTD Press, 2002.

————. *Beyond Telling Ain't Training Fieldbook.* Alexandria, VA: ASTD Press, 2005.

————, eds. *The Handbook of Human Performance Technology: Improving Individual And Organizational Performance Worldwide.* San Francisco: Jossey-Bass Pfeiffer, 1999.

————, eds. *The Handbook of Human Performance Technology: A Comprehensive Guide for Analyzing and Solving Performance Problems in Organizations.* San Francisco: Jossey-Bass, 1992.

Stone, N. J. "Exploring the Relationship Between Calibration and Self-Regulated Learning." *Educational Psychology Review* 4 (2000): 437-75.

Sugrue, B., and J. Fuller, eds. *Performance Interventions.* Alexandria, VA: ASTD Press, 1999.

Sugrue, B., and R. J. Rivera. *State of the Industry: ASTD's Annual Review of Trends in Workplace Learning and Performance.* Alexandria, VA: ASTD Press, 2005.

Surowiecki, J. *The Wisdom of Crowds: Why the Many are Smarter Than the Few and How Collective Wisdom Shapes Business, Economics, Societies and Nations.* New York: Doubleday, 2004.

Torraco, R. J., ed. *Performance Improvement: Theory and Practice.* Advances in Developing Human Resources series, no. 1. San Francisco: Berrett-Koehler, 1999.

Vam Tiem, D., J. Moseley, and J. C. Dessinger. *Performance Improvement Interventions: Enhancing People, Processes, and Organizations Through Performance Technology.* Silver Spring, MD: ISPI, 2001.

Villachica, S. W., and D. L. Stone. "Performance Support Systems." In H. D. Stolovitch and E. J. Keeps, eds., *Handbook of Human Performance Technology: Improving Individual and Organizational Performance Worldwide.* San Francisco: Jossey-Bass/Pfeiffer, 1999.

Yates, B. J. *Analyzing Costs, Procedures, Processes, and Outcomes in Human Services.* Applied Social Services Research Method series, vol. 42. Thousand Oaks, CA: Sage Publications, 1996.

About the Authors

Harold D. Stolovitch and **Erica J. Keeps** share a common passion—developing people. They have devoted a combined total of more than 80 years to make workplace learning and performance both enjoyable and effective. Their research and consulting activities have involved them in numerous projects with major corporations, such as Alcan, Bell Canada, Canadian Pacific Railway, The Coffee Bean & Tea Leaf, DaimlerChrysler Academy, General Motors, Hewlett-Packard, Prudential, Merck & Co., and Sun Microsystems. Their dedication to improving workplace learning and performance is reflected in the workshops they run internationally—workshops that focus on training delivery, instructional design, and performance consulting. Stolovitch and Keeps are the principals of HSA Learning & Performance Solutions, specialists in the application of instructional technology and human performance technology to business, industry, government, and the military. Together, they edited the first two editions of the award-winning *Handbook of Human Performance Technology: A Comprehensive Guide for Analyzing and Solving Performance Problems in Organizations* and *Improving Individual and Organizational Performance Worldwide,* published by Jossey-Bass/Pfieffer. They are also the authors of the award-winning bestsellers *Telling Ain't Training* and *Training Ain't Performance,* and of the *Beyond Telling Ain't Training Fieldbook,* all published by ASTD Press. Stolovitch and Keeps are co-editors and co-authors of the Learning & Performance Toolkit series published by Pfeiffer.

Stolovitch (CPT) is a graduate of both McGill University (Montreal) and Indiana University (Bloomington), where he completed a PhD and post-doctoral work in instructional systems technology. With one foot solidly grounded in the academic world and the other in the workplace, Stolovitch has conducted a large number of research studies and practical projects aimed at achieving high learning and performance results. In addition to creating countless instructional materials for a broad range of work settings, he has written almost 200 articles, research reports, book chapters, and books. He is a regular columnist for *Workforce*

Performance Solutions magazine. He is a past president of the International Society for Performance Improvement (ISPI), former editor of the *Performance Improvement Journal,* and editorial board member for several human resource and performance technology journals. He has won numerous awards throughout his 45-year career, including the Thomas F. Gilbert Award for Distinguished Professional Achievement; ISPI's highest honor, Member-for-Life; ASTD's 2003 Research Award; and the Canadian Society for Training and Development's most prestigious President's Award for lifetime contributions to the field. Stolovitch is an emeritus professor, Université de Montréal, where he headed the instructional and performance technology programs.

Keeps (CPT) holds a master's degree in educational psychology from Wayne State University (Detroit) and a bachelor's degree from the University of Michigan (Ann Arbor), where she later became a faculty member in the Graduate Business School Executive Education Center. Her 35-year professional career has included training management positions with J. L. Hudson Co. and Allied Supermarkets. She has consulted with a wide variety of organizations in the areas of learning and performance. Keeps not only has produced and supervised the production of numerous instructional materials and performance management systems but also has published extensively on the topic of improving workplace learning and performance. She has provided staff development for instructional designers, training administrators, and performance consultants. Keeps has been acknowledged by many learning and performance leaders as a caring mentor and major influence in their careers. She is a former member of ISPI's executive board, a past president of the Michigan Chapter of ISPI, and a Member-for-Life of both the Michigan and Montreal ISPI chapters. Among her myriad awards for outstanding contributions to instructional and performance technology is ISPI's Distinguished Service Award for her many leadership roles.

The authors live in Los Angeles and can be reached through their Website, www.hsa-lps.com.